Islam and Nationalism

Series Editors
Umut Ozkirimli, Center for Middle Eastern Studies, Lund University
Spyros A. Sofos, Center for Middle Eastern Studies, Lund University

International Advisory Board

Seyla Benhabib, Eugene Meyer Professor of Political Science and Philosophy, Yale University

Sondra Hale, Research Professor and Professor Emerita, Departments of Anthropology and Gender Studies, University of California, Los Angeles (UCLA)

Deniz Kandiyoti, Professor Emerita, Development Studies, School of Oriental and African Studies, University of London

Saba Mahmood, Associate Professor, Sociocultural Anthropology, University of California, Berkeley

Jørgen S. Nielsen, Danish National Research Foundation Professor, Center for European Islamic Thought, University of Copenhagen

James Piscatori, Head, School of Government and International Studies, Durham University

Gayatri Chakravorty Spivak, University Professor in the Humanities, Columbia University

Bryan S. Turner, Presidential Professor of Sociology and Director, Committee on Religion, The Graduate Center, the City University of New York; Director, Religion and Society Centre, University of Western Sydney

Peter van der Veer, Director, Max Planck Institute for the Study of Religious and Ethnic Diversity, Göttingen

Nira Yuval-Davis, Director, Research Center on Migration, Refugees and Belonging, University of East London

Sami Zubaida, Emeritus Professor, Department of Politics, Birkbeck College

One of the main objectives of this series is to explore the relationship between Islam, nationalism and citizenship in its diverse expressions. The series intends to provide a space for approaches that recognize the potential of Islam to permeate and inspire national forms of identification and systems of government as well as its capacity to inspire oppositional politics, alternative modes of belonging and the formation of counterpublics in a variety of local, national or transnational contexts.

By recognizing Islam as a transnational phenomenon and situating it within transdisciplinary and innovative theoretical contexts, the series will showcase approaches that examine aspects of the formation and activation of Muslim experience, identity and social action. In order to do justice to, and make better sense of contemporary Islam, the series also seeks to combine the best of current comparative, genuinely interdisciplinary research that takes on board cutting-edge work in sociology, anthropology, nationalism studies, social movement research and cultural studies as well as history and politics. As research on Islam as a form of identity is rapidly expanding and as interest both within the academia and the policy community is intensifying, we believe that there is an urgent need for coherent and innovative interventions, identifying the questions that will shape ongoing and future research and policy and exploring and formulating conceptual and methodological responses to current challenges.

The proposed series is intended to play a part in such an effort. It will do so by addressing a number of key questions that we and a large number of specialist interlocutors within the academia, the policy community, but also within Muslim organizations and networks have been grappling with. Our approach is premised on our understanding of *Islam* and the concept of the *nation* as resources for social identification and collective action in the broadest sense of these terms, and the need to explore the ways in which these interact with each other, inform public debate, giving rise to a diversity of experiences and practices.

We would like to thank The Center for Middle Eastern Studies, Lund University, for their support in initiating the series.

Titles include:

Olivier Roy and Nadia Marzouki (*editors*)
RELIGIOUS CONVERSIONS IN THE MEDITERRANEAN WORLD

Spyros A. Sofos and Roza Tsagarousianou (*editors*)
ISLAM IN EUROPE
Public Spaces and Civic Networks

The Islam and Nationalism series
Series Standing Order ISBN 978–0–230–30492–5 (paperback)
and 978–0–230–30491–8 (cased)
(*outside North America only*)

You can receive future titles in this series as they are published by placing a standing order. Please contact your bookseller or, in case of difficulty, write to us at the address below with your name and address, the title of the series and the ISBN quoted above.

Customer Services Department, Macmillan Distribution Ltd, Houndmills, Basingstoke, Hampshire RG21 6XS, England

---

Islam in Europe

Public Spaces and Civic Networks

Spyros A. Sofos

Center for Middle Eastern Studies, Lund University, Sweden

Roza Tsagarousianou

Communication and Media Research Institute (CAMRI), University of Westminster, UK

First published 2013 by
PALGRAVE MACMILLAN

Palgrave Macmillan in the UK is an imprint of Macmillan Publishers Limited, registered in England, company number 785998, of Houndmills, Basingstoke, Hampshire RG21 6XS.

Palgrave Macmillan in the US is a division of St Martin's Press LLC, 175 Fifth Avenue, New York, NY 10010.

Palgrave Macmillan is the global academic imprint of the above companies and has companies and representatives throughout the world.

Palgrave® and Macmillan® are registered trademarks in the United States, the United Kingdom, Europe and other countries.

ISBN 978–1–137–35777–9

This book is printed on paper suitable for recycling and made from fully managed and sustained forest sources. Logging, pulping and manufacturing processes are expected to conform to the environmental regulations of the country of origin.

A catalogue record for this book is available from the British Library.

A catalog record for this book is available from the Library of Congress.

To Iason and Roxana

Contents

Figures

Acknowledgements

Looking back in time, it is really hard to pinpoint the exact time this project was conceived. Our interest in issues pertaining to the relationship between Europe and Islam has emerged out of our broader work on Western discourses, attitudes and practices vis-à-vis the 'Rest' as Stuart Hall aptly has named the ensemble of cultures and societies that are constructed, not only as alien, but also as belated and backward (1992). Research on South Asian Diasporas (Tsagarousianou) in the early 2000s and on the debates on the Bosnian War and the place of Islam in a Bosnian state in Europe (Sofos) a few years earlier was crucial in helping us formulate some of the underlying questions of the work presented in this book. The aftermath of the September 11 attacks, the widespread and uninhibited islamophobia that ensued and its convergence with anti-immigration discourses made these questions more urgent.

This book would not have been possible without the generosity and tolerance of hundreds of ordinary people who have given their time to help us understand how Islam features in their everyday lives, what meanings and shapes it assumes as they go about their work and interact with neighbours, classmates, friends and relative strangers. Their contribution is even more valuable as they had to overcome suspicions and fear at a time when Muslim communities in Europe have been subjected to severe criticism and, often, insult and aggression. We are really grateful for the trust and help they have extended to us.

We are also grateful to a number of organizations and individuals who helped us with the logistics of the project, who brought the project to the attention of potential interviewees, helped us with snowball sampling whenever this was necessary and provided practical and interpretation help. We would like to thank the Afghan Association of London, the Bangladeshi Parents and Carers Association, Ali and his friends from the Bangladesh Youth Movement, London, the East London Mosque, the Islamic Cultural Center, Frankfurt, the Islamic Students Association at the Vrije Universiteit in Amsterdam, the Kingston University Islamic Society, the Lambeth

Somali Community Association, the London South Bank University Islamic Association, the Moroccan Muslim Association of Amsterdam, the Muslim Community & Welfare Centre, the North London Muslim Community Centre, the Pakistani Islamic Community, Frankfurt, the Somali Refugee Action Group, the South London Somali Community Association, the Southwark Muslim Women's Association and the Turkish Islamic Center, Frankfurt.

We are indebted to the members of the Al Ummah Mosque congregation, Ahmed, Ali Yildrim, Aynur Oran, Azedinne, Cengiz, Iffat Shabaz, Layla, Mert, Mohammed, Mussadika, Mustafa, Nadia, Osman, Rana, Sabah, Shehina, Tarik, Yusuf M., Yusuf K. and the many more people who chose to remain anonymous in London, Paris, Amsterdam, Antwerp and Frankfurt, who have offered all sorts of practical help, brought us in touch with potential interviewees and helped us overcome suspicion and mistrust. Without you, this book would have not existed.

In this long journey, we were fortunate to meet and exchange views with many people who have provided fresh perspectives and gave us the opportunity to rethink many of our assumptions and interpretations. The late Fred Halliday had subjected our ideas to what, at the time, we had perceived as savage criticism at a very early stage of the project. His comments allowed us to avoid logical traps that made our argument appear to be yielding to the lure of essentialism despite our best intentions. His interest in the project and encouragement, our subsequent discussions on his work on the Yemeni diaspora and its relevance to our work, as well as the broader topic of Islam in Europe have inspired us and helped us to develop and refine our argument. We feel privileged to have benefited from his observations and our exchanges. Umut Özkırımlı has been an invaluable colleague, friend and interlocutor. In the course of our numerous discussions and through his reading of several drafts of this book, he has provided astute criticism and generous encouragement, pinpointing the weaknesses and strengths of our argument. What is more, his encouragement kept us going during times when the task in hand seemed enormous and unwieldy. Other colleagues and friends who have discussed with us, or allowed us to rehearse ideas or aspects of our argument, include Jon Anderson, Severin Carrell, Rafey Habib, Catharina Raudvere, Satwat Rehman, Paddy Scannel, Iffat Shahnaz, Leif Stenberg and Sami Zubaida.

The arguments of this book have been tested in front of a number of audiences: earlier work from this project provided the basis of presentations to the Digital Diasporas: Migration, ICTs and Transnationalism Conference, organized by the Centre for Research in the Arts, Social Sciences and the Humanities, University of Cambridge, the International Communication Association and the International Association for Media and Communication Research Conferences, the International Organization of Migration Conference on Migration and Religion in a Globalized World in Rabat, the Nordic Society for Middle Eastern Studies Conference, the Understanding Islam Conference at Kingston University and two workshops of the International Network for the Study of Islam and Nationalism in Barcelona and Damascus. We are indebted to the participants for their questions, comments and suggestions.

Our classes on 'Multiculturalism and the Media' and 'Approaches to Social and Cultural Diversity' at the University of Westminster and 'Debates on the Middle East' at the Center for Middle Eastern Studies at Lund University have provided us with the opportunity to explore some of the themes we examine in this book. On such occasions, the lively debates that ensued reminded us of the timeliness of our endeavour and helped us recalibrate our argument so as to make it more accessible and also to incorporate insights that emerged in the discussions. We would like to thank our students for their enthusiasm and insightful observations.

Amber Stone-Galilee, senior editor for politics at Palgrave Macmillan has seen through this project from inception to fruition, always supportive and immensely tolerant and patient. Andrew Baird, has also been extremely helpful and responsive to our continuous queries and requests in the course of the production of this volume, while Devasena Vedamurthi and her colleagues at Integra Software Services have patiently and efficiently taken this book to production.

Roza would like to acknowledge a University of Westminster Communication and Media Research Institute-funded sabbatical leave that allowed her to conduct part of the fieldwork upon which this volume is based.

Spyros A. Sofos and Roza Tsagarousianou
Lund and London

Introduction

In a thought-provoking essay written in 1996, Roger Ballard explains how the geographical entity known as Europe became the product of a long process of 'imagination'. Ballard suggested that the continent was effectively imagined out of a disparate group of peoples, speaking different languages, often pitted against each other in protracted and devastating wars. Not the product of a common history, or even of a common culture, the emergence of Europe was not as obvious a development as it might appear. As many commentators suggest (Ballard 1996, Delanty 1995, Neumann 1999), Europe, at the time of its inception as a cultural and geopolitical signifier, was a loose collection of Christian peoples. Christianity, of course, was by no means confined within the boundaries of today's Europe as further to the East, in Asia Minor, Syria, Palestine, Egypt, and the rest of North Africa flourished old, established Christian communities. What provided the impetus for the emergence of Europe was the rise and spread of Islam. As the new religion started appealing to the populations of traditional centres of Christendom, and Muslim armies spread the rule of Islamic leaders in the East and then further West to North Africa, Southern Europe and later on in the Balkans and beyond, Europe started taking shape largely with reference to the Muslim threat that lay just beyond its boundaries.

Europe became 'the Christian continent' through its fight against an expanding – in territorial and religious terms – Islam. In this context, Muslims have become 'outsiders' and Islam has been defined as 'alien' to European culture. This assumption, of course, has relied on a long process of suppressing an important part of Europe's past that entailed close encounters and exchanges with Muslim societies and states that were not banished, as the dominant narrative suggests, outside Europe's boundaries in Africa and Asia, but were present within it, having established significant centres of culture, commerce and technology. It has been premised on the construction of a worldview that posits Europe in an ahistorical, antithetical relationship to Islam. This transformation has been so pervasive and so significant in European self-representations that throughout the career of the idea of Europe, Islam has become its alter ego, a threat that is largely constitutive of the continent, its culture and the social imaginary that sustains the latter two.

Several centuries after the expulsion of Muslims and the eradication of most traces of Islam from Southern and parts of East-Central Europe, Islam still remains significant in this relationship. The carefully managed representation of Islam as 'a temporary exception, a momentary lapsus in a predominantly and historically Catholic country' in Spain; the neglect of remnants of an Islamic past spread throughout Southern and Southeast Europe and obscured through the force of organized forgetting; and the uncomfortable realization after the end of the Cold War that Muslim majorities call home a number of European countries despite past totalitarian suppression and more recent genocidal conflicts are a testament to the uneasy relationship between Europe and Islam, between Europeans and the Muslim world. But, perhaps one of the most controversial issues that have given rise to a heated debate relates to Europe's relationship with its large Muslim minorities largely comprising migrants from the Middle East, North Africa, Southeast Asia, Turkey and beyond and their descendants, and also including sizeable numbers of converts. After centuries of systematic demarcation of the boundary that separates Europe and the Muslim world, of the meticulous construction of European self-representations 'cleansed' from the presence of Islam and infused with a sense of mutual incompatibility of the two religions, cultures and worlds, European societies have to come to terms with the breakdown of the physical and mental boundaries that separated them from all things Islamic.

Islam is regularly described as the 'second largest religion' in Europe, after Catholicism, its adherents numbering some six to eight million, depending on one's sources. The continent's Muslim populations, whose bulk settled originally as industrial workers, beginning in the 1950s, increased during a period of family reunification and, more recently, by the arrival in Europe of migrants largely driven from their homes by conflict, oppression and poverty, include a substantial number of younger people who were born and brought up in Europe. Some of these second- and third-generation European Muslims have known only Europe as their home, as have the little-researched population of converts.

Europe's Muslims have been attempting to make a home in Europe, in what often appears to be an alien environment, lacking familiar signs and sounds that they can use as 'signposts' in their everyday lives. They have largely been engaging in a long process that involves the adaptation of their communities to their new societies, to new ways of dealing with social issues and challenges, while they have also tried to sustain and reproduce distinctive cultural values in a non-Muslim setting. What is quite interesting and pertinent as far as this book is concerned is that, in many cases, they have been doing so in the company of fellow Muslims whose practices originated in homelands different from theirs. These diaspora Muslims now find themselves in countries that vary demographically, economically and juridically. Despite this variety, their shared experiences have produced some commonalities in their engagement with the Islamic tradition and their modalities of creating late-twentieth-century communities. They have, moreover, not negotiated such issues in isolation: Muslims today are tied together globally through a range of institutions and media so much so that, as Tsagarousianou (2007: 27–30) has elaborated elsewhere, referring to diasporas and other transnational phenomena, we can no longer ignore the conceptual move 'from the more essentialist notions of *homeland*, national, ethnic or even religious identity and geographical location to deployments of the notion of diaspora conceptualized in terms of transnationality, imagination, ambivalence, hybridity or *mestisage* and heterogeneity'. Thus, instead of adopting uncritical definitions of European Muslims as looking back (both in temporal and geographical terms), this volume constitutes an attempt to focus more on the complex processes of cultural translation, negotiation and social construction that they are engaged in. As Mandaville points out:

> The estrangement of a community in diaspora – its separation from the 'natural' setting of the homeland – often leads to a

particularly intense search for and negotiation of identity: gone
are many traditional anchor points of culture; conventional hierarchies of authority can fragment. In short, the condition of
diaspora is one in which the multiplicity of identity and community is a key dynamic. Debates about the meanings and boundaries
of affiliation are hence a defining characteristic of the diaspora
community. (p. 172)

This, essentially novel opportunity for self-invention inherent in
diasporic cultural politics, is clearly reflected in Brah's claim that
'diasporas are ... the sites of hope and new beginnings' (1996: 193). In
this context it is important to recognize the 'opportunity structures'
that the combination of migrancy and connectivity that the diasporic
condition entails give rise to. This is largely, though not entirely,
uncharted territory; empirical, mainly anthropological research has
started to shed some light in this area. Through his study of the politics of identity among migrants from the Balkan region of Macedonia
in Australia Loring Danforth (1995) has demonstrated the potential
for cultural creativity that can be unleashed by the opportunity structures that processes of deterritorialization and reterritorialization of
populations entail. By examining how, once detached from traditional, territorially based networks of power and authority, the ethnic
identification and ecclesiastical affiliation of Australians originating
in the region of Macedonia varied even among members of the same
family, Danforth very convincingly argues that diasporas effectively
discover (or construct) notions of 'who we are' and 'what home is,
or has been' by essentially looking forward. What must be stressed
above all is the sense in which the construction of diasporic identity, as is all identity, is inherently a socio*political* process, involving
dialogue, negotiation and debate as to 'who we are' and, moreover,
what it *means* to be 'who we are'. These 'new beginnings' that Brah
talks about, or the cultural creativity Danforth identifies, can take
various forms, from the questioning of boundaries and the development of identities that challenge monoculturalism to the creation of
closed understandings of identity akin to what Benedict Anderson
calls 'long distance nationalism' (1992) or to the development of
an 'authentic' and 'pure' sense of Muslimness premised on notions
of cultural separatism evident in the practices and discourses of a
small yet not negligible number of informants we encountered in the

course of the research this volume draws upon. But, even in the latter case, authenticity, purity and separateness are largely the product of responses to 'being in Europe' and to the challenges this presence generates and the opportunities it affords. As we will see in Chapter 6, the authentic and pure cultures putatively unearthed are in fact social constructs, product of present needs and aspirations.

In some way, the term we chose to describe Europe's Muslim population – 'European Muslims' – connotes this complex process of making space, or making a home in Europe. The condition of being a European Muslim constitutes a veritable laboratory of identity, marked by polyphony, convergence and contestation, looking for alternative sources of inspiration, developing new meanings and repertoires of collective action. Anecdotal evidence confirming this is slowly being complemented by concrete research findings. Indeed, there are a number of studies that indicate that a shift is taking place in the identification of Muslims in Europe, especially the younger ones, primarily moving away from an emphasis on ethnic identity towards prioritizing Islam, or, more generally, as we will argue later on in this volume, a sense of being Muslim that occupies an important position in their identification.[1]

Our own research has revealed such signs of a shift towards an overarching Muslim identity as the following representative statements suggest:

I am Arab but most of all I am Muslim. These are names the colonizers gave us to divide us and they keep on doing it over here. Nations are not about values... they are not of the soul.
(Isa, 18 years old, British/Palestinian as he defines himself)

I appreciate my parents tried to raise us as Pakistani as... they did the best they could... they thought we needed a link to our culture and tradition. But what is Pakistan? What does being Pakistani mean if not being Muslim.
(Syeda, 21 years old, British Muslim of Punjabi origins)

Being Turkish is being Muslim, part of a family of peoples who carried the banner of Islam... that spread Islam.
(Tugce, 21 years old, of Turkish/German origin in
response to a question of whether she feels
Turkish or Muslim foremost)

Unlike (earlier migrants) we are not looking back to their villages, we do not try to preserve (a world) that has passed away. Young Muslims in this country are struggling to be recognized, to meet the challenges of the future.

(Mohammed, 25 years old, Belgian of Syrian origin)

My parents came from India but I was never in doubt that what mattered for me was that I am Muslim. India may be where my family has its roots.

(Adil, 21 years old, British of Indian origin)

But, a note of caution is in order. What is unclear is the meaning that the act of identifying oneself as 'Muslim' has. We should not assume that anyone identifying herself/himself Muslim focuses wholly on Islamic cultural expressions – indeed research findings (Dassetto 1996; Sander 2004) indicate that people define themselves as Muslim even if they are not practicing, or even religious – in place of all other loyalties. Muslims in Europe are enmeshed in a web of loyalties and networks that may well take on different emphases in different contexts and at different times, and that typically change in the very processes of social and political life. A Muslim identity has, however, been important and has entered into public life at both local and national levels. So, without underestimating the significance of other, alternative or parallel identifications associated with places or cultures of provenance or of abode, with socio-economic position, work or education, to name but a few potential resources for the construction of identity, we think that the time is ripe for the exploration of what such trends mean, what identifying as Muslim in Europe today means and, equally importantly, what processes underpin this shift in identification. This book is intended to understand the processes of Muslim identity construction in contemporary Europe. It is not intended to replicate other books which expertly provide detailed accounts of Muslim associational life in Europe or discuss in detail Muslim politics. What we are more interested in is to examine in some detail aspects of the complex way in which European Muslims relate to each other, construct and populate spaces they call home and create spaces of dialogue and debate.

In order to situate these shifts in terms of the socio-political environment in which they take place, we explore the current controversies about the place of Islam and of European Muslims in contemporary Europe in Chapter 1. Although this is not a comprehensive exercise – a separate volume could be dedicated to such an endeavour – peering into the complex public and 'expert' debate, our discussion suggests that the current exchanges, even when they assume the guise of academic discourse, are highly politicized. This politicization of public discourse on Islam and Muslims in Europe has contributed to a broad moral panic about European Muslims and has done very little to facilitate a better understanding of key aspects of their lives and the complexity of their position.

Chapter 2 attempts to question some of the dominant assumptions in contemporary public debate on the place of Islam and of Muslims in Europe. Challenging the systematic positing of Islam and Muslims as external to Europe, it aims to reintegrate it to the European dominant historical narrative. The argument deployed in this chapter constitutes an attempt to sketch the outlines of a genealogy of Muslim presence in Europe and of the historically complex relationship between Islam and Europe. Furthermore, it focuses on the ways in which quarters both in 'European' and 'Muslim' public debate (to the extent that we can have such a distinction) have made sense of this relationship as a challenge as well as on the various ways solutions for a modus vivendi have been sought.

To Chapter 3 is left the unenviable task to navigate through the maze of attempts to define, demarcate, categorize and, not least of all, count European Muslims. After a critical examination of the relevant literature, of the limitations and breakthroughs it comprises, we suggest that Muslim identity, its meanings and its potency can best be studied in the context of social action. In this chapter, therefore, we explore the ways in which we can incorporate aspects of the relevant debate into a social action-centred approach and briefly outline the contours of the methodology we have adopted in our own study.

In Chapter 4, we turn to the examination of ways European Muslims inhabit local and translocal social spaces. Drawing upon theoretical contributions from transnational, globalization, cultural and media studies and premised on the recognition that the complex webs of interaction that make up European Islam and underlie European Muslim lives are multilocal phenomena, we look at how 'Muslim space' is constructed through face to face and, more importantly, interaction mediated through the deployment of Information and Communication technologies (ICTs). In this context, we examine space-making processes situated at the centre of sets of intersecting translocal or transnational flows and linkages that bring together geographically remote locations. We, furthermore, examine the construction of landscapes and soundscapes and their investment with emotions which, we argue, are crucial in the construction of a sense of 'home' and, by extension, of belonging.

Chapter 5 casts a look at another aspect of social action of European Muslims, notably the various ways in which they mobilize in order to construct their own experiential frameworks. We look at local forms of collective action around issues pertaining to their visibility and audibility, and ultimately the validation of their presence in their broader societies. We also focus on how, again through the use of media and ICTs, particular ways of interpreting life in Europe and beyond are constructed, with special emphasis on the construction of what William Gamson (1995) calls 'injustice frames'. Drawing upon our earlier discussion of emotional investments, we argue that these processes of construction of experiential and injustice frames are crucial for the process of formation of European Muslim identities as they open spaces where different experiences of other Muslims become translatable and are integrated into a common stock of 'knowledge' shared by members of a European Muslim 'imagined community' – to borrow a term coined by Anderson (1983).

But these instances of social and cultural creativity that we examine in Chapters 5 and 6 are not just central in the construction of a European Muslim identity, and definitely not one that is fixed, monolithic and reified. Chapter 6 is dedicated to a discussion of the various practices that constitute instances of (re)fashioning Islam (as both a religion and, more broadly, identity). We look at how mobility and connectivity have provided opportunities for European Muslims to 'vernacularize' Islam, to adapt it to their own particular needs and to initiate debates and exchanges on what Islam means to them. These practices, we argue, underline the cultural strength, creativity and inventiveness of European Muslims and open up new public spaces from which European Muslims explore their identities and their place in Europe as well as vis-à-vis other Muslims.

The concluding chapter contains our reflections on this journey of discovery, where encounters, the identification of shared concerns and the engagement in collective action slowly set in motion processes of convergence among European Muslims. We cast a last look at European Islam as both a European and multilocal phenomenon, situated at the centre of sets of intersecting translocal or transnational flows and linkages that bring together geographically remote locations, on the processes that provide the connecting tissue that unifies it, and we propose ways of further exploring it by focusing on the category of 'experience'. It is the experience of feeling 'out of place', of finding oneself straddling the boundary between the *local* and the *translocal*, that plays a formative role in the processes of European Muslim identity formation, and more research should be directed towards the ways in which this experience is constructed and is framing the ways in which Europe's Muslims translate their everyday realities and even their relationships with 'others like them'.

1
Muslims in Europe: Balancing between Belonging and Exclusion

An Overview

Over the past decade, Islam has gradually assumed an unenviable position in European public debate as it has been represented and understood as equivalent, or conducive to, cultural and religious fundamentalism, political extremism and terrorism. This has affected significantly European Muslims and their communities as, by being systematically posited at the antipodes of Western culture and the values of liberal democracy; in domestic debates, it has been seen as a religion and culture that stubbornly hinders the cultural and social integration of Muslims in European societies. In addition, the ongoing debates on the desirability and usefulness of immigration have often converged with those focusing on Islam, giving rise to discourses defining Muslim immigration as a problem and contributing to the formulation of distinctions between 'manageable' and 'unmanageable' immigration, the latter often comprising immigration from Muslim countries.[1] Seen as a threat to social cohesion (in the United Kingdom), or to the secular character of European societies (in France but also elsewhere), adherence to Islam or declaration of some sort of Muslim identity by Muslims in Europe has come to be viewed as a deficiency, as something that had to be rectified through adaptation to European cultures or to be contained through various forms of exclusion. Featuring prominently in the processes of construction of societal insecurity in most European societies, Islam, and more specifically, Europe's Muslims, have unavoidably borne the brunt of public scrutiny and condemnation.

10

Although in the 1980s and early 1990s, the encounter of European populations with Islam was rather localized, soon, Islam and European Muslims acquired broader visibility in European societies and presence in public debates. In areas of settlement of Muslim migrants their initially 'exotic' presence gradually gave way to closer interaction, cooperation and, not uncommonly, competition between Muslims and non-Muslims in various public spaces dedicated to work, education, welfare and consumption. Different approaches to an array of issues such as gender relations, aspects of schooling and the creation or use of buildings and public spaces informed, or perceived to be informed, by Islamic principles, especially in domains characterized by scarcity of resources, often were construed in terms of a clash of cultures and led to disputes and confrontations. Instances of such perceptions of cultural clash and incompatibility are discernible in the various disputes around the construction of mosques or community centres in European cities, the visibility of Muslims in public spaces through the construction of minarets or the wearing of headscarves or the face veil, the provision of *halal* school dinners for Muslim students or the negotiation of acceptable school attires taking into consideration Muslim sensitivities.

As migrants of Muslim backgrounds became more settled in Europe and as the predominant pattern of settlement shifted from that of single guestworkers to families, these, initially localized, disputes progressively gave their place to more general debates and, not surprisingly, confrontations between Muslims and non-Muslims. The settlement or formation of Muslim families confirmed in many ways in Muslim and non-Muslim minds alike that their presence in Europe was no longer temporary and brought to the foreground a number of issues, concerns and aspirations linked to their social and cultural reproduction. Interaction between European Muslims and the broader societies which they formed part of, eventually revolved around symbolic issues such as blasphemy and the limits of free speech, the visibility of Islam as an element of European societies and cultures, as well as more practical matters such as the right to religious schooling or to sharia governing personal status law. Whereas conflict between 'the mainstream' of European societies and European Muslim communities has traditionally been latent or of low intensity, only occasionally disrupted by more manifest and widespread disputes, during the past couple of decades or so it became much more visible and pervasive. During this period, together with a host of other themes such as unemployment or immigration, the compatibility of Islamic and European cultures and the alleged 'islamization' of European societies became a staple ingredient in the articulation of societal insecurity throughout the continent.

The 1989 *Satanic Verses* controversy in the United Kingdom that saw British Muslims engage in highly visible and vocal protests calling for Salman Rushdie's novel to be banned for blasphemy, and even some threatening the author and his publishers, constituted an important moment of 'awakening' for many Muslims in the United Kingdom as well as far beyond its borders.[2] More importantly, in the United Kingdom, the controversy prompted a process of rethinking the position of Islam in British society and started a debate on whether their relationship entailed merely the progressive adaptation of British Muslims to the mainstream, dominant culture, or a much more mutual process that involved cultural exchange and dialogue (Parekh 1998). One of the most visible instances of the transformation of the mood among the Muslim community was the campaign for the rethinking of the blasphemy law to encompass Islam in the definition of blasphemy in addition to the Anglican Church (Cesari 2009).

Across the Channel, the *affaire du foulard*,[3] which erupted in France in the late eighties over the alleged threat headscarves posed to the principle of secularity (*laïcité*) in French schools and public institutions, focused on a visible item of clothing and transformed it into a symbol of cultural alterity and of a cultural clash. The controversy lasted several years and subsequently informed public debate throughout Europe; it cast European Muslims in an unflattering light representing their faith and cultures as backward and misogynistic, while giving rise, at the same time, to a more critical approach towards the assumed neutrality of secularism within Muslim communities.

The dress codes observed by some Muslim women in Europe have continued to provide fertile ground for the mobilization of a motley constellation of xenophobic, right-wing forces only too happy to jump into the bandwagon of the secular, liberal and feminist opposition to Muslim women's practice of covering. Over the past decade public attention was directed to the practice of a relatively small minority of Muslim women to use variations of the *burqa* or *niqab* (full body and face cover), again a visible and quite alien item of clothing for the majority of the Western European population. In Spain, campaigns were initiated by local authorities. By 2010 several municipalities introduced bans that effectively prohibit women who wear the *niqab* to enter public buildings. The bans were prompted according to municipal government spokespersons for allegedly security reasons. However, many politicians suggested that one of the main goals of such measures was the protection of 'the dignity and freedom of [Muslim] women' (Sofos and Tsagarousianou 2010) as they considered the *niqab* demeaning and a sign of oppression. In the United Kingdom too, the *niqab*, has been posited in public discourse as the visible symbol of the perceived lack of integration of the Muslim community into British society and has therefore been associated with the whole debate over the perceived failures of multiculturalism as Jack Straw's (who was at the time leader of the House of Commons) 6 October 2006 column in the *Lancashire Telegraph* indicated when he described the veil as 'such a visible statement of separation and of difference'. In all these debates proponents of such bans have used arguments that identify in the veil patriarchal oppressive practices that are detrimental to the dignity of Muslim women, or safety and security problems or, finally, barriers to intercultural communication and social cohesion. As we will argue later on, these discourses are often articulated within the context of xenophobic and indeed islamophobic[4] definitions of the situation, under the cover of concerns over security, community cohesion and women's rights.

In the summer of 2001, a more explicit campaign against the 'belated' and 'barbaric' culture of Islam was unleashed in the Netherlands in the wake of homophobic statements made by the Moroccan imam El-Moumni and became a typical precursor of Dutch (and, more broadly, European) responses towards the 'backwardness' of Islam that were to be rehearsed on several occasions over the past decade. The tension between an otherwise libertarian and tolerant Dutch society and its uncompromisingly negative attitude towards Muslim communities in the country was renewed after the assassination of Theo van Gogh by Dutch-born Mohammed Bouyeri, in November 2004.[5] Close by, the *Jyllands-Posten* Muhammad cartoons controversy that arose in Denmark in September 2005[6] rapidly mobilized Muslims all over Europe and beyond and opened a window of opportunity for some marginal yet vocal minorities within European Muslim communities to express their total rejection of an 'uncompromising' and 'Islamophobic' West as exemplified by the offensive affront of *Jyllands-Posten* against Islam. But the controversy also prompted more moderate Muslims to question the value of unfettered freedom of speech and to draw attention to the need on the part of the media to exercise this right responsibly and, in the process, became the catalyst for the formation of a disparate coalition of political and social forces around the issue of freedom of expression. On the other hand, Muslim protests have been routinely dismissed as irrational and regressive, primarily due to the visibility afforded to the most radical and intransigent views and mobilizations by the media. Indeed, whereas questions about freedom and its potential limits have been posed time and again in debates around the concept of Western democracy by theorists, politicians, jurists and ordinary citizens alike, their articulation within the confrontational and polarized context of the Muslim protests dissimulate the potential legitimacy of such an intervention and stifle moderate Muslim voices that do not manage to compete with their radical counterparts who enjoy public visibility and audibility, reinforcing the perception of an irreconcilable cultural rift in European societies. Ordinary Muslim voices remain thus in a subaltern position, unable to gain a voice in a confrontation between islamophobic mainstream and radical Muslim voices.

In addition to such controversies which were instrumental in representing the diverse cultures of European Muslims as 'backward' and 'unsophisticated', events such as those of the 1995 Paris Metro bombings, the September 11 attacks in the United States, the 11 March 2004 bombings of the commuter train network in Madrid and the 7 July 2005 London bombings[7] or the controversy that surrounded the murder of the Dutch filmmaker Theo van Gogh introduced another crucial element in the public discourse about Islam and have given European Muslims further unprecedented and rather unwelcome visibility.

As Burgat aptly points out, another facet of the progressive transformation of the term *Islamism*, from one merely referring to Islam to one tainted by a 'quasi-criminal connotation', is the misrecognition of otherwise legitimate forms of social action and protest.

Therein perhaps lies the source of the real difficulty experienced by the West in hearing what they [those who assert the right to 'speak Muslim'] have to say. Preceded by an 'Islamic' formula, a protest against some military occupation here, against the absolutism of a leader there, against the American superpower everywhere are so easy to dismiss!

(Burgat 2008: 8)

Although his examples come from instances of protest relating to interstate relations and politics in Muslim majority societies, the kernel of his argument applies equally to attempts to 'speak Muslim'[8] in European and, more broadly, Western societies. These incidents of terrorism and political violence have virtually indiscriminately coupled Islam and Muslims (in and out of Europe) with uncompromising and irrational terrorist violence and given rise to concerns of public safety. They have decisively contributed to the 'securitization' of anything related to Islam as the religion, its followers and the communities and cultures informed by it, are no longer merely viewed as an 'irritating anomaly' in the European social landscape but hitherto seen and 'administered' through the lens of a significant societal threat. Thus *Islamic militancy, fundamentalism, jihad* and *terrorism* have become part of the staple vocabulary used by policymakers, politicians, commentators and ordinary people in everyday contexts when discussing Islam and Muslim communities.[9]

But, it should be stressed that this misrecognition is not accidental or 'innocent'. It is premised on a long tradition of misunderstandings, of selective appropriation of the past, of particular ways of viewing the present, on the construction of particular *regimes of truth* (Said 1978) and ultimately on the exercise of the power to construct and regulate the Muslim world as we will see in some detail in Chapter 2.

This misrecognition posed questions about the place of Islam in Europe (or, more broadly, the West), or the possibility of accommodation of Islam in secular societies and gave rise to intense and broader debates on multiculturalism and its consequences, on the feasibility of integrating European Muslims into contemporary European societies as well as the social and material cost of such an endeavour.[10] And, as the spectre of terrorism cast its shadow over Europe, politicians and commentators pinpointed what they perceived to be inextricable links between Islam and Islamic fundamentalism, anti-Westernism or even terrorism. Islam became a religion of terror, and Muslims were systematically represented as virtually prone to irrational, violent behaviour. Naturally, the particular social–historical conjecture in which such questions were posed and revisited and the urgency attached to them further contributed to the predominantly negative framing of the debate on Islam. In this context, disputes about Islam and Muslims have, more often than not, acquired racist overtones, whereby secularly minded commentators have been readily stigmatizing Islam as a profoundly anti-modern religion and way of life and European Muslims as bearers of the associated burden that this 'unsavoury' cultural baggage entails. It would be fair to say that the dominant perspectives on Islam and Muslims in Europe, reinforced by the visibility and near monopoly of the 'Muslim voice' by radical Muslim activists and groups,[11] have severely undermined the possibility of creating spaces for a constructive encounter and exchange between non-Muslims and Muslims in the current moment.

More importantly though, the process of securitization of Islam is not just a matter of a changing rhetoric but possesses, or generates, its own reality, its own 'materiality' and has the ability to tangibly impact on the relationship between mainstream European societies and their Muslim minorities and define and shape them both.[12]

For one, as Cesari (2009) points out, the discourse of securitization permeates the policymaking process and has tangible effects in a variety of fields ranging from immigration law to minority protection framework, schooling and health provision, security policies and broader processes of inclusion. In other words, contemporary discourse on Islam, and on European Muslims is thus not merely a way of talking about them or representing them but a means of 'constructing' them, making sense of them and developing relevant reactions to their presence and action. Through today's securitized discourse therefore, Muslims in Europe are constructed, not only as culturally different, but as a significant security threat that needs to be monitored and 'administered', whose presence in Europe and membership to European societies is increasingly questioned and subject to terms and conditions, constraints and regulation.

On the other hand, as we will see later on, securitization also provides a lens through which European Muslims themselves see (and shape) their relationship with the broader societies which they are a part of. It impacts on their repertoire of collective representations and actions and on their attempts to gain control over the ways they become visible and they are heard. In a way, policy and societal definitions of European Muslims attempt to curtail their rights in response to the securitization of the way they are seen and understood by authorities and public opinion. These set in motion reactions on the part of Europe's Muslim communities, which often take the form of increased assertiveness, giving rise, in the process, to what amounts to a self-fulfilling prophecy in the eyes of those recognizing in this assertiveness a threat. And, crucially, as we will show later on, these perceptions and actions of European Muslims are constitutive of their very own identities and consciousness as 'European Muslims'.

Clashing timeless monoliths?

Several commentators readily, and we would suggest uncritically, identify in the philosophy that underlies Muslim assertiveness and mobilization in European societies and, by extension, in the values and practice of Islam that is supposed to inspire them, an authoritarian ideology that is seen as deeply inimical to the clear and unambiguous separation between religion and politics that is thought to underlie European traditions of secularism. Quite often, the presence of assertive Muslim minorities in European societies has been perceived and depicted by populist politicians and commentators as a challenge to the norms, values and principles of liberal democracy. The latter see in demands that European Muslims put forward for recognition and voice a challenge to Western liberal (or even Christian, depending on one's standpoint) values and a threat to social cohesion. The succession of controversies and disputes such as the ones we attempted to outline earlier on and the emergence of anti-Western terrorism in the name of Islam have contributed to the construction of a framework of understanding Islam, and European Muslims for that matter, that has given rise to definitions of the situation in Europe along the lines of what Huntington has called *Clash of Civilizations* (1996). Indeed, many of the commentators expressing concern over the presence and rootedness of Muslim minorities in Europe claim that Muslim societies (and, by extension, Muslim communities in Europe) are markedly different in terms of history, language, culture, tradition, and, most important, religion from European societies. At best, they argue, Muslims need to adapt to the Western way of life, while many suggest that Muslims are unwilling or unable to change and therefore have no place in Europe.[13]

Mamdani argues that the implications of this trend which he calls *Culture Talk*, not only posit two opposing cultures but also sustain a hierarchical and unequal relationship between them by representing one of the two as reified, frozen in time, incapable of evolving and adapting to new challenges. As he characteristically points out:

> According to some, our [Muslim] culture seems to have no history, no politics, and no debates, so that *all* Muslims are just plain bad. According to others, there is a history, a politics, even debates, and there *are* good Muslims and bad Muslims. In both versions, history seems to have petrified into a lifeless custom of an antique people who inhabit antique lands. Or could it be that culture here stands for habit, for some kind of instinctive activity with rules that are inscribed in early founding texts, usually religious, and mummified in early artefacts?
>
> (2004: 18)

But does this perceived incongruence of objectives amount to a *clash of civilizations* as many contend, whereby Islam is viewed as a time-less, monolithic social and cultural force which is in a collision course with contemporary European societies and the values they hold dear? Are European societies really under siege, threatened by the assertion of the Islamic identity of a sizeable minority of their citizens? And are the causes of this presumed confrontation between Islam and the West (Europe in our case) inherent in Islam? Although at this point there is no consensus, such questions are posed with an increased sense of urgency and anxiety.

Many reject such a notion of a confrontation as too alarmist or mis-leading. Scholars such as Paul Berman (2003) or Edward Said (2001) argue that such a formulation is highly problematic as, in their opin-ion (a) there is neither an 'Islamic' nor a 'Western civilization' as each of these terms is used as shorthand for an array of disparate and occasionally contradictory sets of practices and values informed by a variety of factors that may emanate from diverse interpretations of Islam and of what is 'Western' and (b) there is no convincing evidence for such a contention. In particular, as Said points out, such an assumption omits the dynamic interdependency and interaction of culture and constitutes an example of an imagined geography, where the presentation of the world in a certain way legitimates particular political objectives.

In his attempt to counter the bipolar logic underlying arguments positing Islam and the West in an antagonistic relationship, Halliday (1996) echoes Said's broader argument by pointing out that the 'myth of confrontation' between the West and Islam cannot be adequately made sense of if one does not focus on the particular political needs it serves. Halliday also explicitly stresses the convergence between what he calls 'anti-Muslimism', that is, 'a diffuse ideology... rarely expressed in purely religious terms, but usually mixed in with other rhetorics and ideologies' (160), with racism. As he very aptly points out, the kernel of anti-Muslimism is not theological objections or religious differences but a 'hostility to *Muslims*, to communities of people whose sole or main religion is Islam, and whose Islamic character, real or invented, forms one of the objects of prejudice' (160).

On the other hand, others ignore such criticisms and recognize in the perceived tensions between Islam and Europe, or more broadly, the West, an antagonistic and mutually exclusive relationship, or a fundamental incompatibility. This alarmist discourse that sees in Islam and the West two largely monolithic and timeless, mutually irreconcilable and contradictory forces has, not unexpectedly, made inroads in the way the presence of Islam and Muslims in Europe has been seen. What is more, it has often led to arguments subjecting Europe's Muslims to relentless public scrutiny. The crux of such arguments is that if Islam and the West are mutually incompatible, then the presence of Muslims in Europe cannot but be a grave problem and their inclusion through economic and political forms of citizenship may be, at the end of the day, incomplete or even impossible. This effective and indiscriminate marginalization of European Muslims is exemplified in the passionate and uncompromising discourse of the French political philosopher and influential commentator Yves Charles Zarka who characteristically criticizes those who adopt a sceptical stance against such assertions and represents the relationship between Europe and its Muslim communities in a highly polarized way:

> in France, a central phase of the more general and mutually con-
> flicting encounter between the West and Islam is taking place,
> which only someone completely blind or of radical bad faith, or
> possibly of disconcerting naiveté, could fail to recognize.
>
> (Zarka 2004: 5; our translation)

When it comes to speculating as to what the outcome of this apparently conflicting encounter is going to look like, the answers are
rather bleak. Bassam Tibi, an academic of Syrian origin who lives
in Germany, echoing Bernard Lewis (2002, 2007) claims that we are
faced with an unequivocal dilemma: 'Either Islam gets Europeanized,
or Europe gets Islamized' (2006: 217). Tibi and other proponents of
this argument clearly accept an ahistorical model of civilizations akin
to that of Huntington's. Civilizations, according to such formulations are monolithic and for all intents and purposes immutable.
The possibility of 'civilizational' interaction and exchange, of cultural
translation, domestication and hybridization is either non-existent
or undesirable. This simple, clear, binary *either-or* schema leaves no
other option but confrontation. In this context the European or
Western civilization is in a collision course with Islamic civilization due to their *a priori* mutual incompatibility. What is more, this
simplification of the social and political field is conducive to the
formation of a binary antagonistic relationship between *them* and
us (Laclau and Mouffe 1985), in this particular instance between
Muslims and *Europeans*. The simplicity of this representation of the
relationship between Islam and European Muslims on the one hand,
and European societies on the other, has contributed considerably
to their 'homogenization' and essentialization in public discourse
and has made such formulations appealing to European media as it
provides an easy-to-understand and 'newsworthy' interpretive framework. As Shawn Powers (2008) suggests in his analysis of the media
reporting of the Danish cartoons affair,

> Western mainstream media outlets drew heavily on Samuel
> Huntington's 'clash of civilizations' narrative, increasing public
> fear of Islamic culture, obscuring public understandings of the

geopolitical and cultural realities underlying the affair, and further entrenching assumptions that have become barriers to productive cross-cultural dialogue (339)...by drawing from the deeply entrenched clash of civilizations narrative in describing the events of the affair, many media organizations intentionally deployed culturally inscribed solidaristic appeals – particularly those that invoked fear – in order to appeal for public support and construct collective public cohesion behind their cause. (356)

Interestingly, some intellectual circles even go as far as to attribute agency and purpose to the increase of the visibility and presence of Islam in Europe, suggesting that the particular, confrontational way in which Muslim communities encounter and interact with European societies constitutes part of a strategy designed to achieve the 'takeover' of Europe. This perspective can be clearly exemplified in the work of Zarka, Taussig and Fleury,[14] who discern in the politics of organization and self-representation of Muslims in France a strategy for the takeover of the country. This process entails, in their opinion, the creation and promotion of an Islamic religious orthodoxy that would in turn sanction and promote relevant modes of behaviour and action. In this way, they argue, the scholars and clerics that represent this orthodoxy work towards the effective purification and homogenization of the French Muslim community by suppressing moderate and secular voices and eliminating alternative viewpoints and identifications. Zarka et al. go on to suggest that through a combination of the ideas they propagate and physical force and coercion, representatives of this orthodoxy aim to create Islamic public spaces inhabited by Muslims. As part of this 'Islamization of public space', they consider aspects of contemporary identity politics such as the various mobilizations and lobbying in support of the construction of mosques, or for the recognition of Islamic holidays, and devolution of political functions to religious authorities. More importantly, Zarka et al. give an additional geopolitical substance to this 'cultural threat' as they argue that the 'conquered territories of the [French] Republic' will become a base for fundamentalists whose aim is the Islamization of France and, eventually, all of Europe. Resorting to the idiom of conquest and evoking images of territorial threat is a common and highly effective rhetorical strategy that invests talk on European Muslims communities with a sense of urgency as well as threat and strengthens the overall narrative thread of an impending hostile 'takeover' of Europe by Islamic fundamentalists.[15]

Without underestimating the validity of some of their remarks, such as the current competition of élites and counter-élites within Europe's Muslim communities for the attainment of hegemony and leadership, the representation in this competition of various aspiring orthodoxies, the existence of discourses that are antagonistic to the West, the increasing importance of identity politics and of various forms of collective action among Europe's Muslims for the attainment of the right to recognition, it is hard not to object to their particular framing within a discourse whose *point de capiton*,[16] or narrative thread revolves around the themes of conspiracy and conquest, especially when Zarka et al. fail to provide any substantiation of such claims. We would argue that such arguments advance particular, oversimplified and arbitrary interpretations of a situation that is much more complex, nuanced, often contradictory and ambiguous than we are led to believe. It is important to stress at this point that what Zarka et al. consider rather unproblematically to constitute part of a planned 'takeover of Europe' is at best a constellation of processes which are the product of cultural and social strategies and conjunctures, often unrelated to each other, even accidental. The editors are selective in their identification of what makes up Muslim activity in France and in Europe, ignoring instances of adaptation, dialogue and cultural translation and, more importantly, retrospectively constructing an underlying narrative of threat.

What should be pointed out is that the invocation of this 'threat' to Europe and its culture, the process of externalizing or 'othering' European Muslims is instrumental in the construction of this very Europe. As Said (1993) suggested, conflating Islam with fundamentalism is implicitly positioning 'Europe' in such a way as to uphold the 'moderation, rationality, executive centrality of a vaguely designated "Western" ethos'. Again, the construction of a Europe that is largely defined through an antagonistic relationship to its Muslim 'other' entails the latter's reification, imagining it both as highly homogeneous and monolithic. It is no accident therefore that islamophobic attacks are often taking place in conjunction with attempts to delegitimize and silence voices that are critical of the alleged neutrality of contemporary European democracies and – the also alleged – universality of the values that underpin them. Drawing on the rhetoric that was used to describe the bipolar world of the Cold War era conservative, liberal and Left-wing commentators and politicians have been launching attacks to those advocating the respect of human rights accusing them of betrayal.

Islamist fellow-travelers' and useful idiots...weaving a climate of opinion today that advances the purposes of radical Islam and is deeply damaging to the prospects of reconciliation. Just as every Soviet aggression was once defined as an act of self-defense against the warmongering west, today terrorists of al-Qaeda, or the Chechen terrorists who killed children in the town of Beslan, are described in the media as militants, activists, separatists, armed groups, guerrillas – in short, as anything but terrorists. Dozens of apologists pretend that there is no connection between the religion of Islam and those who practice terror in its name, or suggest that western leaders are no better or are indeed worse than Islamist murderers.

(Pryce-Jones 2004)

A similar idiom is adopted by the left-leaning British commentator Polly Toynbee who accused the Trotskyist-leaning British Socialist Workers Party of being 'fellow travelers with primitive Islamic extremism' in July 2005 ('In the Name of God', *Guardian*, 22 July 2005); while a few days later, Nick Cohen, another left-leaning British political commentator and founding member of the *Euston Manifesto*[17] accused the Left of having 'become the fellow travelers of the psychopathic far-right' ('I Still Fight Oppression', *Observer*, 7 August 2005). Although highlighting not unimportant concerns over the tendency of parts of the European Left to uncritically forge solidarities with dubious Islamist partners motivated by a shared 'anti-Americanism', the discourse of such critics rarely focused on the diversity of Islam and Muslim lives in Europe, or the tangible issues that made imperative the construction of solidarities that addressed the threats posed by racism, islamophobia and the marginalization of Europe's Muslims. In Germany, in a book entitled *Hurra, wir kapitulieren* (Broder 2006), Henryk Broder, a critic of what he sees as concessions to Islam by the state and the political

class, accuses them of pursuing 'appeasement' politics towards totalitarian Islam. Broder's choice of language is deliberate and specific
to his country's political culture and collective memory as he refers
to a different past, that of the appeasement of National Socialism
prior to the Second World War. In this way, he both attempts to
undermine the credibility of the German and European political class
that, in his opinion, refuses to stand up to Islam, and to draw par-
allels between National Socialism and Islam which he considers a
totalitarian religion.[18]

Despite the different historical periods with which the choice of
language is associated, the *idiom* utilized in both cases is telling. Being
a 'fellow-traveller' or 'practicing appeasement' conjure an imagery of
severe political misjudgement and even more so an aura of treason.
They also reify Islam and European Muslims as they effectively and,
we would claim, intentionally conflate a few radical anti-Western
movements with an entire, highly diverse community. The absence
from this language of any reference to the existence of Muslim communities that share very little, if anything, with the radical Islam
such commentators flag as the face of Islam in Europe is telling of
the biases and prejudice inherent in their discourses.

The construction of European Muslims

It should therefore come as no surprise to find that discourse on
Islam and European Muslims has considerably been coupled with the
highly emotional and xenophobic politics of terrorism and migration and has cast Muslims as external to all things European. As
Poole (2002: 259) points out, representation of Muslims and media
discourse on Islam 'legitimize current social relations of dominance,
power structures and therefore continuing patterns of discrimination'. They exclude Muslims from European culture and identity and
discount their claims to citizenship and equality. Or as Deltombe eloquently puts it, the imaginary Islam constructed in (French) public
discourse is an evanescent one,

> disappearing from the television screens as suddenly as it had
> appeared, just as the events that seem to have put it in the spot-
> light. It is also a partial Islam, seen through the lens of the 'prob-
> lems' and the crises that are not linked inextricably to it.... Those

who consider themselves to be Muslims can feel dispossessed and rejected by this amputated and deformed gaze.

(2005: 9; our translation)

Public 'debates-cum-panics' almost invariably exoticize European Muslims, focusing on what appears to be mysterious, alien yet seductive about their cultures and practices. As a result, the veil or, more generally, the attire of women appears to be one of the central elements in discourses on European Islam echoing the earlier Orientalist obsession of Westerners encountering Near Eastern cultures with peering through the (veil-like) curtains of the harem. The very same public gaze carries within it assumptions that these exotic cultures are inferior to Western culture. European Muslims and their ways of life are represented as partial and belated, incomplete and desperately left behind in time by Western modernity. And, not surprisingly, European Muslims are seen as threatening, both as they are perceived and represented as being 'so different' and as they are associated with religious and political intolerance and as they are represented as having allegiance to external religious and political centres (Deltombe 2005; Poole 2002).

Such representation strategies drew and keep on drawing upon 'extreme' behaviour among Muslims (personalities such as the notorious Abu Hamza or – now outlawed – organizations such as *Al-Gurabaa*). By doing so, they have conflated Muslims and Islam with an extreme and possibly extremist minority within it and, impatiently and unsympathetically have refused to engage in processes of translation between 'us' and 'them', in attempts to comprehend the other's individual and collective standpoint before passing judgement on them. Such constructions of the other tend to dress in the straitjacket of homogeneity diverse and polyphonic 'communities' and to anchor public definitions of Islam around extremes.

But even the cases of sympathetic engagement with the plight of particular minorities may often not entail empowerment but dependency and 'other-determination', whereby others determine how and when minorities can 'speak' and what they can say. For example, the public concern that has emerged on different occasions in several European countries regarding the plight of Muslim women finding themselves suffocated within the confines of their patriarchal communities have not always been sincere and even in cases where this was genuine has not always succeeded in providing more opportunities to Muslim women but has been subsumed to broader anti-immigration or islamophobic discourses within the universe of public discourse and patriarchal discourse within the targeted communities.

As a result, such concern rather contributed to the stifling and muting of the voices of those on whose behalf their self-appointed advocates have been talking; their own concerns and preferred ways of action are rarely really addressed as someone else is speaking for them and they become part of a broader process of minoritization. The result of all of this is a generalized feeling of 'aporia' and powerlessness and the potential reorientation of Muslims towards alternative political, educational and cultural institutions and alternative media infrastructures and contents as research over the past few years, including the findings that will be presented later on in this volume, and also of many others, clearly indicates.[19]

In the midst of this intense debate and public as well as academic interest lies a paradox: while so many have and are still dedicating considerable time and energy in discussing the position and impact of the growth of populations of Muslim background as well as of the practice of Islam in Europe, the debate is politically and emotionally charged and largely informed by widespread societal insecurity. This unprecedented degree of public visibility of Islam and Muslims in Europe is matched by the invisibility of the actual people, of the majority of ordinary European Muslims whose real life concerns, whose everyday life, whose encounters with practices of exclusion are obscured by this intense, yet ideologically loaded, debate. Within this highly charged universe of public discourse, it is extremely difficult to develop ways to better know this sizeable part of the western European population, their collective standpoints, their aspirations and experiences of living in European societies. It is hard to gauge the experiences gained from encounters between what run the danger of becoming parallel societies, from daily contacts with what European Muslims perceive as regimes of exclusion and discrimination. This reduction of the Muslim 'other' to invisibility, to being inconsequential and negligible further contributes to their minoritization, to exclusion from the mainstream and, in a way we would add here, from having a stake, a claim to citizenship. Although academic debate has already contributed to the elucidation and demystification of aspects of public discourse on Islam and Muslims in Europe, or to a better understanding of aspects of Muslim lives, values and attitudes throughout the continent,[20] there is still a lot that needs to be done in areas such as better understanding of the meaning of being Muslim in Europe and how this impinges on key aspects of the daily life, collective action and self-expression of Europe's Muslims at local and translocal level. In some ways, this volume attempts to peer through the veil of historically conditioned mistrust and fears and of the charged contemporary public debate and focus on the voices, some of which are not always heard, that make the complex phenomenon of European Islam.

2
Islam in Europe: A Genealogy

Geographies

The presence of Islam in Europe is not new, indeed, shortly after the establishment of the Muslim Caliphate, and the Muslim expansion of the eighth century, much of Europe lay under Muslim rule. Islam and the religious, philosophical, scientific and political innovations it fostered not only influenced but also became part of Europe, and the collective memory and consciousness of European societies.

As we will argue in the course of this chapter, vibrant Muslim communities and polities have known European territories as their homes for numerous generations and have left their indelible mark in the landscape, culture and memory of European societies. More recently, migrant communities, part of a global and transnational Muslim diaspora have settled in western Europe and given the mantle to subsequent generations of European Muslims. Finally, to add to the diversity of European Muslim experiences, not negligible numbers of converts have also impacted or are impacting on the cultural and political make-up of European societies.

Despite this undeniable presence of Islam and Muslims in western Europe, the Muslim communities that live there and the presence of Islam there as a religious, cultural and, possibly, political force have become the focus of attention only relatively recently. As Esposito points out, it is only 'in recent decades [that] Islam has gone from being invisible in America and Europe to being a prominent feature in the religious landscape' (2002: 2). In the next few pages, we will take a closer look at the interrelationship between Islam and Europe as it has evolved historically.

Islam is the second largest of the world's religions, numbering in excess of 1 billion faithful (Horrie and Chippindale 2003; Hunter 2002; Nielsen 2004). The vast majority of Muslims is more or less concentrated in 56 countries that are generally considered to comprise the Islamic world (Esposito 2002: 2), or, more literally, the 'Land, or Abode, of Islam' – *Dar-al-Islam*. Nowadays, this term often refers descriptively to the countries where Muslims represent the majority population and includes countries as populous as Indonesia, Bangladesh, Pakistan, Egypt, Nigeria and Iran. *Dar-al-Islam* is thought to extend from North Africa and parts of sub-Saharan Africa to the Middle East, and beyond, to Central and South East Asia. In addition, significant Muslim populations also live in India (comprising one of the largest Muslim communities in the world living alongside a non-Muslim majority), China (East Turkestan or *Xinjiang* Uyghur Autonomous Region) and several republics of the Russian Federation. The presence of Muslim populations in these territories and the influence of their religion and cultures is such that, they too, are readily associated with Islam and often feature in Islamic geographical and political imaginaries. Indeed, the *Barelvi* school of Islamic thought – representing one of the most influential intellectual traditions in Islam – originates in India where Muslims form a minority, albeit a very large one, while parts of the Russian Federation with a majority Muslim population, such as Chechnya, Dagestan, Ingushetia and Tatarstan are often seen by Muslims as an integral part of the Muslim world.[1]

Not unusually, references to *Dar-al-Islam* acquire political dimensions and overtones as, in the context of particular interpretations of Islam, they evoke the 'memory' of the Islamic *Caliphate* (Arabic *khilāfa*) and rekindle the desire for its reestablishment as a potentially vast and united religious, moral and political entity (Horrie and Chippindale 2003: 157; Hunter 2002; Nielsen 2004).[2]

Trajectories

European societies have, both in the past and today, defined themselves in juxtaposition to Islam. From the very early stages of Islam's expansion westwards, it has assumed the role of Europe's significant 'Other', an 'Other' that has been instrumental in the crystallization of the borders of Europe and, more importantly perhaps, in the definition of Europe as a Christian, and more recently secular, continent (Delanty 1995). In most accounts, the encounter of Islam with Europe has been dramatic as Europeans had to stop and repel Islamic aggression both in Central and Southeastern Europe and in the North Shores of the Mediterranean. It has also been remembered as a traumatic one as significant centres of Christianity such as Jerusalem and Palestine and the major Christian centres of the Byzantine Empire have been lost to the advancing Islamic armies. Whereas these territories were incorporated irretrievably to the Islamic world, as Europe was taking shape in the imagination of its inhabitants as a 'Christian' continent, the presence of Muslims in it has been seen as mostly temporary and exceptional.

The presence of Muslims in Europe is not a new development; in fact it is almost as old as the history of Islam itself. Soon after the death of the prophet Muhammad in AD 632 , the Muslim world expanded in the form of the Caliphate beyond its original Arabian territories to include, initially, lands that had a significant place in European Christian imagination (and, more broadly, in the cultural and political geography of what was to become Europe) and, soon after, encompassed sizeable parts of what today is considered Europe. The capture between 630 and 640 of Palestine (Christendom's 'Holy Land') and of Mesopotamia, both areas criss-crossed by the major trade routes that linked Europe with the East, provided the ground for the first encounters between European Christians and the Muslim populations of the Near East and for the development of relevant narratives both in Europe and the Muslim world. And although it was still remote to most Europeans, Islam soon became a reality to the 'border' populations in the Byzantine east as well the inhabitants of southwestern Europe.

Between 634 and 638, in the wake of a prolonged and destructive war between the Byzantine and Persian empires which resulted in their military decline, Muslim forces easily prevailed over the Byzantines in the crucial battles of Ajnâdayn (634) and Yarmûk (636) and wrested control of the province of Syria from them. Resistance to the Muslim advance was sporadic and weak as the populations of the Near East were weary of the prolonged Byzantine wars and Byzantine persecution of the numerous monophysite 'heretic' Christian churches of the region and wanted to see an end to the corruption that accompanied Byzantine decline in the region.

Indeed, ten years later, the caliphate had established its control over Egypt, Mesopotamia and most of what is now Iran. Over the next 70 years, the westward push of the Muslim armies resulted in the incorporation of the entire region of North Africa into the Islamic world.

Consolidation of the hold of Islam in North Africa was soon to be followed by expansion into what is now Europe as Muslim armies initially attempted raids and eventually conquered territories leading to the establishment of Muslim states on the European continent, some of which were quite long-lived. From the eighth century to the fifteenth, Muslims ruled large parts of the Iberian Peninsula and areas of southern Italy, southern France and, more generally, the western Mediterranean, while in the East, incursions into a much reduced in territory and weakened Byzantine Empire continued unabated.

As early as 711, when, in the east, Muslim troops were pushing through Iran and across the Oxus and Indus rivers, in the west, Muslim armies were landing in the Iberian Peninsula. In the midst of dynastic infight and widespread famine in the Visigothic kingdom of Spain, the Berber general Târiq ibn Ziyâd leading a north African Muslim army crossed the straits of Gibraltar to the Iberian Peninsula and easily defeated the army of the Visigothic Kingdom, killing its last king, Roderic at the Battle of Guadalete. Expansion was rapid and by 720, Arab and Berber Muslim armies had subjected most of the Iberian Peninsula to Umayad rule. In the 720s and 730s Arab and Berber forces fought and raided north of the Pyrenees, well into what is now France, reaching as north as Tours where they were eventually defeated by the Franks in 732 and repelled to their Iberian and North African strongholds. After the Umayyad Caliphate was overthrown by the Abbasids, the deposed caliph Abd al-Rahmân I fled Damascus – the seat of the Caliphate – in 756 and established an independent emirate in Córdoba. His Umayyad dynasty put an end to the wars that had tormented the population of the Iberian Peninsula and further consolidated the presence of Islam in Al-Andalus – the name by which Spain was known to Muslims – by uniting Muslim Spain and centralizing power in Córdoba. By the time his great-grandson, Abd al-Rahmân II ruled over the emirate (822–852) Córdoba was becoming one of the biggest and most important cities in Europe and Umayad Spain was progressively transformed from a mere province of the vast Caliphate into a centre of the Muslim world that rivaled the traditional centres of Damascus and Baghdad. The emirs of Córdoba built palaces reflecting the confidence and vitality of *Andalusī* Islam, minted coins, brought to Spain luxury items from the East, initiated ambitious projects of irrigation and transformed agriculture, reproduced the style and ceremony of the Abbasid court ruling in the East and welcomed famous scholars, poets and musicians from the rest of the Muslim world. But one of the most astounding changes of the time related to the appeal of Arab and Muslim culture to the local population. In the emirate of Córdoba, Muslim faith and Arab culture exercised a powerful attraction to the local population, especially when Christian Europe's alternative was a decaying Latin culture. Christian writers of the period were alarmed by the radical transformation of the high and popular cultures of Spain. They documented the ascendance of an 'elegant Arabic' as the preferred language of the educated – Muslim, Christian and Jewish alike – the increasing readership of Arabic books, the popularity of Arabic romance and poetry (Paulus Alvarus, *Indiculus luminosus*, in Southern 1962: 21–26; also Tolan 2002: 86).

Even those who remained faithful to the Christian religion often adopted the Arabic language and recognized the superiority of Muslim culture as Eulogius, one of the most important Christian chroniclers of the period, notes with disdain:

> Córdoba, however, once called Patricia, now called the Royal City, because of his ['Abd al-Rahmân's] residence, has been exalted by him above all, elevated with honors, expanded in glory, piled full of riches, and with great energy filled with an abundance of all the delights of the world, more than one can believe or express. So much so that in every worldly pomp he exceeds, surpasses, and excels the preceding kings of his race. And meanwhile the church of the orthodox groans beneath his most grievous yoke and is beaten to destruction.
>
> (Eulogius, *Memoriale sanctorum* in Colbert 1962: 194)

Such was the extent of the Arabization of the Christians of the Iberian Peninsula that the populations in question were being referred to and are remembered as Mozarabs (*mozárabes* in Spanish; *moçárabes* in Portuguese – from the Arabic: *musta'rib*; 'like Arabs', 'Arabicized' (Burman 1994)). The establishment of Islam and Muslim principalities in the Iberian Peninsula has therefore been much more pervasive and influential than the other forays of Islam into European territories as the former were much more long-lived and became closely intertwined with Christian and Sephardic Jewish Iberian culture. Although tolerated and, to a considerable extent, incorporated in the court and state organization of the emirate, the Catholic Church was not in a position to rival a confident Islam and its vibrant culture, or the elegance and vitality of Arabic language, literature, art and science.

Muslim presence in the Iberian Peninsula did not comprise a mere array of cultural and geographical outposts of the Muslim world but a number of veritable centres where theology, science and art flourished. Iberia became one of the centres of Islamic civilization of the period and its influence extended far beyond its borders. Crops produced using irrigation, along with food imported from the Middle East, provided the area around Córdoba and some other *Andalusī* cities with an agricultural economic sector by far the most advanced in western Europe at the time. Among European cities, Córdoba under the Caliphate, with a population of perhaps 500,000, was second only to Constantinople in size and prosperity. Within the Islamic world, Córdoba was one of the leading cultural centres. The work of its most important philosophers and scientists such as Ibn Rushd (Averroes) and Ibn Sina (Avicenna) had a major influence on the intellectual life of medieval Western Europe. Muslims and non-Muslims alike often came from abroad to study in the famous libraries and universities of *al-Andalus* and transmitted aspects of the Iberian Muslim civilization to medieval Europe This transmission was to have a significant impact on the formation of the European Renaissance.[3]

At the time of the Moorish invasion of Spain (eighth century) and over the course of the next several centuries, Moorish, Arab and Berber military units and navies based in Spain and North Africa conquered most of the major islands of the western Mediterranean (Sicily, Sardinia, Corsica, the Balearics) as well as a large portion of Puglia on the Italian mainland.[4] Of considerably greater importance in this connection was Sicily, which had been conquered by the Muslim Aghlabid dynasty of North Africa in the course of the ninth century. Within just over a decade after the first landing of the Aghlabid troops in Mazara in 827, the big cities of Palermo and Messina in Sicily itself and Taranto in the Italian mainland became part of the emirate, Naples was threatened and Muslim troops advanced north only to be stopped when their fleet was destroyed at Ostia in 849 (Setton and Baldwin 2006: 40–53). Sicily, in particular, enjoyed a period of stable and orderly Muslim government from c.950 until it was conquered towards the end of the eleventh century by the Normans, thus returning to Christian rule. Muslim Saracen presence in, and rule over, Sicily lasted from 827 to 1072. Although not as long-lived as Moorish rule over the Iberian Peninsula, the presence of Islam in Sicily remained part of the 'collective' memory of the island and other parts of the Italian Peninsula as part of its baroque architecture, Sicilian puppet theatre, a diffuse recollection of the binary division of the world into Saracen invaders and native or Norman Christians preserved in children's stories and popular culture, place names, the Sicilian language itself and, interestingly, in the buildings commissioned from Muslim architects by the Norman rulers of the island.[5]

In particular, the establishment of the Kalbid emirate in 917, with Palermo as its capital was a significant event in the history of the island. Land redistribution, innovation in agriculture, stable and relatively equitable rule contributed to the island living up to its former reputation as the granary of Rome as agricultural production brought a new period of prosperity in an island that had hitherto suffered a protracted period of decay and frequent change of overlords. Following the Norman conquest that was completed in 1072, Islam and key aspects of its cultural contributions continued to persist creating a hybrid culture on the island that has informed considerably the character of modern Sicily. The Norman kingdom of Sicily, initially at least, was reconciled with the presence of Muslim populations in its territory and Norman rulers showed an intense interest in Islam and the arts and sciences cultivated within the Islamic world until 1243 when they, then masters of the Mediterranean, expelled them from their last refuge on Sicilian soil several centuries before their last Iberian coreligionists were to follow their move to exile (Tolan 2002).[6]

Back in Spain, by the thirteenth century all that remained of the erstwhile flourishing Islamic civilization was the Kingdom of Granada, which eventually capitulated to the Catholic Kings Ferdinand II of Aragon and Isabella I of Castile in 1492, bringing the entire peninsula under Christian leadership. The year 1492 not only marks the fall of the Muslim city of Granada and the end of the *reconquista* but also the beginning of a concerted campaign of the Christian rulers of Castille to drive the Muslims (Moors) out of Spain and western Europe. By the seventeenth century, most Muslims, along with Iberian Jews, who were also persecuted as heretics, had fled to North Africa and the Ottoman Empire, carrying with them the memory of *Al-Andalus* and its loss for centuries to come.

And, although Western European Muslim civilization was coming to an end, in the East, Islam was to become inextricably linked to both the idea and the reality of Europe; the expansion of the Ottoman empire through the Balkans and its incursions into 'European' territories as far as Vienna in 1529 and 1683 ensured that Islam would continue to be present in Europe and occupy a central place in European imagination. Indeed, after a string of major victories against Byzantium from 1387 (capture of Thessaloniki) onwards, important centres of Eastern Christendom became Ottoman cities and, in time, sizeable Muslim convert and settler communities called them home. Even the capital of the once vast Byzantine empire, Constantinople, became the Ottoman imperial capital, eventually renamed Istanbul, several centuries after its capture in 1453.

Over the next few centuries, large numbers of Muslim settlers or converts lived alongside Christians and Jews, many of whom had fled the persecution of the Catholic kings of Spain after the *reconquista*. As the whirlwind of modernity reached the region and destabilized the Ottoman empire, new visions of political organization and identity started emerging throughout the region. Despite the processes of ethnic and religious homogenization that took place during the retreat of the Ottoman empire in the nineteenth and twentieth centuries and the establishment of new independent nation states (Özkırımlı and Sofos 2008: 145–178), Muslim populations still form part of the cultural mosaic of contemporary Southeastern Europe. Indeed, Muslims constitute the majority in Albania and Kosovo/a and the largest community in today's Bosnia and Herzegovina. It is also worth noting that Bosnia and Herzegovina, just over 30 years after its occupation by Austro-Hungarian forces in 1878, had already effectively become a Habsburg imperial province. As Nielsen (2004: 3) notes, the dual monarchy of Austria-Hungary even before the annexation of Bosnia and Herzegovina had given legal 'concessions to Muslim law regarding the family', while in 1912 it recognized 'the followers of Islam of the Hanafite rite as a religious community', thus rendering Muslims a legally recognized community of one of the largest European states with a multiethnic and multi-religious tradition and institutionalizing Islam in Central Europe. Indigenous Muslim populations can also be found throughout Southeastern Europe and further north into the Russian Federation.

Nevertheless, the 'liberation' of the Christian subjects of the Ottoman Sultans from the yoke of a Muslim empire inspired European Romanticism whose various proponents viewed Islam as a source of tyranny, backward and alien to Europe that oppressed the freedom-loving European Christians. The establishment of new Christian states in Southeastern Europe was considered to be the result of the prevalence of justice, as was the progressive ejection of the Ottoman Empire from European soil, and the inclusion in these of Muslim minorities was ignored or at best seen as a minor anomaly in the greater scheme of things. After 12 centuries of encounter, conflict and coexistence we have come full circle. Islam became ejected from European imaginaries, although not quite from its territories, and Europe was cast in contrast to it.

Imagining Islam and Muslims

As Delanty (1995: 23–24) points out, from its first encounter with Europe, Islam became a potent symbol of adversity, the virtual antithesis of Europe; in a way, it was rendered its constitutive other:

> [F]rom the seventh century the idea of Europe came increasingly to be articulated against Islam.... With the rise and consolidation of [the] Muslim world-system, the west was put on the defensive.... The threat was no longer from the barbarian tribes of the north who had been attacking the Roman Empire since the fifth century, but from Islam.

But why were Islam and its followers perceived in such antithetical terms against Europe, whereas previous Germanic, Slavic and other invaders had not occupied such a prominent place in European imagination. Why was coexistence deemed impossible even in instances when the Muslim newcomers displayed considerable openness and tolerance of their new Christian subjects?

One answer lies in the antagonistic character of Islamic expansion. As the tribes and armies that claimed Near Eastern and European territories in the name of Islam were challenging the then dominant ideology of Christendom, they could not be seen as mere 'barbarians' but as a threat to the reproduction of Christendom, its political, ecclesiastical and cultural elites. The migration and settlement of the various Germanic and, later, Slavic tribes in what is now Europe did not preclude the possibility of their accommodation and conversion as they were not advancing a vision antagonistic to that of Christendom. Indeed, many of the 'barbarian' German and Slav notables who had filled the vacuum of the collapse of the Roman empire adopted Christianity and accepted the primacy of the Papal authority in the West and sought some sort of accommodation with the Byzantine Empire in the East. The very same 'barbarians' later posited themselves as defenders of European Christendom against an advancing 'alien' Islam and were welcomed and recognized as such. In contrast to their Muslim counterparts, they were not challenging the Christian ideology underpinning Europe but were willing to integrate into Christendom and the ecclesiastical and political architecture of the continent.

Islam, however, was by definition a force that threatened the hold of Christianity in 'European' imagination and the authority structures that were derived by it; its iconoclasm, its potential appeal to the various dissenting segments of Christianity, its claim to be the true religion constituted a potent threat that could not be ignored by the ecclesiastical and political elites of Christian Europe. What is more, the fact that Islam had often assumed the form of a religious, social and political liberating force in the imaginaries of disaffected or repressed Christians throughout the Byzantine empire, the Mediterranean Sea and Southern Europe and the awareness that Muslim armies were often invited or greeted as liberators in the formerly Christian heartlands of Spain, Sicily, Syria and the Balkans coloured negatively its representations in the official and eventually popular Christian European discourse.

Not surprisingly, Europe's encounter with Islam has been cast in this unflattering light and subsequently burdened by the heavy baggage of centuries of Orientalism; the exoticized, negative and antagonistic way in which the – primarily Muslim – Orient was constructed through western European discourse. From the frontier discourse in the East and West to the impressions of medieval and early modern tourists in the highly diverse Muslim lands, an imagery and imaginary of a Muslim world whose culture was backward and partial, whose mindset was irreconcilably different from the European slowly took shape and form and largely framed – and still frames – the ways through which Europeans see Islam and the Muslim world, including their Muslim compatriots.

As Europe underwent the cultural, political upheavals brought by the Reformation and the age of revolution and experienced a period of technological innovation and as capitalism started to emerge, it was driven towards a period of colonial and imperial expansion that was also directed towards the Islamic world. In this context, overt or covert colonialism dominated the way in which European states related to the Muslim world. What is more, the colonial context which regulated interaction with the Muslim subjects of the European colonial empires and the concomitant belief in the 'completeness' and superiority of European culture and civilization has left its indelible mark on the ways in which European societies organize their relationship to their Muslim minorities.

Towards the twentieth century

Until the late eighteenth century, most of the Muslim territories that made up the Near East and North Africa remained tied to the Ottoman Empire with the exception of the Alaouite kingdom of Morocco in North Africa and, eastwards, the Kingdom of Iran. Central Asian Muslims lived primarily within the Russian Empire and the Caucasus constituted a borderland contested by the Russian and the Ottoman Empire as well as the Kingdom of Iran. British and Dutch colonial expansion in India and Indonesia brought these two European countries in direct contact with the Muslim populations of these territories. By the late eighteenth century, Napoleon's 1798 expedition to Egypt and, perhaps more importantly, France's invasion of Algeria 40 years later, in 1830, signalled a transformation in Europe's relation to the Muslim world as it marked a more aggressive attitude. Algeria's 'military pacification' lasted nearly 50 years and was coupled with the settlement of the territory by tens of thousands of immigrants from around the Mediterranean basin who seized land and resources from the Algerians. France adopted what was considered at the time to be a *mission civilizatrice* (civilizing mission) that entailed educating the local population according to Western standards (ignoring in the process the local culture which was seen as inferior and severely restricting educational opportunities for local children) but also allowing Christian missionaries to convert the native Muslims and Jews. France eventually invaded Tunisia in 1881 and Morocco in 1912 (where Spain had already established a presence since 1860), forcibly incorporating these states into the project of French imperialism albeit in a different way to that of Algeria, which was annexed. In contrast, the two countries retained the appearance of limited sovereignty with local rulers remaining in place and religious courts retaining jurisdiction over matters relating to personal status or family affairs for the Sunni Muslim majority and Jewish communities. These two new protectorates were also settled by Europeans who, just as in the case of Algeria, gained privileged access to the best land and resources at the expense of the local populations. In 1860 France established its hold over Lebanon, effectively continuing a legacy of intervention since the 1500s, under the pretext of protecting the local Christians from the Druze.

During the nineteenth century, the British established their presence in Egypt and the Sudan. Further east, having forged a series of economic pacts with Gulf region sheikhs in 1820, they annexed Aden in 1839. In collaboration with the French, they built and operated the Suez Canal, which opened in 1869. And, in order to ensure that it had unimpeded access to India and East Asia via the Middle East, Britain fought a war with Iran in 1856 confirming its dominance in the region.

The Muslim-populated territories of sub-Saharan Africa became the next target of European colonial expansion at the Berlin Conference in 1885 where Zanzibar became a British protectorate in 1890 and Dar es-Salaam a German protectorate a year later, while the French took over Senegal in 1890, Timbuctu in 1893, and destroyed the Rabah empire in Chad in 1900. In 1911 Italy claimed Libya and inaugurated a period of aggression and brutal occupation.

Despite differences in style, all European empires ruled parts of the Muslim world pursuing similar policies, dividing resources at the expense of the colonized populations, often co-opting and collaborating with indigenous political elites in order to quell popular resentment and administer the local populations. This co-optation strategy did not always succeed as the 1881 *Urabi* uprising in North Africa indicates (Safran 1961: 35–49). Nevertheless, with European powers being dominant in the Middle East, North and sub-Saharan Africa, this was a period where the ideology of European technological superiority became prevalent in tandem with the development of a discourse that posited the 'Orient', of which the Muslim world formed a substantial part, as an alien, mysterious but also inferior region and sustained a sense of moral, cultural and racial superiority and of a natural right to dominate other peoples. Oriental cultures were seen as decaying, as cultures that were situated at the antipodes of the civilizations that had erstwhile flourished in the very same places that were now witnessing decline and neglect. David Roberts, a Scottish painter whose works featured aspects of the 'Orient', wrote:

> Splendid cities, once teeming with a busy population and embellished with temples and edifices, the wonder of the world, now deserted and lonely, or reduced by mismanagement and the barbarism of the Muslim creed to a state as savage as wild animals by which they are surrounded. Often have I gazed on them till my heart actually sickened within me.
>
> (quoted in Kabbani, 1986: 11)

Within this context, the apparently benevolent 'burden' of the *mission civilizatrice* that accompanied colonialism served to provide a moral justification from an aggressive endeavour of displacement and exploitation of the colonized. Positing the Oriental, largely Muslim populations that the European expansion encountered and subjugated as 'in need of being civilized' defined their cultures as deficient, as lacking the crucial characteristics that would enable them to encounter Europeans as equals and that would no longer necessitate European tutelage. A concise rendition of this argument was offered by Jules Harmand, a staunch apologist of French colonialism, who in 1910 said:

> It is necessary, then, to accept as a principle and point of departure the fact that there is a hierarchy of races and civilizations, and that we belong to the superior race and civilization, still recognizing that, while superiority confers rights, it imposes strict obligations in return. The basic legitimation of conquest over native peoples

is the conviction of our superiority, not merely our mechanical, economic, and military superiority, but our moral superiority. Our dignity rests on that quality, and it underlies our right to direct the rest of humanity. Material power is nothing but a means to an end.

(quoted in Edward Said 1993: 17)

This perspective on the relationship between Europe and the 'Orient' required evidence. To this end, an array of Orientalist descriptions of the inhabitants of the region as savage, degenerate, hostile and even deformed, largely drawing on earlier imagery from the era of the Islamic expansion, served as metaphors for the cultures of the 'Orient' and the capacity (or lack of) of those living there to participate in the world shaped by European modernity. The cultures of the 'Orient' became a spectacle in the search of visible markers of difference and inferiority, so much so that even the very act of colonial aggression and subjugation of the 'Oriental Other' became the object of detached curiosity; in 1830, almost 200 years before the live televising of the Gulf War, and the visual and mediated routinization of human suffering of the inhabitants of the Orient, a number of businessmen from Marseilles saw the attraction of this very spectacle and converted a steamer into a cruise ship for a new type of tourism that would allow passengers to watch the French bombardment of Algiers from offshore (Mitchell 1991: 57).

This lens through which European societies have grown accustomed to view the Muslim 'Orient' largely remained in place since then. The imagery, the language and the narrative became part of the way Europe and Europeans encountered Islam and Muslims. The scene was set for a next phase of this relationship between Islam and Europe, this time not one of European expansion but one marked by the implosion of the European colonial empires and the migration of people from the colonial periphery to the former colonial centre.

From Islam *and* Europe to Islam *in* Europe

Although, as we have already seen, Muslims have lived for over six centuries in the southeastern part of Europe and despite their earlier presence in the Iberian Peninsula and in Sicily for centuries until their eviction by the two Catholic Kings of Spain and the Normans respectively, the presence of Islam in Western Europe has not been continuous.[7] Indeed, the largest part of the current Muslim population in western Europe arrived to its current places of settlement as migrant workers. At the dawn of the postcolonial era, European societies, exhausted by the Second World War and focused towards rebuilding their economies, attracted migrant population flows from the territories that had until recently formed part of their imploding colonial empires.[8]

Today, Muslims may be found in significant numbers in most western European countries. The largest Muslim populations are to be found in France, Germany and the United Kingdom, followed by smaller communities in such countries as Belgium, Spain, the Netherlands, Sweden, Denmark, Norway and Austria.

A first wave of Muslim migration relates to the move to Europe of relatively skilled migrants who, having cooperated with the European colonial powers, upon independence of their home countries, or soon after, chose to emigrate. Such are the cases of the Algerian Harki (Cesari 2004: 12) or of the South Asians who had to leave Africa as a result of policies of *Africanization* of the economies and of the civil service of several former colonies. Although not part of the mainstream of the Muslim migration process to western Europe, these professionals and skilled labourers from former European colonies in Africa, South Asia and the Arab world were some of the first Muslims who emigrated to Europe seeking a better life.

As the war-ravaged continent required additional labour to rebuild its economy, from the late 1950s onwards, migrants and guestworkers from predominantly Muslim countries such as Algeria, Pakistan (but also from India's substantial Muslim minority), Turkey as well as the rest of Northern Africa and West Africa moved to Belgium, France, the Federal Republic of Germany, the Netherlands, Switzerland and the United Kingdom arrived in Europe.[9] It soon became evident that western European societies and their political classes were not adequately prepared to comprehend the impact and magnitude of the social transformations that this phase of migration was to have. For a start, migration to Europe was seen in crude economistic terms. Overlooking the broader social and human dimension of immigration, European discourses on immigration at the time were governed by an emphasis on its instrumental character which was clearly reflected in the economic and labour policies initiated by western European governments during the 1950s, a period of rapid industrialization and reconstruction. Thus, European governments tried to frame migration within the logic of temporarily needing labour for the purposes of the reconstruction and eventual take-off of the economies of the continent: bilateral and multilateral agreements were signed with countries which had a 'surplus of labour' – and which, indeed, were homes to Muslim populations – such as Turkey and Yugoslavia – to encourage and manage migration to western European countries. Germany, for example, devised the 'guestworker scheme' and signed agreements on labour recruitment with Turkey. In 1973 the policy was stopped, as a direct result of the 'oil crisis' in Europe (Mehrländer 1978: 116). This affected the legal routes which migrants were to take in subsequent years as family reunification and asylum provided the legal basis of entry for many migrants in Germany as well as the rest of western Europe. In all cases, the presence and, eventually, settlement of Muslim, and other, migrant populations in major European and other developed societies was seen as 'temporary' as the German term to describe such migrants, *Gastarbeiter* (guestworker) indicates. These 'guests' were expected, upon the expiry of their contracts and their usefulness for western European economies, to return to their countries and families; if they proved to be unwilling to do so, 'generous' relocation packages were envisaged to curb their resistance[10] as the possibility of using various types of coercion such as the revocation of their residency and employment status. The legal frames governing immigration were modified over the years, but the basic, underlying, concept of the immigrant as foreign, temporary and spatially displaced have remained. European societies and governments have persistently and almost invariably refused to embrace even established migrant communities.

Western European societies and their governments were unprepared and, one could argue, unwilling to face the new reality of mass migration. Germany, the home of a very large Muslim minority and a possibly extreme example, considered Muslim (and, more generally, migrant) presence in the Federal Republic a temporary phenomenon. Successive governments were unprepared to recognize the sea change that immigration was bringing about in German society and did not plan for the integration of the country's large migrant population. This attitude reproduced a state of denial and a reality of segregation in social, religious and educational terms.

As Nielsen (2004: 25–26) points out, it is true that government funding was channelled towards the establishment of cultural associations and that the authorities supported broadcasting in Turkish; the German Government also initiated in 1973 a policy of integration that earmarked even more funds for the integration of new migrants (mostly Turkish). Nielsen (p. 26) also points out, however, that the oil crisis of the 1970s brought these short-lived initiatives to an abrupt end as *gastarbeiter* recruitment was restricted, recognition of the *gastarbeiter* as migrants was refused and a host of positive or punitive measures (financial inducements or restriction of access to welfare respectively) were adopted to encourage them to return home. Indeed, we would suggest that some of the integration initiatives launched by the German government were often reactive (e.g. followed the short recession of 1966) and not necessarily the product of a long-term vision. The fact remains that the authorities remained inimical to the idea of extending basic civic rights to foreigners and local societies have often objected to other forms of integration such as the recruitment of Turkish migrants by the police. In these areas progress has been very slow; premised on extrapolations from data on the origin of the German population, Blaschke (2004: 41–197) suggests that the number of Muslims (comprising people of Turkish but also Bosnian, Iranian, Moroccan and Afghan origin as well as an estimated 100,000 converts) in the country may be approaching 3.2 million of which close to 80 per cent do not have German citizenship. Indeed, the persistent denial of the German authorities and society to recognize the reality of migration and settlement has led to migrant activists and intellectuals to reclaim and use the term *guest* in deliberate and subversive ways.

Similarly France, the home of the largest Muslim population in Europe, including a sizeable minority of converts, has not followed a substantially different path. French Muslims are settled in most major cities and towns, quite often tucked away in the suburban satellite cities (*banlieues*) that were planned and constructed in the 1960s to house parts of the French working class, including migrants, away from the 'civilized' city centres reserved primarily for the 'indigenous', white French population. Segregation has been a central aspect of French Muslim experience as, apart from housing, educational and employment opportunities have not been readily available to its vast majority. The French Muslim population has grown considerably over the years and it now outnumbers Protestants and Jews while it is second only to Roman Catholics. This demographic reality is reflected in the increasing visibility of elements of Muslim presence in the urban landscape, most notably the existence of *Grand Mosques* in major cities like Paris, Lyons or Marseille and a multitude of mosques, prayer rooms, specialist Islamic or other relevant centres and shops throughout the country. Muslim communities have continued to grow because of their high birth rate, regulations that permit additional immigration to reunite families and a continual flow of legal and illegal entrants from North Africa although subsequent French governments have attempted to stem the flow of migrants. In the absence of concrete information on religious affiliation in France one has no choice but to extrapolate from statistics on ethnicity/ethnic origin. Using this highly unreliable method, one can trace the build-up of France's Muslim population by starting from the first half of the 1950s when the French census registered 212,000 Algerians (who until then constituted the overwhelming majority of North African – primarily Muslim – migrants). By 1990 over 614,000 Algerians, just under 600,000 Moroccans and 200,000 Tunisians had settled in the country. To these one should add at least 200,000 Turks and 100,000 West Africans and close to half a million *Beurs* – French citizens of Algerian descent. Nielsen (2004: 11), referring to estimates by French social scientists, suggests that the actual Muslim population of France could be in the region of five million, accounting for almost 10 per cent of the population while Cesari (2004: 10 and 183) estimates it to be around four or four and a half million.

Just across the Channel, although the 2001 UK census included, for the first time, a question on religious affiliation, the data it produced are not entirely reliable, as we discuss in more detail in Chapter 3. Although the data indicate that approximately 1.6 million of Britain's population are Muslim, the actual number may be much higher – possibly in the region of two million – if one takes into account various reasons for underreporting religious affiliation.[11] Britain's Muslim population is fast growing, young and quite diverse. Britain's Muslims come primarily from the Indian subcontinent – the majority of South Asian Muslims to arrive in Britain after the war were Pakistanis, with smaller numbers of Indian Muslims and, in the 1980s, a new wave of Bangladeshi migrants – although a not negligible part of the country's Muslim population comes from Africa, Turkey, Malaysia

and the Arab world. Peele (2006: 197) estimates that Britain's ethnically diverse Muslim population includes two-thirds of South Asian
origin, about 8 per cent of African origin, while about 12 per cent are
white. British Muslims have been traditionally concentrated in the
northern industrial cities of Yorkshire, Lancashire and the Midlands
and in the East End of London although, as the Muslim population
became more diverse and more mobile, their visibility and tangible
presence outside these areas have increased substantially over the
past couple of decades. Mosques, education and community centres
are now visible in all big British cities and Muslim communities have
left their imprint in the areas they inhabit. Muslim experiences in
the United Kingdom are not uniform as they largely depend on the
time and mode of migration as well as the degree of integration of
particular groups. So, whereas Pakistani Muslims, for example, have
made more inroads in British society in terms of access to education,
entrepreneurial and employment opportunities, other Muslims such
as those originating in Bangladesh or, say, Somalia have not yet had
similar success.

Today, Britain's Muslim communities are concentrated in London
and a number of cities in the Midlands and the North (including
Glasgow). In London, there are a number of clusters of concentration of Muslim communities of particular ethnic origin but, with the
exception of the borough of Tower Hamlets which has a substantial
concentration of Bangladeshis and Sylhetis, other boroughs of settlement are more ethnically and religiously diverse. In the North of
England, Muslims tend to be concentrated in particular areas and the
topography of their settlement indicates patterns of urban divide.

In Belgium, settlement of Muslim migrants was initially the product of the *gastarbeider* policies designed to ensure a sufficient supply
of labour for the country's mining, iron and steel industries. A series
of migration agreements with Morocco, Turkey, Algeria and Tunisia
in the 1960s were used primarily by the Moroccan government
to channel surplus labourers to Belgium. Turkish and other North
African workers followed soon. Shortly after their arrival Muslims settled in Brussels and the industrial areas of the French-speaking south
where demand for labour was pressing. In Flanders, similarly, Muslim settlement was concentrated in the industrial and sea port regions
around Antwerp, Ghent and Limburg. The oil crisis of 1973 prompted
a fundamental rethink of Belgium's immigration and guestworker

policies; in 1974 legislation considerably restricted labour immigration but the country did not radically change its family reunification policies which effectively enabled the dependants of Muslim guest-workers to join them in Belgium. As the closest exercise to a census conducted since 2001 in Belgium has been its *2001 General Socio-Economic Survey*, there are no comprehensive data to allow us to get reliable estimates of the country's Muslim population. Nielsen (2004: 70), drawing upon a number of estimates, suggests that by the end of the 1990s Belgium's Muslim population could have been in the region of 370,000 while a European Parliament report (European Parliament 2007) estimated Belgium's Muslims to be between 320,000 to 450,000, that is between 4 and 5 per cent of the total population of the country. Due to Belgium's relatively liberal citizenship legislation, the majority of Muslim migrants have Belgian citizenship unlike their German counterparts who have remained disenfranchised for the most part. In addition, Belgium's consociational principles of social and political organization have facilitated the recognition of Islam as one of the officially sanctioned religions in 1974 and the representation of Muslim organizations in government bodies since 1998. Yet, despite the state's attempts to co-opt Islam, discrimination and segregation have been persistent. As Muqtedar Khan (2005) reports, a dialogue between 32 American Muslim scholars and intellectuals, community leaders, journalists and activists and 70 of their counterparts from the Belgian Muslim community between 16 and 18 November 2005, co-hosted in Belgium by US Ambassador to Belgium Tom Korologos and Ambassador Claude Mission, the Director General of the Royal Institute for International Relations, identified systematic discrimination in the marketplace and housing as issues of primary concern among Belgian Muslims.

In the neighbouring Netherlands, although one would have expected the colonial ties that linked the country to Indonesia to have resulted in migration flows from the former colony, the first considerable wave of Muslim immigration originated in Dutch Guyana and took place between the mid-1960s to 1975 when the former colony gained its independence as Suriname. As Nielsen (2004: 62) points out, a bilateral agreement signed after Surinamese independence and expired in 1980, allowed continued migration and provided opportunities for family reunification. In the 1960s, agreements between the Netherlands and Morocco and Turkey lead to some 250,000 Moroccans (many Berbers among them) and 300,000 Turks and Kurds arriving into the Netherlands as *gastarbeider* (Fassmann and Munz 1992). Although many of the *gastarbeider* returned to their countries of origin within a few years after their arrival to the Netherlands (one-third of the total by 1965 according to Fassmann and Munz 1992), most remained in the Netherlands and were later offered the opportunity to be naturalized. A relatively relaxed family reunification legal framework enabled, here too, the families of many of the migrants to move to and settle in the Netherlands.[12] A new survey method employed in 2006 by Statistics Netherlands, the national bureau of statistics, where respondents themselves report what religious denomination they belong to, resulted in calculating Muslims in the Netherlands as 5 per cent of the Dutch population, that is 850,000 persons in 2008 (van der Bie, R. 2009: 16).

Recent conflicts and economic pressures have given rise to legal (mainly, but not exclusively, asylum) as well as illegal migration from countries such as Afghanistan, Iran, Iraq, Somalia and many West African countries where Islam is predominant or at least widespread. In addition to these, new migration flows originate in European countries with substantial Muslim populations such as Bosnia and Herzegovina, Kosovo, Albania and Macedonia due to a combination of conflict, societal insecurity and scarcity of economic resources. Alongside North Africa, South Asia and Turkey, which have been the traditional places of origin of Muslim migrants, a host of new places feature in the topography of Muslim migration to Europe.

Changes in migration patterns over the past couple of decades mean that, apart from the traditional western European destinations of Muslim migrants, more European countries have become places of settlement of sizeable Muslim communities. Austria, a relatively early choice destination for Muslim immigrants is estimated to be the home of 200,000–300,000 people of Turkish origin (Minority Rights Group 2005), while smaller immigrant and naturalized minorities include people of Afghan and Kosovar Albanian origin. Scandinavian countries have also been popular among asylum seekers and economic migrants as well. In 2006, according to estimates, approximately 175–200,000 Muslims live in Denmark (Ministry of Integration 2006) and 250–350,000 in Sweden (The Open Society Institute 2007). Finally, the littoral countries of Southern Europe have experienced a sea change as they have been transformed from traditional societies of emigration into societies of settlement of new migrants from Asia, North and sub-Saharan Africa, with many Muslims among them. It is estimated that over 250,000 Muslims live in Greece – most of them from neighbouring Albania – in addition to the indigenous Muslim minority that numbers approximately 120,000. Spain, whose proximity to North Africa has made it an important place of settlement as well as a transit station to other European destinations, is home to 500,000 Muslims. Italy, itself a transit route connecting North and sub-Saharan Africa to Northern and Western Europe is estimated to be home to more than 700,000 Muslims (European Monitoring Centre on Racism and Xenophobia 2006: 30). As Muslim migrant communities are relatively new in these countries they have often been received with fear or hostility. Instances of religious hatred and racism are widespread[13] and include both corporeal harm and damage to property. There is evidence that, as Southern Europe's Muslim communities take roots, they are developing institutions of sociability and solidarity and make inroads into local and national politics, but clearly the process is long and painstaking.

Focusing on the perspective of the migrants themselves, overall, the main reasons for migration were economic and, during the period of early settlement of Muslim migrants in Europe, religion had not occupied a central position in the visible concerns of the migrants. During the 1960s and 1970s, the belief of many that they were indeed guestworkers, temporary sojourners in Western Europe whose eventual return to their birthplaces was considered to be not only an inevitable but also desirable prospect, impacted on the way in which the first Muslim migrants interacted with mainstream European societies: being primarily male and having left families and dependants behind, their life was dominated by work, their earnings were sent back into the countries of origin to support those depending on them and very little time was dedicated to longer-term considerations. The devout were content with fulfilling their religious duties often in makeshift prayer rooms and rarely articulated demands for the building of mosques; the demographics of the migrant populations were such that concerns about their longer-term social reproduction as *communities* (schooling, cultural institutions, etc) did not emerge until migration under the various family reunification policies in place from the 1970s onwards altered the make-up of Europe's Muslim population. The arrival of families and of dependants – many of school age – impacted considerably on the way in which the former guestworkers and their families were making sense of their presence in Europe. The logic of subsistence which was intertwined with the experiences of solitary guestworkers gave progressively way to the logic of cultural reproduction of the new Muslim migrant communities, encompassing their education, religious and welfare needs. As a new generation of Muslims was growing up in Europe, looking back towards 'home' was no longer a viable option; their needs could not be suspended and their return to a home that many of them had no recollection or experience of was becoming even more implausible and remote. In this, new, context concerns and demands about education, the establishment of cultural and religious institutions and a new politics of recognition emerged. A combination of statistical and anecdotal information indicates that a smaller but increasing part of Europe's Muslim population is made up by recent converts to Islam (Brice 2011).

Overall, estimates of the number of Muslims now residing in Western Europe range from 10 to 20 million, depending on the source one uses.[14] The ethnic diversity of Muslims in Europe is extremely broad, representing most of the major ethnic groups of the Muslim world. Among the most numerous minority groups are those of South Asian, followed by Algerian, Turkish and Moroccan origin. Because of this great diversity, despite a common religious bond, it is difficult to speak of a homogeneous Muslim community in any individual country, let alone across Europe without qualifying such claims.

Leaving the issue of the accuracy of the population figures temporarily aside, it is evident that the relationship between 'Europe' and Islam is a difficult one. This 'difficulty' is also in evidence when Europeans reflect on the relationship between Europe and Islam and the position of Muslim minorities within European societies. Indeed, as pointed out in the previous chapter, an increasingly vociferous portion of the European political elites and intelligentsia have been arguing that Islam is incompatible to European civilization and Muslim minorities are, therefore, particularly hard to adapt to life in 'secular' European societies.[15]

Several factors can be said to have contributed to this perception of Muslim citizens and residents as outsiders, or as a culturally and politically marginal section of the societies in question. Presumed cultural 'incompatibilities' between Muslim and European culture are not uncommonly used to justify various modes of exclusion of Muslim presence in Europe. It is often argued that the Christian heritage of European societies makes it difficult for those professing another religion such as Islam, or having been socialized within cultural contexts informed by the latter to integrate into European societies. Similar arguments are usually advanced with particular reference, not to the religious heritage of European societies but to what is perceived to be the largely secular character of European institutions, be they political or cultural or economic. Indeed, both such lines of argument seem to converge to the view that Muslim presence in Europe is often perceived to be at odds with core definitions of Europe and Europeanness. Indeed, the President of the European Constitutional assembly and former President of the French Republic, Valery Giscard D'Estaing, referring to the potential admission of Turkey to the European Union, brought forward arguments drawing upon such historically conditioned perceptions of Europe[16] and disregarding the complex historical, as well as current, interrelationship between Europe and Islam. The role of Islam as a notable 'other' in the process of definition of late medieval and modern Europe is particularly relevant here and has been researched and discussed reasonably well (Neumann, Delanty, Said).

Another, not negligible line of explanation revolves around the argument that the memories or current experiences of the European imperialist and colonial intrusion or presence (perceived or actual) in territories and societies considered to be part of *Dar-al-Islam* have almost indelibly erected mental boundaries between Europe and the Muslim world and that these boundaries obviously affect the ways in which European Muslim citizens or residents are incorporated, if at all, to public and social life. In a way this composite argument blames colonialism for having created irreconcilable differences between the two cultures and rendered Muslims unwilling or unable to adjust to life in Europe. Interestingly, such interpretations, however elaborate, tend to ignore the cultural complexity of both Europe and Islam, or Muslims, and to reify the two in an antagonistic or mutually exclusive relationship. As we will demonstrate in the remainder of this book, this conscious or subconscious misrecognition turns the continuum of cultural experience and expression into a fragmented terrain where cultural contact and exchange is inconceivable. This is indeed not a neutral process, devoid of power and desire. As Mary Douglas points out so eloquently:

> It seems that whatever we perceive is organized into patterns for which we, the perceivers, are largely responsible. Perceiving is not a matter of passively allowing an organ – say of sight or hearing – to receive a ready-made impression from without, like a palette receiving a spot of paint....It is generally agreed that all our impressions are schematically determined from the start. As perceivers we select from all the stimuli falling on our senses only those which interest us, and our interests are governed by a pattern-making tendency, sometimes called a schema. In a chaos of shifting impressions, each of us constructs a stable world in which objects have recognizable shapes, are located in depth, and have permanence....Uncomfortable facts which refuse to be fitted in, we find ourselves ignoring or distorting so that they do not disturb these established assumptions. By and large anything we take note of is preselected and organized in the very act of perceiving. We share with other animals a kind of filtering mechanism which at first only lets in sensations we know how to use. (1966)

The presence of Islam and of Muslims so 'uncomfortably' close to European citizens, who have been inculcated in a representation of the cosmos revolving around understanding Islam and Europe as mutually incompatible, can be disorienting and may have the effect of 'filtering out' of dissimulating all that is recognizable and familiar in the values and lives of ordinary Muslims behind what features like an unknown monolithic 'Other'.

On the other hand, the rise of right-wing neopopulism (Meny and Surel) has recognized in this historically conditioned fear of Islam a veritable means of mobilization and legitimation. Neopopulist discourses draw on and reproduce a potent combination of islamophobia, the socially constructed and historically conditioned sense of collective trauma of the retreat of Christendom in the face of a violent Islamic expansion and forced conversion and the durable Orientalist tradition of the modern era. As we already saw in the previous chapter, the alarmist discourse that sees in Islam and the West two largely monolithic and timeless, mutually irreconcilable and contradictory forces has gone as far as to attribute agency and purpose to the increase of the visibility and presence of Islam in Europe, suggesting that the particular, confrontational way in which Muslim communities encounter and interact with European societies constitutes part of a strategy designed to achieve the 'takeover' of Europe. What is more, such discourses have deployed a topography of a shrinking Europe facing its annihilation by the advancing fundamentalist forces represented in the Muslim population of Europe. Presence becomes conquest, coexistence becomes Islamization, acceptance becomes capitulation in this simplistic schema.

Making sense of the presence of Islam in Europe: Muslim perspectives

The presence of not negligible and dynamic Muslim communities in Europe (as well as in North America), a region that has been traditionally recognized as located outside – and indeed represented as culturally and politically antagonistic to – *Dar-al-Islam*, has often been seen as something of an anomaly both within the Muslim world and in European (and North American) societies. Particular traditions and schools of thought within Islam have tried to make sense of this 'anomaly' by adopting different views on the relationship between the Islamic world and Europe, ranging from outright rejection and denunciation of the latter to more or less selective acceptance of it. Thus, within the broad spectrum of opinion, following the classical juridical binary positing 'the Land of Islam' (*dar al-Islam*) versus the 'Land of War' (*dar al-harb*) or the 'Land of Unbelief' (*dar al-kufr*), strict *Wahabbist* or *Salafi* revivalist organizations (such as Hizb ut-Tahir) tend to denounce European cultures and civilizations as 'unislamic' and 'corrupt' and would therefore, in principle, discourage Muslims to migrate and settle in Europe; those who have already settled are expected to actively reject any attempt or possibility of integration to European life. Others such as the followers of the Islamic theologian Bediuzzaman Said Nursî would eagerly embrace the 'advantages of Europe' – such as its technological and industrial civilization – but would reject 'the sins and evils of western civilization', thus adopting a selective approach towards the West premised on a binary division between spirituality and material civilization.[17] More recently, more mainstream organizations and some prominent Muslim scholars have attempted to navigate through this difficult question by suggesting that European Muslims need to display a flexible approach to the relationship between the demands derived from Islamic sources and the practicalities of life in European societies. Thus, organizations such as the *Union des organisations islamiques de France* (UOIF) or the *Islamic Foundation* in the United Kingdom, while not questioning the binding character of the guidance derived from Islamic sources, advocate a moderate and flexible approach that essentially means that Muslims in Europe should not reject participation in broader social processes and interaction whenever this would not compromise their faith and values. A more flexible approach has also been adopted by scholars affiliated to the Muslim Brotherhood such as al-Qaradawi and Faysal Mawlawi. Interestingly, these scholars and their followers have introduced a new Islamic topography that implicitly rejects the binary division between *dar al-Islam* and *dar al-harb*; in this context, the West is not regarded through the prism of confrontation that is inherent in the classical binary schema but as a land of potentialities, as the 'Abode of Proselytizing' (*dar al-da'wa*). In essence, the language of the *dar al-da'wa* still asserts the superiority of Islam over the West and retains an element of the classical binary schema, but it does so in ways that can allow Muslims to live in the West without having to constantly confront the dilemmas posed by *Salafi* ideologues. Europe thus is seen as not 'the enemy' but as a potential convert to Islam. In principle then, pluralism and liberalism are not wholeheartedly embraced in such a formulation, they are rather seen as temporary features of European life, features that Europe's ultimate Islamization (*da'wa*) would make redundant. Such a formulation obviously combines the best of both worlds. According to some interpretations it does not constitute a call to Muslims to proselytize non-Muslims but it allows them to continue living in a non-Islamic society having faith in the superiority of Islam and in the eventual conversion of non-Muslims, while, others believe that living in the *dar al-da'wa* entails the obligation to spread the faith to non-Muslims.

Others, such as the prominent Swiss Muslim scholar Tariq Ramadan have developed a more complex approach premised on the decoupling of these issues from the context of the intractably antagonistic relationship between Islam and the West that radical and revivalist movements in the Islamic world have often adopted. In contrast, however, to the formulations of scholars representing

the current Muslim Brotherhood approach, Ramadan further mod-
ifies Islamic topography in a way that permits and enables Muslim integration within European societies and promotes a sense of
responsibility for European Muslims.

> [T]he European environment is a *space of responsibility* for Muslims.
> This is exactly the meaning of the notion of *'space of testi-
> mony'* [*dar al-shahada*] that we propose here, a notion that totally
> reverses perspectives: whereas Muslims have, for years, been won-
> dering *whether and how they would be accepted*, the in-depth study
> and evaluation of the Western environment entrusts them, in
> light of their Islamic frame of reference, with a most important
> mission.... Muslims now attain, in the *space of testimony*, the
> meaning of an essential duty and of an exacting responsibility:
> to contribute, wherever they are, to promoting good and equity
> within and through *human brotherhood*. Muslims' outlook must
> now change from the reality of 'protection' alone to that of an
> authentic 'contribution'.
>
> (Ramadan 1999: 150)

Ramadan (1999: 55–56) argues that the view that

> the Islamic juridical frame [is] *entirely immutable*, fixed once and
> for all, because it is from God or because our previous *'ulama'*
> have already formulated all that has to be known and fol-
> lowed... reveals a profound lack of knowledge and, above all,
> tends to define what Islam is not in light of its own principles,
> but in contrast with what it is not, namely Western civilisation. If
> the latter accepts change, evolution, freedom and progress then,
> *logically*, *reasonably* and *as opposed to it*, Islam does not. More-
> over, in their [revivalists, radical] minds, the more one – whether
> an individual, group or society – refuses change, freedom and
> progress, the more he or they are genuinely Islamic.... this kind of
> reflection, even if understandable in a time of social and political
> weakness, crisis and acute pressure, has no justification within the
> fundamental Islamic frame of reference.

In this context, explaining Islam within 'the framework of a specific
relation of protection from an environment which is perceived as

too permissive and even hostile' (1999: 5) is a reactive attempt to stifle the vitality and currency of Islam. Without compromising the core principles of Islam and the laws of worship (*'ibadat*), Ramadan suggests that the Islamic social code (*mu'amalat*) should be the object of 'constant reflection and adaptation in order to permit their faithful enforcement in light of the global principles of *Shari'a*' (p. 43).

Clearly, Ramadan leaves the door open to a flexible reading of the position of Muslims in Western societies, but, what is more, acknowledges that some aspects of Islam not pertaining to its core values and rituals are subject to social change. Such articulations constitute attempts to render Islam and cultural and political pluralism compatible by undermining perceptions of the relationship between Islam and the West premised on the logic of antagonism and intractability. However, they retain the importance of the Islamic faith which provides the guiding principles for Muslims' integration and contribution to Western societies.[18]

The diversity of opinion and the intensity of the dialogue and ideological struggle on the issue of the place of Islam vis-à-vis Europe, and of the place of European Muslims within European societies among Muslim scholars and activists are indicative of the highly contested terrain that European Muslims have to traverse in order to preserve aspects of their religious or cultural identity while making Europe a home for them. One thing is certain; the debate is far from over and, as it does not take place in a social-historical vacuum, it will continue to generate controversy for as long as the Islam–West nexus is built on antagonism and mutual suspicion.

3
Who Are the European Muslims?

Conceptual issues

So far we have attempted to outline the current debate regarding the presence of Muslim communities in Europe and sketched a genealogy of the relationship between Islam and Europe. But, so far, perhaps the most important question – in fact, set of interrelated questions – has remained unanswered in the background of our discussion.

The first question concerns our choice of terminology. One might wonder on what grounds one can talk about *European Muslims* as a meaningful category of enquiry. We have indeed talked extensively about Muslims living in Europe using, for the most part, a particular term – *European Muslims*. This was a deliberate choice as, despite the view of many Europeans who seem to have difficulty in accepting that Muslims are part of Europe and of the societies that comprise it (Ahmed 1999; Bednarz and Kreuel 1998; Roy 1999), we wanted to suggest that Muslims who have 'made their home' in Europe, or whose residence in Europe is not temporary and, of course, the sizeable number of converts to Islam as well as of the descendants of Muslim migrants, are not simply found *in* Europe but they are *European*. As Leggewie (1993: 3) points out, 'Islam is an integral part of Europe, not its antipodes or eternal antagonist.' To be more precise, our hypothesis here is that living in Europe, they have to, and, as we will later on discuss in some detail, they do develop particular relationships with institutions, individuals and groups and they have to participate in shared activities to solve problems and pursue their individual as well as shared aspirations. We, therefore, suggest that we are not dealing with sojourners, foreigners or 'guests' but with an integral part of European societies, sharing goals, problems, fears and aspirations with their non-Muslim fellow citizens. And, indeed, millions are already European citizens through residency, birth and/or nationality (Anwar 1994; Dassetto 2000), or are choosing to become through the process of naturalization (Ramadan 2000). To be sure, this does not mean, of course, that their Europeanness cancels or displaces their 'Muslimness'. It is true that, in addition to the common ground that European Muslims may have with their non-Muslim fellow citizens, they do face challenges and opportunities that may be unique to them, largely because they relate to their 'being Muslim'. Again, we would suggest that many of these challenges and opportunities may have a European dimension. For example, concerns over the rise of Islamophobia may have a local, national but also a pan-European facet. Indeed, as we are going to demonstrate in the following chapters, this is very often the case as many European Muslims actively and intentionally look to Muslims in other European countries in order to generate examples of practice, or ways of solving problems, and to establish emotional or 'material' solidarities.

Still, another important question that has yet to be answered is who these 'European Muslims' that this volume claims to be focusing on are. Is it possible to identify a 'core' element in the identities of European Muslims that can justify the relevant academic discourse (which this book constitutes part of), as well as the political and policy debates, journalistic discourse on, and common sense understandings of Islam in Europe? Indeed, can we speak about European Muslims without falling into the trap of promoting and reproducing what Dassetto very aptly calls 'une appréhension globalisante ou abstraite des réalités musulmanes' – a globalizing or abstract understanding of Muslim realities (Dassetto 1996). And although it is extremely difficult to come up with unambiguous answers to such questions, it is clear that posing questions like these is very pertinent – we would argue, central – to any attempt to explore Islam and Muslim lives in Europe.

So, let us begin to address these points. There is nothing novel in asserting that when we speak about European Muslim identities, we are not referring to something homogeneous and uniform. Indeed, as Anthias and Yuval-Davis argue in their discussion of the complex relationship between race, nation, gender, colour and class (1992: 157), people do not possess one monolithic identity. Instead, they are positioned in terms of the intersection or articulation of these identities. It is therefore clear that European Muslim identities intersect with other forms of social division and differentiation such as class, nation, ethnicity or gender, to mention but a few.

For it is undeniable that Muslim populations in Europe are highly diverse, multifaceted and polyphonic. This diversity is premised on a vast array of factors: it is the product of the different languages, ethnicities and sects or schools of thought that Muslims in Europe are associated with; it is reflected in the different class positions and cultures of Muslims in Europe; it is permeated by the distinctive outlooks that gender and generation bring to daily life and longer-term orientations; and it is coloured by the inflections of locality of settlement and dailiness. What is more, the different challenges and opportunities that distinct national frameworks present to Europe's Muslims as well as the diverse claims that countries of putative origin are making over 'their diasporas' complicate the picture even more.

Their diverse origins and ethno-linguistic backgrounds – one can identify Gujarati, Punjabi, Bengali, Sylheti, Middle Eastern and North African Arab, Berber, Turkish, Kurdish, Pashtun, Baluchi, Malay, Indonesian, Iranian, Somali, West African Ibo, Yoruba, Wa'kuri, Wangari, Hausa, Fulani as well as Bosniak, Albanian, Macedonian or Central Asian Muslims, to mention but a few – have given rise to a highly polyphonic, segmented and often disparate universe. There is no doubt that ethnic and national identifications play a very important role in the self-definitions of Europe's Muslims, as they provide genealogies, narratives of provenance or belonging, frames of reference sustaining values and practices and providing the crucial idiom and grammar of cultural reproduction of communities and individuals. When one looks closer at the organization of community life, it is not uncommon to find mosques, cultural and community centres or welfare associations that are ethnically defined and often treated as a particular ethnic or sect group 'property'. In Britain, for example, studies of Muslim associational life have documented the ties between mosques or community associations and institutions or governments in the countries of origin of Muslim populations, as the cases of Kashmiri and Bangladeshi Muslim communities (Lewis 2002; Werbner 2002) indicate, while, in Germany, Schiffauer (1999a) has drawn attention to the links between German Muslim organizations and Turkish political parties and their political agendas.

In such instances Islam is articulated with ethnicity in a variety of ways, some of which we will explore later on, in Chapter 6. What is more, it should be noted that the idiom of ethnicity has often been used by at least some European Muslims in the context of their institutional representation vis-à-vis the authorities and as part of their broader collective action repertoires: where ethnicity, or nationality for that matter, represents a resource or a particular means of accessing financial, political and symbolic resources, Muslim communities have on occasion tapped into it by adapting their self-representation and identification strategies and practices to reflect this.[1] Conversely, European governments have often found in the idiom of ethnicity a useful and preferable tool for their interaction with, and administration of Muslim populations and have addressed them as such.[2]

To add to this, localism and other affinities and relationships imported from the countries of origin of many of Europe's Muslims also contribute to subtle, often hard-to-detect fissures and divisions as local and kinship networks have been found to be reconstituted in the diaspora (Baumann 1996). The further complications that divisions along the line of sects, schools of thought, or styles of worship – Sunni, Shia, and Wahabbi, Salafi, Sufi, Barelwi, Deobandi – introduce, make clear that any reference to European Muslims and/or Islam has to be carefully qualified.[3] Indeed, if one looks again at mosques, these are, or have been, associated with particular sects and schools of thought (often replicating the situation in the countries of origin of the communities in question, while Muslim cultural centres bringing together people from particular localities or even tribal or kinship groups (Baumann 1996: 122–126)). To add to this, everyday life, basic contexts of sociability such as clubs, coffee or tea houses, or even local markets are often organized on the basis of the same principle of ethnic or local affinities and assumed commonalities. As Metcalf points out:

> Islamic practice and behavior take place largely in milieux defined by language, ethnicity, and sect. Indo-Pakistanis meet in one another's homes to sing, recite, and pray. North African and West African workers in France tend to interact separately; mosques are often ethnically defined. A metaphor for such difference is the design of the mosque in Lorraine... which explicitly joins North

African and Turkish motifs (New York Times, 29 November 1990). This at once underlines the fact that there are two distinctive communities involved, but that, in this context, they unite as 'Muslim'.

(Metcalfe 1996)

Among those Muslims who migrated to Europe, another not negligible factor of differentiation relates to the 'routes' of migrations they have followed to reach localities of settlement. Whereas it is true that ethnicity may generate common experiences, memories and repertoires of action, it is equally important to acknowledge that the particular reasons that prompted the migration of individuals or groups (asylum, other forms of forced migration, economic need) and the actual routes followed (legal, illegal, etc) can give rise to distinct experiences that cannot simply be reduced to ethnic identity/provenance alone and can often give rise to fissures and distinct outlooks within particular ethnic groups.

Class differences among Europe's Muslims are also significant as are issues pertaining to the differential access to educational and employment opportunities. Clearly, the experience of being a Muslim in the *banlieues* of Paris or the working-class estate of Malmö's Rosengård, deprived of opportunities of social mobility and access to work is quite different from that of a Muslim professional who lives in a more affluent middle-class suburb of West London, or in the centre of Frankfurt. Indeed, our sample represents a population with a variety of socio-economic and educational backgrounds and, by extension, experiences and life chances.

What is more, as Werbner points out in her study of Manchester Muslims, gender and generation activate different performative spaces and contribute to differential empowerment and identification processes (2002: 217–230). Indeed, different perspectives on social hierarchies, authority structures, ingroup and outgroup relationships as well as on the meaning and importance of Islam are coloured by gender and the different generational experiences of Muslims in Europe and this obviously affects the action repertoires available to or preferred by them.

More specifically, the gendering of Muslim experience in Europe is hard to ignore as, apart from the different perspective that gender in itself brings to daily life, the context of European, more or less secularized, societies brings additional challenges. For example, as the various headscarf and *burqa* debates demonstrate, apart for having to negotiate through the maze of patriarchy within Muslim communities, Muslim women have often to confront an inimical state that selectively targets them and victimizes them by effectively turning them into 'battlefields' on which it launches assaults against the difference and 'backwardness' of Muslim cultures by introducing stigma, prohibitions, sanctions and forcing them to make choices that may subject them to further stigma or communal sanctions. Throughout the 1990s, for example, the exposure of French female high school students to the effective prohibition of the headscarf by some school councils meant that a relatively small, though not negligible, number of young female students faced what amounted to a de facto exclusion from the right to education and the potential opportunities opened up by it. What is more, it forced them to make a choice that could put them at the centre of a confrontation between those forces within French Muslim communities that advocate the wearing of the scarf on the grounds of the value of modesty, or for other reasons, and a secular state schooling system. In such a highly polarized situation, young women often found themselves unable to articulate their own views about the importance and meaning of the headscarf, or on education, or about the experience of attending school without what might or might not be a significant element of their belief system or identity.

Similarly, the withdrawal of translator services for 'immigrants who do not want to learn English'[4] currently debated in the United Kingdom, has the potential of trapping women in the confines of a domestic sphere circumscribed by the power of patriarchy, isolating and leaving them voiceless and helpless. Whereas the availability of interpreters could provide a lifeline for women who might otherwise be facing isolation and invisibility, the assumption that Muslim women, because of being Muslim, do not want to learn English and, therefore should not be a burden on public resources is highly likely to lead to the withdrawal of their last communication channel to vital services. On such occasions, Muslim women can experience a profound aporia as they become the object of contestation and of demands from family, community and the state.[5] Despite their potential vulnerability, they become easy targets for both islamophobic campaigns and Muslim responses to these and are subjected to more intense scrutiny and state regulation than Muslim men. These are admittedly extreme cases that, nevertheless, expose some aspects of the distinct challenges, experiences and life chances associated with gender. It is clear that, in such contexts, men and women experience 'being a Muslim' in markedly different ways and develop distinct responses to the way they are defined and addressed.

Generational differences and rifts also generate diverse perspectives and experiences, and make an important contribution in shaping distinct outlooks towards life, coexistence, or, as we are going to see later on, interpretations of religion and authority, especially as first-generation Muslim immigrants and their second- and third-generation offspring in Europe obviously face particular, but often distinct, problems and challenges with regard to their integration in the host society. Indeed, younger generations draw upon different raw materials and experiences in the process of constructing identities and solidarities, making sense of their environment and interacting with others in comparison to their parents as we will later see. Whereas the former were most often migrants born and socialized in a country of origin outside Europe, the latter have mainly been born and educated in Europe and develop their own sense of belonging that defines Europe as their home (Cesari 1999), albeit a home that largely denies them a place in it and resists the creation of spaces of belonging as we have already seen.

And then, one needs to take into account the many facets and degrees of Muslim affiliation and religiosity. A multitude of radical and fundamentalist Muslims of different hues share and lay a stake on this polyphonic universe together with more moderate voices, the devout meet the less religious or even 'secular' Muslims as our research reveals, or the cultural Muslims according to Dassetto[6] in a variety of everyday, vernacular and more formal or official contexts. Faith finds itself alongside a more diffuse sense of cultural heritage or of political exigency or ideology in the face of adversity and prejudice, and all these factors give rise to a complex constellation of attitudes, motivations and practices that contest, redefine and make what we call European Islam and Muslims.

It is also undeniable that there are occasions in which European Muslim communities have developed strong local cultures which are based on solidarity and local pride and constitute responses to local conditions of life. Everyday life largely unfolds within particular localities and local spaces are invested with the meaning produced by their inhabitants, and as we will discuss in more detail in the next chapter, this is true for European Muslims. Locality acquires even more importance in the case of Muslim communities as there tend to be clusters of Muslim settlement throughout Europe where daily experience may be inflected with the experience of being Muslim. Thus the city of Bradford, or areas of the East End of London or Glasgow, or the cities of Antwerp, Lyon, Grenoble and Berlin, are clear examples of such, often rich and internally diverse Muslim local cultures which provide a sense of solidarity and a source of pride and identity for their inhabitants. Indeed, as both our research and research conducted by others (e.g. Open Society Institute 2010; Schmidt 2012) indicate, local identities are very strong among European Muslims who feel more *Berliner* than Germans, more *Londoners* than English and more *Parisiens* and *Parisiennes* than French.

But as Europe comprises a rich array of different polities and civil societies, each one of which has developed over time distinct institutional and cultural responses to diversity, minorities and religion, it is not surprising to encounter a complex mosaic of Muslim strategies, responses and attitudes towards different European policy frameworks. Corporatist or statist or more liberal political cultures and policies not only affect Muslims' lives by introducing particular rights and obligations, expectations, opportunities and constraints but often play a role in shaping the ways in which Muslims will engage in associational life and develop representation strategies and practices. The vast array of responses to difference, ranging from the assimilationism or integrationism, traditionally, though not entirely accurately, linked to the French republican model, to the different ways multiculturalism is understood and practiced in countries such as the United Kingdom or Sweden, or consociationalism as practiced in the Netherlands, Belgium or Northern Ireland have also informed the ways in which European Muslims have been responding to the institutional and cultural frameworks that they encounter in their everyday lives. The varying degrees of institutionalization of secularism in different European societies, or of recognition of official or state religions have given rise to different opportunity structures for the organization and self-expression of European Muslims.

To add to this the complexity of experiences that inform the organization, self-identification and collective action of European Muslims, one cannot overlook the variable relations and lines of communication between countries of origin and 'their diasporas'. Whether seen as valuable resources for states of origin, or a threat to their security, 'homelands' develop complex institutional apparata to generate valuable flows of money and investment from Europe to them, to mobilize political support and to monitor and, occasionally, discipline potential critics and political 'deviants'. Various governments of 'Muslim' countries are often involved in attempts to promote national identifications or particular versions of Islam, or even suppress Muslim activism, depending on their particular interests at a given time. Turkish government involvement in the religious and associational life of Turks in western Europe has, for example, in the past sought to keep under control the spread of religious movements such as Millî Görüş that were seen as a threat to the country's secular system and tutelary democracy.

In addition to 'concerned' or 'interested homelands', third countries, such as Saudi Arabia or Iran, also utilize Islam as a powerful weapon that allows them to gain the allegiance and support of European Muslim constituencies and spread particular versions of religious and state ideology. The long-standing division of French Muslim associations and mosques into those affiliated to the Paris Mosque, which is in turn financed and controlled by the Algerian government, and those associated to the FNMF (*Fédération Nationale des Musulmans de France*), which is largely controlled by Morocco, is a prime example of how 'homelands' of Muslim populations may have agendas that extend beyond their 'own' diasporas, into the broader European Muslim populations. Indeed, such is the degree of this involvement of countries of origin and other third countries in the affairs of Muslim communities in Europe that some commentators suggest that an end to it would be tantamount to the achievement of emancipation for those affected by such interventions (Ramadan 2000).

Finally, another important, though less studied, dimension of Muslim experience in Europe relates to the considerable variety of state-sponsored versions of Islam advanced or encouraged by different governments and state apparatuses in Europe as documented in

Blommaert and Verschueren's study of Belgian institutions and their approach to Islam (1992) but also indicated in the various attempts of European governments to influence or control the training of European imams and regulate the activities of mosques. And as Roy points out, there is a tendency in Europe for governments to 'push for some sort of "official Islam" (for example, the Conseil Français du Culte Musulman)' (2004: 95). Needless to say that such intervention often has a divisive impact among Muslims as it affects existing authority and community and solidarity structures and associational life.

In view of this astonishing diversity of inflections, variants and nuances of Muslim lives and experiences in Europe, it is not surprising that any attempt to explore the meaning of the term *European Muslims*, or to talk about *European Islam*, almost certainly entails venturing in a conceptual and theoretical, as well as political, minefield. During such an endeavour one has to navigate through the murky waters of political wrangling inspired by different agendas among various community activists, policymakers and politicians and an academic debate that, with a few notable exceptions, has yet to come, or is just coming to terms with the significance – local and transnational – of the presence of Muslims and Islam in Europe.

Perspectives

If one looks at the development of academic interest in Islam in Europe and the lives of European Muslims it becomes immediately obvious that the past decade has witnessed a veritable boom in research and publications. Before this period, published work on Islam in Europe took the form of collections of essays, quite often bringing together the work of researchers with no unified agendas or the proceedings of conferences. Although many of these constitute most useful contributions to better understanding a largely uncharted territory, they often lack the focus that is needed in order to approach the phenomenon rigorously and comprehensively.[7] By the mid-1990s, the field of research had acquired more discernible contours and directions and this was increasingly reflected in the publication of more sharply focused and systematic attempts to explore European Islam and European Muslim communities (Abumalham 1995; Antes and Hewer 1994; Bistolfi and Zabbal 1995; Lewis and Schnapper 1994; Maréchal 2002; Metcalfe 1996;

Nielsen 1995 and 1999; Nonneman et al. 1996; Vertovec and Peach 1997).[8]

From then on, publications primarily focused on either broad overviews of the phenomenon of Islam in Europe (Nielsen 1999, 2004) or even the exploration of the possibility of the emergence of a particular variant, European Islam, emerging in organizational, ideological and cultural terms (Alsayyad and Castells 2002; Amiraux 1997; Dassetto 1996, 2000; Douwes 2001; Ramadan 1999). In addition, research focused on gender and youth cultures (Vertovec and Rogers 1998) and the politics of urban planning and the building of mosques and the negotiation of the functionality and semiology of space involved in these processes (Allievi 2009). Very interesting comparative work is also contained in Allievi's examination of the phenomenon of conversion (Allievi 1999a, 1999b, 1999c).

But sifting through the vast literature, it is evident that there is no consensus on what is meant by *European Muslims* or *European Islam*. In addition, we would argue that most of the literature attempting to explore aspects of the presence of Muslims or of Islam in European societies in both the media and the academia does not cast a critical look on the use of these terms and does not do justice to the complexity of these phenomena. These are important questions that need to be addressed as they have conceptual, methodological as well as practical, policy-related implications.

The first point of contention relates to the use of the adjective *European*. The various contributions to the debate adopt highly diverse positions. Some do not employ the term explicitly or use it in a merely descriptive way, merely as a tag of convenience to refer to Muslims living in Europe. It is not often clear whether one is talking about *European* Muslims or European *Muslims*. Shifts in emphasis might give rise to considerably diverse lines of reasoning and paths of investigation. Does stressing the 'Europeanness' of Europe's Muslims imply the success of processes of integration or even assimilation, or could it refer to the cross-fertilization of the respective cultures and identities? And, does muting the importance of *Europe* in the combination of these two terms suggest an assumption that, apart from the geographical coincidence the coming together of these terms denotes, Europe and Islam, or Europe and the cultures of its Muslim populations run on parallel and non-intersecting tracks? Or, in other words, is the presence of a large Muslim population in Europe significant insofar as the make-up of European as well as of Muslim cultures and identities are concerned, or is it inconsequential, accidental and unimportant? And, finally, does the usage of both terms together indicate primarily geographical realities (i.e. that Europe is the home of 10–16 million Muslims, depending on the different calculations available) or does it connote a dimension of membership, citizenship or identity? These questions are addressed in a variety of ways, not only by academics alone, but also by activists and politicians as both the academic and public debates on the relationship between Islam and Europe are in full swing.

Counting and naming

Attempts to determine the number of Muslims in Europe have almost invariably been intertwined with implicit definitions of who they are. This should come as no surprise as 'counting' presupposes an 'object', a 'reality' to be counted and made sense of. Indeed, the various methodologies of 'counting' are inextricably linked with discourses that, at the end of the day, circumscribe or demarcate the very object of the 'counting' exercise, give it shape and substance. Enumeration of Muslims as members of religious or cultural associations, as worshipers or believers or as people who share a particular heritage or culture, is part and parcel of particular economies of knowledge and power as it also 'talks' about Muslims and advances particular understandings of what it means to be a Muslim before the very act of counting. What is more, any counting exercise is inextricably linked with particular objectives; this is obvious in the case of census data which are used by state agencies in order to administer populations, to adjust electoral and political representation maps, to plan public services but also to facilitate population surveillance and monitoring and to support state revenue-generation policies.[9] It is with this premise in mind that we will focus on the different ways in which researchers, institutions and agencies have attempted to calculate Europe's Muslim populations and the assumptions underlying them.

European governments, governmental agencies and intergovernmental organizations have opted to approach and engage with Muslim minorities in a variety of ways. Occasionally they have done so by stressing the ethnic divisions among them[10]; at times their preferred policies have revolved around emphasizing their common Muslim backgrounds and purported faith[11]; sometimes they sought to address issues related to the presence of Muslim minorities by tending to ignore their ethnic, religious or cultural specificity, usually, though not exclusively, under the guise of secularism.[12] Given the complexity and diversity of European governmental approaches to Islam and their Muslim populations, our understanding of who is a European Muslim, as well as how many Muslims there are in Europe, is the product of a notoriously imprecise science. Censuses across the continent have almost invariably failed to give us any clear information regarding the religious/cultural affiliations of European populations as the problems identified in Chapter 2 are inherent in their planning and execution.[13]

Indications of the potential size of Europe's Muslim population have often been extrapolated from information on the origins of census respondents[14] although obviously such methodologies do not take into account processes of subjective identification or the fact that a not negligible part of Europe's Muslim population has been born in a European country either coming from a migrant background or belonging to increasing numbers of converts. In most of these cases, it could be argued that the discourse on the Muslim communities and networks in Europe is framed in such a way that the emphasis is placed not on their potential Europeanness, the ways in which these may be rooted and participating in European societies, but on their being associated with *Islam* and processes of *immigration*. At policy level, these discourses are prevalent as often in the absence of census data, the Muslim population estimates are premised on calculations of, and extrapolations from the number of migrants from countries where Islam is the predominant religion. In this context, voices have emerged against government and other efforts to map Muslim populations in this way. Some suggest that the collection of statistical information on migrants in general, including those relating to the European Muslim population in particular – their deficiencies identified in the previous chapter notwithstanding – is producing an atmosphere of polarization that essentially reduces immigrants to the status of the outsider and contributes to their exclusion and isolation (Gunner 1999). In the case of European Muslims, this is more so as the relationship between immigration and Islam is not as straightforward as the statistical data produced would have us believe. Indeed as pointed out above, a small but increasing number of Europe's Muslims are not the descendants of migrants but converts to Islam. What is more the establishment of a link between immigration and Islam is ideologically biased; by identifying Islam and Muslims as immigrants, essentially foreign to the societies in which they have taken roots,[15] it externalizes Islam and Muslims from the body politic and everyday cultures of European societies. In many ways, such discourses need to be examined in the light of the impact the complex nexus of Orientalism, imperialism and decolonization, discussed in more detail in Chapter 1, has had on the contemporary debates on Europeanness and European identity.

Alternative attempts to define European Muslims have been premised on arguments drawing upon what one could call associationist principles. In the debate on who is a Muslim in Sweden for example, it has been argued that it can be reasonably assumed that Muslims are only, or perhaps mainly, those individuals who join Muslim associations since participating in such associations constitutes a visible expression of one's free will to be counted as such and the realization of the freedom to be a Muslim (cf. Gunner 1999). One of the major advantages of such approaches is undeniably the fact that it draws attention on an aspect of the expressive repertoire of individuals in the sense that it focuses on an act that constitutes an instance of self-definition.

But here too, similar objections against efforts to determine who is a Muslim as in the case of the use of government censuses have also emerged. Additionally, one might argue that such practices are restrictive as they conflate Muslim identity with participation into particular, formal institutions. Despite the fact that this may give us confirmation of the self-identification of those who are members of such associations, it does not offer us any clue as to the self-identification of many others, say members of the families of participants in these institutions (especially female or others who might be primarily confined to the domestic sphere), or those who may feel alienated by the domain of formal, public institutions and could possibly prefer to express and formulate their identity in the context of much more flexible spaces that such analyses might not take into account. Such methodology of identification and definition of European Muslims does not take into account, as our research has revealed (see Chapter 4 onwards), the potential effect of alienation towards such institutions and their politics, fear towards and withdrawal from mainstream public spaces especially, though not exclusively, after the events of New York in September 2001, Madrid in March 2005, London in July 2005 but also the numerous terrorist incidents in France during the past decade. In addition, membership might be the result of complex motivations that might include the hope of access to government funding and support, the provision of facilities and vital support (translation, mediation) and not so much an expression of one's free will to be counted as a Muslim and the realization of the freedom to be a Muslim as the argument cited in Gunner above postulates.

In other instances, the terms *Muslim* or *Islam* are usually considered to relate or to refer to religious phenomena, such as the followers of a religion, a faith and its spiritual, moral, normative and institutional dimensions, or, more frequently, are not scrutinized and are used fairly loosely and descriptively to denote the part of the European population that, as in the attempts to demarcate statistically European Muslims discussed earlier, has its origin in the greater Middle East and other parts of the Muslim world.

Focusing on religiosity and religious practice, one way of thinking about Muslim communities in Europe is by exploring the extent to which, and the way they organize the 'everyday' according to Islam – seen as a system of norms and values providing direction for this. According to this view, wherever Muslims, both in the Muslim world and in the diaspora, may be and whenever they live, they will constantly strive to arrange their lives in accordance with this normative system as much as possible, because Islam prescribes an array of appropriate behaviours. It is hardly surprising that the adherents of this formalistic view of Islam are primarily concerned with the formal aspects of religion. However, such perspectives are susceptible to criticism for a number of reasons: we would suggest that their underlying conceptualization of Islam is limited and inflexible and, accordingly, deterministic, ahistorical and largely isolated from its social context.

Indeed, 'religiosity' has proved to be a quite difficult concept to define and therefore unreliable as the core of identification of European Muslims. Studies attempting to 'measure' Muslim religiosity have relied on various different methodologies, have been premised on different questions and working hypotheses and have yielded markedly different results. Focusing on French Muslims, Tribalat concluded back in 1996 that approximately 60 per cent of Muslim men and 70 per cent of women, while engaging in practices which would normally be associated with religiosity such as fasting during the month of Ramadan, not eating pork and not drinking alcohol, are not observant. In this context, she argues that maintaining what she calls 'cultural attachments' to Islam does not constitute evidence of being a practising Muslim (Tribalat 1996). A study of Turkish migrants in Nordrhein-Westphalia (Sauer and Goldberg 2001) found that 40 per cent were not, or a little religious, while 49 per cent described themselves as religious and 9 per cent as very religious. In contrast, a study of Dutch migrants of Turkish and Moroccan origin has concluded that 88 per cent of the former and 98 per cent of the latter define themselves as believers (Maliepaard and Phalet 2012). These differences indicate that in the absence of an 'objective' and 'reliable' criterion of religiosity this line of investigation may be marred with pitfalls.

Within the Muslim communities themselves, activists and leaders stress the element of religious attendance and practice, as their agenda reflects a preoccupation with building and representing a religious community. Thus, in the writings of leading Muslim commentators on Islam such as Tariq Ramadan and, even more so in the interventions of religious figures or activists, Islam is consistently considered to be a faith and European Muslims are represented as those who follow this faith and live in European societies. Ramadan for example argues that 35 per cent of the total Muslim population could be considered religious in a fairly exclusive sense of term – that is on the basis of the frequency of visiting prayer halls/mosques – while an additional 18.5 per cent of less frequent worshippers (i.e. a total 53.5 per cent) could be said to be religious (Ramadan 2001). Clearly, the motivation behind such estimates is related to Ramadan's own project of reinvigorating an integrated religious community in Europe and his ensuing agenda of engaging with European Muslims as a faith community. From markedly different quarters, but in a similar vein, research such as Åke Sander's study of Swedish Muslims has also been quite unequivocal in its linkage between religious practice and the designation of 'European Muslim' and has thus been preoccupied with determining the extent of religiosity among European Muslims (Sander 1993, 1997, 2004). Despite the usefulness of this methodology, and practical considerations notwithstanding, focusing on the numbers of Muslims or even of those who regularly participate in Muslim associational life (and are probably registered members of mosques or community organizations) might not be sufficient for determining who is a Muslim. For a start, Islam does not require attendance of a mosque as prayers and worship can be conducted in a variety of mundane contexts. What is more, participation in a community's associational life can take informal expressions that may not easily be detectable from official membership records.

On the other hand, some Muslim associations and activists such as the Muslim Council of Britain adopt a diametrically different claim that seeks to be as inclusive as possible. They effectively argue that everyone coming from a Muslim background is a Muslim and should be counted as such. Such eagerness to see tentative or even non-existent associations with Islam as a sufficient basis for identification, partly at least, reflect a practical and pragmatic recognition of the power of numbers in the pursuit of cultural, political and material demands vis-à-vis the state and in the context of competition with other stakeholders for scarce symbolic and material resources.

In both such cases, it is clear that political and practical considerations give rise to either too exclusive and restrictive, or too broad and inclusive definitions and understandings of *Islam* and *Muslims*. As we have already argued, exclusive definitions associated with the *formal* and public display of adherence to Islam are useful but also potentially misleading as they do not focus on the diversity of ways in which Islam is made sense of, internalized and practised. On the other hand, broad definitions end up in the formulation of unfocused concepts that may have little critical value and little or no use in policymaking, advocacy as well as in theoretical and conceptual analysis.

Attempting to offer a flexible, yet workable solution to this conceptual conundrum, Sander, in one of his later studies (2004: 213–218), suggests what essentially amounts to a multilayered definition, comprising and organizing most of the key aspects of the definitions one encounters in the debate. Sander is distinguishing between four main dimensions: an *ethnic*, wide definition, a somewhat narrower *cultural* definition, an even narrower *religious* definition and, last, and narrowest, a *political* definition. According to this schema, an *ethnic Muslim* is anyone born in an environment dominated by a Muslim tradition, belonging to a Muslim people, of Muslim origin, with a name that belongs in a Muslim tradition and/or who identifies her/himself with, or considers her/himself to belong to this environment and tradition. This definition is quite broad and independent of cultural competence, attitudes towards Islam as a cultural, political or religious system and its various representatives and leaders, religious beliefs and whether or not the individual actively practices Islam as a religious system and attempts to reflect the multidimensionality of Muslim experience in Europe that had largely been neglected in similar earlier but also contemporary exercises.

A *cultural Muslim* is anyone who is socialized into, and has to some extent internalized, the Muslim cultural tradition – the Muslim 'cognitive universe' to borrow from Berger and Luckmann's phrase – and who has relevant cultural competence. In this sense someone is a Muslim if the *Islamic cognitive universe* functions as her/his frame of reference (1971: 213–218) and is central in the construction of meaning. Being a *cultural Muslim* does not imply homogeneity in terms of identity, values or repertoire of social action as *cultural Muslims* can have diverse norm and value systems, political opinions, attitudes towards Islam as a religion and very different degrees as well as ways of practising religion from one another. But, and this is what is important, they all have a certain common knowledge, in the wide sense of the term, they share a *common universe of discourse* or *structure of feeling*. Stated differently, they understand each other, and they relate to shared narratives, memories and experiences.

The narrower category of *religious Muslim* refers to the possession of specific beliefs, participation in worship and other religious practices, personal piety and other elements of personal lifestyle or, in other words, depends on one's degree of religiosity. Finally, a Muslim in the *political* sense essentially, according to Sander, refers to the degree of politicization of religion that one accepts. if one has specific ideas about the place, role and function of Islam in society, that is, if one claims that Islam (in its various manifestations such as doctrine, the idea of the *Ummah* informs or dominate politics or sees Islam as a total way of life for the individual as well as for society at large cf. Choueiri 1990; Esposito 1992, 1997; Esposito and Voll 2001).

The definition that, explicitly or implicitly, is the most commonly used in the compilation of statistical data about the number of Muslims in a particular country relates to Sander's ethnic definition, as this is easy to operationalize and can serve as a practical guide to one's research. Nevertheless, for all the practical advantages this definition

presents us with, it is admittedly laden with an inbuilt bias as it asso-
ciates Islam and Muslims with migrancy and migrants respectively
and therefore implicitly sees Islam as something foreign to western
European societies and considers it identifiable on the very basis of
this foreignness. Indeed, Sander explicitly refers to this foreignness as
he discusses the practical problems of researching Islam in Sweden:

> When trying to answer this question we face the empirical prob-
> lem just mentioned: how to find what we want to count when
> the only available statistics are based on nationality, which, for at
> least some national groups, admittedly is a poor indicator of which
> religious tradition people from there belong to, even in the ethnic
> sense? Here the only feasible method – given a reasonable amount
> of money and work – we can see is to start out from the number
> of people with foreign backgrounds from countries we know have
> sizable Muslim populations and adjust that with what we know
> from other sources about these countries, their populations, the
> structure of immigration from the various countries, etc. The obvi-
> ous fact that this procedure of estimating the number of Muslims
> in Sweden is open to criticism in many respects and that its results
> will be afflicted with a considerable uncertainty and a large margin
> of error – the populations in most countries are, just to mention
> one problem, made up of several different ethnic and religious
> groups – is something we have to put up with, at least until we
> find an alternative procedure that is feasible and practicable.
>
> (Sander 2004: 215)

The practical problems of such a definition also relate to the fact
that it overlooks one large constituency of European Muslims that
we and others have identified in our research (also see Cesari 2003),
notably the convert Muslim population that defies this type of ethnic identification and for which, admittedly, there are not sufficient
statistical data. If, or rather, to the extent to which the findings of
our research can give an indication of trends within European Islam,
there is no doubt that this is a trend that has eluded statisticians and
social scientists for a long time and needs to be addressed.

The definition of *religious Muslim* that Sander proposes seems to
be going a long way towards addressing this problem as converts
are almost by definition adopting a religious and moral system and

way of life. According to this categorization a Muslim in the religious sense is anyone who fulfils a set of criteria set by Muslim religious leaders and adapted by social scientists (cf. Mandaville 2002; Sander 2004). Religious Muslim, according to Sander thus is whoever:

> (i) accepts (claims to accept) the words of the Islamic declaration of faith (the *shahadah*) that there is no God but Allah and that Mohammed is his ultimate messenger, (ii) believes and has faith in Allah as the highest authority, (iii) believes and have faith in his Angels, his books, his prophets, the day of judgment and the final resurrection and, as a consequence of (i – iii,) (iv) claims to have as her/his, at least long term, goal in life to try, to the best of her/his ability, to realize the commands and intentions of the Qur'an and the example of Mohammed (the *sunna*) (as (s)he understands it) in her/his life, and (v) that because (s)he, independently of how (s)he at the moment *de facto* is living his/her life right now, seriously believes (claims to believe) that it is a life in accordance with the Qur'an, etc., as (s)he understands it, that constitutes the meaningful, the right, the good, the correct or the most valuable life. Included in this goal in life should be, among other things, that (s)he, to the best of her/his ability, shall perform the daily prayers (*salat*), visit the mosque with reasonable regularity, fast (*sawm*) during Ramadan, perform the pilgrimage (*Hajj*) and follow the basic rules of Islam in matters of food, dress, ethics, family relations, etiquette and so on as (s)he understands them.
>
> (Sander 1993)

Such a detailed and prescriptive definition combines both attitudinal and behavioural aspects and can provide a reasonable basis for calculating the religious population that participates in worship in the ways outlined above. Thus, Sander et al. concluded in a study, using both survey questionnaires and counts of visitors to local mosques and prayer-halls in the early 1990s (Sander 1993) that 40–50 per cent of the ethnic Muslims in Sweden could reasonably be considered to be religious. Sander commenting on the situation in Sweden (2004: 213–218) argues that given what the researcher knows about changes in the Muslim population since then – for example, that Iranian Muslims, then the largest and by far the least religious group, at the time of writing made up a smaller part of the total Muslim population, and that Muslims from some of the 'newer' groups, such as those from Bosnia-Herzegovina, Somalia and Ethiopia, manifest a relatively high adherence to Islam and Islamic practices – it seemed reasonable to conclude that the relative proportion of religious Muslims should (in 2004) not be less than in the early 1990s. We find this claim highly problematic as it is premised on a chain of arbitrary assumptions and shaky extrapolations. What is more, it is based on a very prescriptive and rigid understanding of religion and does not allow for processes of cultural change and transformation to feature anywhere in such a framework. Second, it uncritically lumps together diverse ethnic groups and, rather arbitrarily assumes that Bosnians and Somalis, for example, have a relatively high adherence to Islam and Islamic practices. As a matter of fact there is little, if at all, evidence to substantiate such a claim – to the contrary, Bosnians seem to display a considerable array of attitudes towards Islam, from the ultra-religious to the staunchly secular, with some identifying their self-designation (*Musliman* – Muslim) to their ethnic and often secular identity. In addition, there is a considerable difference between religious Muslims who simply adhere to the letter of the religious code of practice and those who are characterized by an intensity of religious feeling and this clearly poses serious challenges to the researcher who attempts to gauge aspirations, attitudes, the degree of inclusion or alienation of Muslims in Europe and a host of other issues. Such attempts are premised on a high degree of abstraction, simplification and distance from the actual lives and self-definitions of Muslims themselves.

Another special problem here relates to the second and subsequent generations of Muslims born and raised in European countries. How many of these can be considered, or consider themselves, Muslims in a religious sense, is difficult to establish. Indeed, from interviews Sander's team had with Muslim leaders among others, it did not seem that the percentage they consider to comprise the category of religious Muslims in a more qualified sense exceeds 15 per cent, if anything it is less. However, our research indicates that a substantial percentage of young Muslims identifies itself as 'Muslim', although not necessarily in the religious sense of the term. Although our sample is not statistically representative of Europe's Muslim population in a way that can allow us to provide the data that the use of probability sampling techniques might do, we think that we can identify trends that are developing. Out of a total 735 informants, 149 articulated definitions of being Muslim that emphasized 'culture', values, 'ways of doing things' in a way that echoes Dasetto's designation of part of Europe's population as 'cultural Muslims'. A further 82 have opted for what we could describe as a secular 'political' definition, that is, have described themselves and other Muslims as a primarily or exclusively racialized category, as the underdog, as victims of racism and islamophobia, but also as subjected to socio-economic and political discrimination – we chose to call these 'secular' Muslims in order to differentiate them from those who emphasize culture, or religion for that matter, as the premise of Muslim identity. Nevertheless, a not insignificant proportion of these would value Islam as a religion and, indeed, they would consider themselves religious albeit in ways that do not always meet the criteria set by Sander and others that are premised on mosque membership and religious attendance. The fact remains that such definitions of religiosity are rather prescriptive and rigid and thus are incapable to grasp the changing nature of Islam in general, and European Islam and Muslims in particular.

And, indeed, other sophisticated approaches stress the obvious diversity of Islamic religiosity and its visible markers by pointing out the importance of concentrating on the interaction between Muslim immigrants and their host societies. According to proponents of this approach, practising Muslims do not shape the development of Islamic religious communities in isolation, but through their interaction with the society around them which also influences the process. The final form, which Islam – in all its variants – assumes, is the result of the interaction, negotiation and conflict between all the different parties involved. In this context, the extent and ability of Muslims to engage in their self-definition, religious practice and to build up their own institutions is the by-product of political interactions in particular local or national contexts. While acknowledging the existence of a universal Islam (and also the dynamic character of the receiving society), these researchers focus on the emergence of *local Islams* in Europe (Rath et al. 1991).

A way forward?

The preceding discussion has demonstrated the polysemy of the terms *Islam* and *Muslim* and the existence of a multitude of hues of experience and practice that make up Muslim identities in Europe. But alongside this polyphony and diversity, trends of convergence, coexistence and closer interaction between Muslims from different backgrounds and from remote localities are slowly but unmistakably emerging. The signs of this convergence can be seen in a variety of contexts. Research on the de-ethnicization of mosques (Cesari and McLoughlin 2005; Maréchal et al. 2003), community initiatives and our own research have pointed out significant shifts in identification processes whereby Islam and 'Muslimness' are explicitly or implicitly 'claimed' by diverse groups with varied experiences and different perspectives and understandings of what it means to be a Muslim. And as early as in the late 1980s, referring to the search for non-ethnic forms of authenticity among young Muslims, Waardenburg (1988) also predicted a future 'Islam without ethnicity' in large part as a result of the heterogeneity produced by migration. Waardenburg documents this shift by pointing out the growing trend of discarding national or regional traditions and focusing upon the Qur'an and Sunna. The felt need to establish a distinction between truly 'Islamic' culture from other, 'secondary', ethnic traditions is, according to Schiffauer (1999), often what prompts young people in diaspora situations to join so-called fundamentalist movements. And as we will discuss later on in some detail, quite often, the shift detected in such studies consists of re-designating, or translating practices, hitherto linked to ethnic identity, as practices intrinsic to 'being Muslim'.

And, at another level, with a view to the translocal dynamics of contemporary Islam that overcome the potentially divisive power of locality, Mandaville points out (2001: 109) that for many Muslims there is a diasporic yearning beyond national geography not to return to the *Ummah* of Medina in the first half of the seventh century but to reconstruct Islam's very first journey, the *hijra*, the migration from ignorance (*jahiliya*) to unity in God (*tawhid*) to construct the *Ummah* and partake in the experience of being immersed in the feeling of membership, belonging and solidarity the latter conveys. What is effectively argued is that the traditional universalism of the Islamic belief system and of the *Ummah* is nowadays, in the context of increased connectivity that transportation and communication technologies bring about, coupled with the transnational and translocal dynamics that are emerging in the era of intensified globalization.

Regardless of whether people yearn for the reassurance and organic warmth of fundamentalist religious movements or the solidarity of a more diffuse identity based on broader understandings of Islam, to be sure, this is a long, painstaking process that relies largely on the construction of shared experiential frames that, as earlier work on diasporas (Tsagarousianou 2007) has demonstrated, provide a fertile ground for collective attempts to 'form new forms of association, articulate new grievances, construct new identities' (to use Hannigan's words 1991). In other words, we suggest that the reality of Muslim lives in Europe in all the complexity that our brief outline of the theoretical debate has revealed can best be glimpsed at through the adoption of an emphasis on collective action (as defined by Melucci 1995), that is the study of the complex process of construction of action systems, of the relevant cognitive definitions concerning the ends, means, and field of action and of the emotional investment (Moscovici 1981) necessary for the development of a sense of unity, empathy and solidarity; ultimately through focusing into the process of construction of a European Muslim collective identity.

This contour of our preferred definition,[16] it needs to be stressed, does not imply the development of uniform and coherent cognitive definitions about what it means to be a Muslim, or a Muslim in Europe. As Billig has so clearly demonstrated in his discussion of the imagination of nationhood (1995: 74–77), contradictory themes, definitions and understandings can coexist within the same experiential framework and context of continuous interaction and negotiation that makes possible, sustains and reproduces social action systems. Collective identity should therefore be approached bearing in mind that it constitutes 'work in progress', an interactive and shared definition produced by several individuals and groups that is continually negotiated, tested, modified and reconfirmed. Having said that, we do not advocate a definition that focuses on the creativity of groups and individuals but is oblivious to the various structural and institutional constraints to collective action and, in this particular case, to definitions of 'European Muslims'. Indeed, self-identification depends on social recognition, as the demarcation of the self (a collective actor) must be recognized by others who are defined as such through this very process. European Muslim identities, as we have already seen, are not constructed in a void following mere cost-benefit calculations and particular choices of action. Interaction with 'others' such as the broader societies and different groups, as well as with institutional frameworks opens up particular opportunity structures and plays a role in determining the breadth and content of the experiential horizons of Muslims in Europe. In addition, as Melucci (1996) points out, cost-benefit calculations themselves are also circumscribed, inflected and limited by emotional investments that constitute an important element of collective identity (also Aminzade and McAdam 2001). What is more, our emphasis on seeing collective identity as 'work in progress' does not imply lack of some sense of fixity of meaning. Indeed identity relies on a fine balancing act between a sense of continuity over and beyond variations in time on the one hand, and its various permutations and adaptations to external stimuli, the subtle underlying process of change inherent in it. And as Tsagarousianou points out (2007), the network of relationships that underpins and is, in turn, underpinned by the processes of interaction and negotiation that are central in the construction of collective identity is made up from an array of languages, communication channels, organizations, authority and leadership models and structures, narratives, experiences and memories.

It is therefore through these attempts to look for, and construct new shared contexts of experience, to produce new narratives, that this type of collective action, that definitions and self-perceptions of European Muslims emerge. In other words, European Muslims define themselves and their relationship to their environment – other social actors, the array of available resources, opportunities and obstacles – through processes of interaction, negotiation, opposition (cf. Melucci 1988). In a way, the forms of collective action which they initiate and carry out play a constitutive role vis-à-vis their identities. Their collective action, however mundane and everyday in character, provides the raw material which eventually shapes who they are, how they are defined and, obviously, it does so incessantly. We would therefore argue that although the various attempts to define European Muslims that we briefly examined earlier provide us with very useful insights, they nevertheless are partial as they do focus on particular aspects of European Muslim life and experience and most are rather prescriptive and therefore restrict our understanding of European Islam almost as much as they are advantageous in certain respects.

As Melucci (1995) aptly suggests:

> Collective identity enables social actors to act as unified and delimited subjects and to be in control of their own actions, but conversely they can act as collective bodies because they have achieved to some extent the constructive process of collective identity. In terms of the observed action, one may thus speak of collective identity as the ability of a collective actor to recognize the effects of its actions and to attribute these effects to itself. Thus defined, collective identity presupposes, first, a self-reflective ability of social actors.

In this context, it is in the field of practice and of interaction, that the diverse experiences of secular and religious, relative strangers from remote localities, or of different ethnic provenance are transformed through interaction, debate, contestation, shared practices, the expression of voice, into elements of shared experiential frameworks which, in turn, provide opportunities for further convergence and the formation of a sense of 'we'. To be clear, as we have pointed out, such processes do not entail the creation of a monolithic, homogeneous identity but contribute to the construction of shared definitions of the situation, action repertoires, and mutual recognition – implicit or explicit – as fellow Muslims.

With this in mind, we suggest that we adopt a more proactive approach that identifies domains or milieus of action that relate to Muslim activity in European societies where European Muslims are likely to be involved in and engaged in interaction with each other and society at large. These may include religious settings such as mosques or community centres, schools and training programmes, local or national or transnational movements involved in rights advocacy, citizenship and inclusion, anti-racist campaigns and, of course, localities and other similar settings where 'Islam' may be incorporated into the fabric of dailiness into even the most mundane aspect of everyday life. Instead of prescribing which modes of action or even thought and cognition and which value systems relate to a 'Muslim worldview and way of life' we need to trace the ways in which the latter emerge and claim to be part of a broader universe of discourse that can be called *Muslim*. And instead of imposing conceptual straightjackets in our analysis we might need to explore processes of self-definition and contestation of what it means to be *Muslim*, and a *European Muslim* for that matter. As Tilly suggests (2004: 78) it is important not to underestimate the importance of self-expression and collective experience as well as the contingency, plasticity, and wilful self-transformation of the identities deployed in collective action.

Following Hannigan's argument that the study of new forms of religious identification can be better explored and understood by drawing on social movement theory, we therefore propose to see European Islam as a broad social movement comprised by several concentric circles which represent different degrees of intensity of experience and practice, different degrees of consciousness identification and belief but which all contribute to the construction of a shared universe of discourse and debate and a sphere of interaction and contestation of sorts. The thread that provides some degree of coherence through this polyphonic and multifaceted universe and that provides a shared language for interaction lies in the process of formation of shared experiential frameworks, of common denominators that turn the diversity of the experiences of European Muslims intelligible and relevant to individuals and groups that would otherwise be 'relative strangers' or 'remote others'. As we will see later on, in this context, distinct *interpretive codes*, *traditions* and local experiences converge and are experienced as *equivalent*, part of a shared, common cultural stock.[17]

In addition, as European Muslims have had to develop appropriate responses to their, perceived, symbolic, and often physical, marginalization, within a highly polarized socio-cultural context, they have formed, over time, particular perceptions of themselves and of their place in European societies. Through the complexity and considerable diversity of the responses of our interviewees, we see emerging an overarching theme in their own self-representations: Our data suggest that Muslims in Europe have been constructing representations of themselves as victims of processes of systematic marginalization and discrimination. We have also pointed out that complementing this widespread view among them, is the overwhelming sense of Muslims throughout the world being subjected to various forms of political and economic injustice by Western states including the European countries they reside in or whose citizenship they have. This self-perception is particularly important as it introduces an explicit link between experiencing, or rather, forming perceptions of marginalization on the one hand, to identification as a 'Muslim' as opposed to particular class or ethnic identities, educational or other socio-economic characteristics on the other. This prevalent sense of injustice provides the raw material for the construction of what, following Gamson, we call injustice frames, that is, a particular lens through which the diverse category we can descriptively call 'European Muslims' view the public debates and practices that relate to them and affect them as such. In other words, these frames constitute a threshold beyond which the term *European Muslims* is no longer merely descriptive but acquires a meaning and significance for those it has been used to describe.

Methodological remarks

This volume largely relies on discussions with 735 informants. The discussions took mainly the form of group interviews (or focus groups) and a small number of individual interviews. Our respondents included 390 men and 345 women between the ages of 16 and 45 years, who described themselves as 'Muslim' or of 'Muslim background'. Of these interviewees, the majority (595) were residents or citizens of Belgium (90), France (130), Germany (115), Netherlands (90) and the United Kingdom (170). A further 145 interviews were conducted online with interviewees from other European countries, notably, Italy (20), Spain (15), Denmark (22), Norway (16), Sweden (22), Switzerland (20) and Austria (25).

The sampling design was intended to avoid replicating uniform and coherent cognitive definitions of what it means to be a 'European Muslim' and the related shortcomings of the previous methodologies discussed earlier on in this chapter. As our aim was to reflect and 'capture' the polysemy of the terms *Islam* and *Muslim* and the diverse experiences and practices that comprise Islam in Europe, using a combination of non-probability sampling techniques would have the potential of better capturing the internal diversity of experience and opinion we wanted to chart and analyse.

As Muslims in Europe tend to be concentrated primarily in cities we decided to focus on residents of conurbations in all the countries concerned. However, the diverse patterns of urban settlement, the distinct urban identities of the various potential focal areas for this research meant that, given the limitations of our research, any choice of cities was unavoidably to entail the exclusion of valuable and unique local experiences from areas that were not to be selected, a shortcoming unfortunately shared by other research projects that study the experiences of European Muslim urban life (cf. Open Society Foundation). Despite the lack of any satisfactory option, we decided to focus on a number of cities that, despite their obvious uniqueness and rich local cultures and identities, could provide a glimpse into the diversity of Muslim lives in Europe. Our choice was determined by a number of factors; (i) the location of considerable and, where possible, diverse Muslim populations in them, (ii) the vibrancy and polyphony of civic, religious and community life and (iii) the accessibility of organizations and informants.

The urban areas selected included London in the United Kingdom, Paris in France, Antwerp in Belgium, Amsterdam in the Netherlands and Frankfurt in Germany in an attempt to obtain a snapshot of a geographically spread population separated by national boundaries.

London

Although it is thought that the UK census data on London's Muslim population underestimates the latter's size, there is no doubt that Islam is London's largest and most significant minority religion. It is estimated that 40 per cent of England's Muslims live in London with particularly high concentrations in the east London boroughs of Newham, Tower Hamlets and Waltham Forest, but also Camden, Hackney and Harringey. The first Muslims to settle in London were sailors from Somalia and Yemen who arrived in the nineteenth century. However, the main waves of immigration followed the Second World War (also see Chapter 2), when many Muslims emigrated to the United Kingdom from Commonwealth countries and former colonies to provide labour for the needs of the rebuilding of the British economy and welfare state. Initially, many of Britain's Muslim migrants came from Pakistan – especially the Pakistani Punjab – and Kashmir as well as the Indian state of Gujarat.

This initial wave of immigration of 1950s and 1960s was followed by substantial numbers of migrants from the Sylhet region of Bangladesh and, later on, from a host of other countries in Africa and Asia. Amongst those from other countries, Muslims from Yemen, Somalia and Turkey have established large communities in London and further afield in the United Kingdom. Today, London's Muslims come from all over the world and they include a small but growing group of converts.

The establishment of Muslim communities in parts of London has, on occasion proved to be controversial, especially in localities where Muslim communities were perceived or represented as contenders for scarce resources. As a result, tensions have arisen in some localities. In the East End of London, the area around East Ham, Barking and Dagenham has experienced such tensions as non-Muslims have perceived the changing demographic makeup of the area as an indication of the Islamization of their localities, while the Muslim community has been gaining confidence and developing a rich associational life. These tensions were exploited by extremist forces in both communities. The British National Party attempted to capitalize from the situation and, after an alarmist and islamophobic campaign that represented local Muslims as invaders displacing the 'original' local population and usurping valuable and scarce resources, gained their highest vote nationwide, 16.9 per cent, in the 2005 General Election in Barking. Although the extreme Right has not sustained its electoral gains in the area in subsequent elections, the issues it has introduced into the public debate have not been effectively confronted – indeed sometimes they have been taken on board – by mainstream parties and thus constitute potent mobilizing factors. Muslim radicals also found in the area fertile ground for advancing divisive demands such as the initiative to turn the nearby borough of Waltham Forest into a 'sharia zone' in 2010 and 2011.[18] It is also in this context of the antagonism cultivated by extremists on both sides that recent conflicts on the erection of mosques in the area should be seen.[19]

Paris

Although it is difficult to obtain accurate data on the population of Muslim migrants and, even more so, the large numbers of their descendants from the French Census, an extrapolation of the available figures of immigrants from countries where Islam is widely practiced indicates that Paris is home to approximately 38 per cent of France's Muslim population (Leveau and Hunter 2002: 8). This includes Parisians originating in Algeria, Morocco, Tunisia and West Africa (part of France's former colonial sphere of influence) as well as from Turkey, Southeast Asia, the Middle East and other parts of sub-Saharan Africa. According to information from the Paris Grand Mosque, there are over 75 registered mosques and prayer areas in Paris but a substantial number of unofficial, often makeshift, halls of prayers representing a polyphonic universe of schools of thought, styles of worship and political affiliations. Paris is home to a number of Muslim organizations with lobbying and representation, charitable, intercultural as well as sectarian focus. The city's Muslim population is primarily concentrated in the north-east – remnants of urban regeneration projects gone wrong – and in some central *arrondisements* of Paris. This de facto geographical segregation of the city's Muslim population has been the source of considerable grievances and friction.

Mostly latent tensions due a feeling of marginalization prevalent among young French Muslims or of Muslim origin have often led to localized conflicts and given rise to a potentially explosive mix of highly politicized religion fuelled by perceptions of exclusion (Kepel 1987). In these microcosms of French Islam, one can note traditional forms of religiosity next to primarily political uses of Islam whereby the latter becomes an idiom of protest and contestation.

In October and November of 2005 the north-east of Paris experienced extensive riots after two male youths of North African origin, allegedly pursued by the police, were electrocuted in an electricity substation in the Parisian suburb of Clichy-sous-Bois. The events culminated in considerable destruction, arrests of hundreds of rioters and curfews in the affected areas and quickly spread to other urban centres throughout the country.

Antwerp

Although, just as in the case of France, official data on religion are not collected in Belgium so there are no accurate data on the size, demographical makeup and origins of Antwerp's Muslim population, researchers estimate there are around 500,000 Muslims in Belgium, with significant higher concentrations in major cities including Antwerp – one of the most diverse cities in Belgium and home to a large Muslim community originating primarily in Morocco and Turkey, with relatively more recent arrivals from Somalia, Southeast Asia and the Middle East.

The city's Muslim population has in the past effectively mobilized against the rise of the *Vlaams Blok* and *Vlaams Belang* far right neo-populism (Coffé 2005; Erik 2005) and has made considerable inroads in gaining high-profile representation in city and regional politics primarily through mainstream parties. Although the city has adopted a number of policies recognizing the increasing diversity of the local population and programmes aiming to improve the inclusion and participation of minorities, including its Muslim population, Antwerp has not been unaffected by the general unease over the assumed foreignness and incompatibility of Muslim cultures and minorities with Belgian culture and the xenophobia and islamophobia expressed by *Vlaams Belang* but also other more mainstream politicians. In recent years, the emphasis on 'integration' (*inburgering*) and secularism and the related implicit assumption of the 'foreignness' of the country's Muslim citizens, has led to tensions in the city. Proposed measures to ban municipal employees who are customarily in contact with the public from wearing Muslim headscarves and other religious or political symbols have also sparked controversy but were eventually found by the Antwerp court of appeal unlawful.

Amsterdam

The majority of Muslims in the Netherlands live in Amsterdam, and, according to some sources, comprise approximately 13 per cent of the city's total population (see, e.g., OSI 2007). According to the calculations of the Open Society Institute Monitoring and Advocacy Programme as of 2004, there were approximately 63,000 inhabitants of Moroccan descent, and 38,000 of Turkish descent – the two largest Muslim communities in Amsterdam – out of the city of Amsterdam's total population of 750,000. In addition, smaller but not negligible communities of Egyptians and South Asian Muslims call Amsterdam their home. To these figures, one should also add the city's Muslims of Surinamese origin although there is no information as to how many of the city's 71,000 Surinamese inhabitants (OSI 2007).

The religious needs of the city's Muslims are met in the numerous mosques of the region – according to our calculations, based on information provided by our interviewees, there are a total of 55 mosques and prayer rooms in the city and the surrounding region, some of which, as we shall see in Chapter 6, have mixed congregations in terms of ethnicity. Having said that, the existing mosques and cultural centres represent a vast range of cultural, ethnic and spiritual diversity characterizing Amsterdam's Muslim communities. Notable within this polyphony is Amsterdam's first women-only mosque which was opened in 2005. Its establishment had caused considerable controversy as it went against the grain of 'conventional practice' and the patriarchal culture that is prevalent among the Muslim communities of the city. As responsibility for the running of the mosque is undertaken by women, including the call to prayer and leading of prayers, its establishment was seen by some as heterodoxy and, more significantly, as a challenge to established authority. Rumours of the mosque being part of a government funded attempt to influence Muslim politics and boost more modern, 'liberal' versions of Islam palatable to the country's libertarian elites meant that this initiative has not made inroads in community life and has been seen with suspicion. On the other hand, advocates of its establishment represented it as a response to the spiritual needs of Muslim women, and as a space free of patriarchal values and power structures.

Muslim associational life in Amsterdam is rich and varied including cultural centres, schools, youth and women's organizations.

Frankfurt

Germany has the largest Muslim population in Western Europe after France. Approximately 3.0–3.5 million Muslims live in Germany, and 80 per cent of them do not have German citizenship; 608,000 are German citizens (Blaschke 2004). Seventy per cent of the Muslim population is of Turkish origin (Blaschke 2004: 78). Turkish immigration to Germany began in the 1960s in response to a German labour shortage as the country's economy was taking off after its reconstruction under the Marshall plan. To this effect, Germany devised the 'guestworker scheme' and signed agreements on labour recruitment with Turkey (1961). In 1973 the policy was stopped, as a direct result of the 'oil crisis' in Europe (Mehrländer 1978:116). This affected the legal routes which migrants were to take in subsequent years as family reunification and asylum provided the legal basis of entry for many migrants in Germany as well as the rest of western Europe. As 'guestworkers' were expected, upon the expiry of their contracts to return to their countries and families, successive governments were unprepared to recognize the sea change that immigration was bringing about in German society and did not plan for the integration of the country's large migrant population. As pointed out in Chapter 1, the number of Muslims in the country may be approaching 3.2 million of which close to 80 per cent do not have German citizenship. Indeed, the persistent denial of the German authorities and society to recognize the reality of migration and settlement has led to migrant activists and intellectuals to reclaim and use the term *guest* in ways challenging the status quo. Muslims settled around the industrial areas of Berlin, Cologne, Frankfurt, Stuttgart, Dortmund, Essen, Duisburg, Munich, Nurnberg, Darmstadt and Goppingen.

Frankfurt is a major centre of Muslim settlement with a rich associational life including community centres, mosques and prayer halls and charities for the region's Sunni, Alevi and Shi'a communities. Although associations and mosques are marked by ethnicity, sect, or even state and religious organization patronage – there are several mosques that are affiliated to the Turkish Government Religious Affairs Directorate (Diyanet) while others are linked to the Turkish Islamic Milli Görus movement. The city also hosts the World Islamic Council, a major non-Turkish organization supported by Saudi Arabia (Goldberg 2002) that restricts its membership to Sunni organizations only. Despite the ethnic and denominational divisions these organizations often work together and have developed shared strategies together with the city's smaller and less organized Bosniak community. Frankfurt is also home to several *ad hoc* and localized initiatives of Muslims independent of the official Muslim community organizational framework.

In search of Europe's Muslims

Taking our cue from Sander's distinction between *ethnic, cultural, religious* and *political* definitions, we therefore resorted to the use of multiple sampling frames relevant to these dimensions of experience. We did so by identifying a number of 'starting points' that could give us access to diverse fields of practice and interaction and enable us to compile a broad and diverse sample that would reflect the polyphonic universe of European Islam. These included mosques, prayer halls, religious associations, community centres with links or affiliations to countries or ethnic groups where Islam is practiced (including many that exclude Islam from their names or self-definitions), youth centres and projects in areas of high Muslim population concentration or in culturally diverse areas with substantial Muslim minorities, or organizations and initiatives against islamophobia or racism.

Potential informants were also located among university and college students with the help of student organizations that put us in touch with members with surnames that are commonly found in countries where Islam is practiced or through visits to student societies with interests in Islam or in the regions where Islam is practiced widely. The population sample that ensued, although not necessarily statistically representative of the Muslim population in the areas covered by our project, was considerably diverse in terms of ethnicity, provenance, socio-economic backgrounds, but also in terms of the intensity of religious belief and practice. What is more, it allowed us to access individuals that more traditional sample framing methods were likely to overlook as they did not necessarily 'fit' into established or widely held research preconceptions as to who is a Muslim and who is not.

In a similar vein, interview questions were also formulated in ways that avoided advancing or reproducing preconceived definitions of who is a Muslim and what Islam represents. Although our interviewees were informed about the subject of our research project at the outset, we felt that research questions should be open and flexible. Interview participants were given numerous alternative identification options as well as opportunities to define Islam or 'being a Muslim' during our discussions both in instances where they were explicitly asked to reflect on their identity, and when they were not directly asked to comment on it. For instance, discussions on current affairs, international politics or gender issues provided opportunities for interviewees to position themselves vis-à-vis Islam or relate to existing definitions of 'Muslimness' or articulate new ones. The interviews covered a variety of themes such as definitions of terms such as *home, Islam, Muslim*, the exploration of their religious feeling and attendance (or lack thereof), the importance of religion, experiences of discrimination, political engagement, media and cultural practices, as well as family, relationships, concerns and aspirations. Interviewees as well as group interview participants were allowed to elaborate on issues they found of particular importance. Both group and individual interviews were designed to generate rich data in the participants' own words and to allow us 'explore the categories which participants use to order their experiences' (Kitzinger 1994).

Discussions focused not only on perceptions and self-definition but also on aspects of collective action such as

i. how interviewees formulate cognitive frameworks concerning their goals, definitions of the situation, means of action (including not only high-profile political mobilization but also more mundane everyday activities that relate to their domestic environment, work, material, cultural and media consumption),

ii. how relationships with others – Muslims and non-Muslims alike – are formed and activated in various social contexts.

iii. how they situate their action in space and place and how their action contributes to the creation and maintenance of local, national and transnational experiential horizons.

iv. the various ways in which interviewees communicate and negotiate aspects of their identity and action as Muslims within particular fields or environments and, finally,

v. the emotional investments which enable interviewees and the broader populations they represent to recognize themselves in each other.

Finally, a combination of participant and non-participant observation in neighbourhoods, shops, mosques, cultural centres and associations prior to our interviews allowed us to gain insights into European Muslim lives, the use of space, or the structuring of dailiness, or of special occasions in the Muslim calendar.

4
Space, Place and Social Action: European Muslim Geographies

The construction of locality: Physical and mediated

If one tried to fashion a map capturing the loci in which European Muslim lives unfold, where European Muslims derive their experiences from, interact with each other and with 'others', engage in various forms of social action and reflect on and construct their identities, they would have to find ways of depicting and making sense of a fluid and continuously evolving, multifaceted and multidimensional terrain that conventional geography would have difficulty to describe. For European Muslim identities clearly derive strength, resilience and a sense of 'belonging' from the relative immediacy of the 'local' but are also very much 'at home' in the midst of complex, more mediated but still strong relationships established at the translocal and transnational fields. At the same time, both *the local* and *the translocal* constitute not only spaces of positive identification but also contexts for the construction and experience of adversity and alterity. These are spaces where European Muslims encounter each other, where their experiences and memory converge, where solidarities are forged, but also arenas of contestation and confrontation where a sense of *self* and *other* is formed and continually tested, confirmed or revised and set in context. In this chapter, we attempt to unravel and make sense of the nexus of physical and virtual spaces, networks and flows that makes up what we could describe as Muslim space in Europe.

Clearly, when asked what place they would call home, about two-thirds of our informants opted for their locality although the extent of this varied considerably, ranging from their neighbourhood, to their city and, occasionally, their region. Indeed the boundaries of home were often intermixed in their responses in a variety of ways. In larger, more impersonal, cities or in areas where the urban space is fragmented or city life segregated, such as in Paris and East London, the neighbourhood is more often than not seen as a place of safety, solidarity and intimacy.

Many younger, mainly male informants, see their neighbourhoods in terms of a safe 'territory', where friends – brothers (and in the case of women, sisters) was often the word used – can 'hang out' together, away from the rest of the urban space which they often describe as inimical and unsafe.

Speaking of his neighbourhood in the north-east of Paris, 17-year-old Noureddine, says characteristically:

> [Y]ou know you can count on your friends, and even people that you know very little.... [In other parts of Paris] you feel out of place. I think everyone is looking at me, telling me with their eyes I do not belong. The police stops you because you don't belong, you don't look right, in the shops they see you as a criminal and you can see they'd rather you left.

Noureddine is not particularly religious – indeed he says that he does not practice and that he has no particular problems with secularism – but he clearly identifies himself and his friends as 'Muslims' as does Ali, a 17-year-old east Londoner from Whitechapel, who distinguishes his neighbourhood from other parts of London which he considers dangerous.

> You hear about people being knifed all the time.... I grew up hearing about this... countless stories; I even knew a couple of people who managed to run away to safety. Racists are always trying to find you where you are alone, away from home. You know, here you can count on your brothers. They will stand next to you if they [racist attackers] come. They will think twice because they know us... they know that we look out for our Muslim brothers.

Echoing this topography of fear and danger as well as of solidarity, Anwar, also 16 years old from East London, makes a point about the violent and dangerous character of places where the help of Muslim friends cannot be relied on.

> So many people I know have been attacked and stabbed. It is dangerous in the street, and it is good to know your mates are there for you and you do not go beyond that ... You simply don't.

Samira, a 19-year-old Belgian woman recounts living in her predominantly Muslim neighbourhood in Antwerp and her venturing outside it somewhat differently as her experience is inflected by the way she sees herself as a young Muslim woman.

> I remember when my mother and I had to travel to see my aunt and cousin in Ghent. It was strange as I could immediately see that people would stare at us as if we were a curiosity. Many times women would whisper while staring, sometimes people would cast angry looks. This made me feel strange, uncomfortable ... Only when I became older and got more directly engaged with racism did I understand why people could not resist showing their disapproval of the fact that we were dressed differently, that we were covering our heads, that we were there ... You did not feel that at all in the old neighbourhood, where we lived a happy and carefree childhood.

Samira, a college student that covers her head and dresses in ways consistent with her sense of modesty derived from being a Muslim juxtaposes clearly her childhood neighbourhood from places outside it, where she remembers being exposed to what she perceived as unkind and often aggressive scrutiny because of her difference.

Such discourses are not uncommon and indicate that the reasons behind the appeal of the neighbourhood are quite complex. Our young informants rely on the local community, especially other young people from it to ensure that their neighbourhood is a safe place to live, work and move about. Many of those who are geographically mobile due to work, study or family obligations, often see their neighbourhood as a place of comfort where they do not enjoy unwelcome visibility, public scrutiny and, on occasion, aggression. Younger informants see it as their 'home turf', a place where they are streetwise and where they can, collectively and individually, assess, control and manage risk. This is not novel as a number of studies on youth (Peterson 2011; Shildrick 2006) that have focused on structural factors of youth cultures, including neighbourhood residence, suggest that locality can be very influential in shaping the cultural identities and experiences of young people. What is pertinent in the case of our young informants is the association of the solidarities forged within the neighbourhood and of the community with 'being Muslim'. To return to Ali's response regarding his neighbourhood, he continuously reminds us that his 'brothers' are Muslim and that this 'Muslimness' is the crucial element upon which trust is built. To be fair, Ali does recognize that his locality is mixed in terms of ethnicities and religions and does suggest that many people he likes and trusts in his everyday encounters are non-Muslim, but still, he stresses that he trusts his friends because 'they are Muslim'.

The neighbourhood clearly represents, according to these accounts, a set of relationships of mutuality and support, of feeling safe and, if necessary, of coming together in a moment of need or of danger. Most informants consider it to be coextensive with their local community and therefore imbued by the spirit of that community that is largely informed by the values associated with being Muslim.

Until the early 1970s Europe's urban spaces were culturally alien to their Muslim residents as, for reasons that we explained in Chapter 1, the majority of Muslim migrants did not see Europe as a new permanent home. The collective dimension of Islam, therefore, was initially confined to personal spaces of private homes, collective immigrant residences, furnished hotel rooms, and shop store-rooms. In view of this lack of a 'proper' Muslim space, for many informants, the recognition of their neighbourhood or of their city as 'home', is the product of what Barbara Daly Metcalfe has described as *making Muslim space* (1996), of 'populating' the localities concerned with familiar markers of their presence, of 'spatializing' with their 'footsteps', as De Certeau suggests when discussing the process of kinesthetic appropriation of space (1986: 97). Indeed, the discourses from our fieldwork reveal aspects of particular geographies of locality that make sense to, and are evoked by, many Muslims. Their topographies contain objects or places that are familiar and relevant to 'being Muslim', such as mosques, community centres, shops, schools, other loci of collective action and sharing, local media and the 'soundscapes' all of these generate and sustain – to use a term that Hirschkind developed in his study of Muslim counterpublics in Cairo (2006). These geographies are not necessarily geographies of concrete landmarks but incorporate personal, family and community narratives bonded to the locality in question.

Mehmet, a 39-year old Hackney resident born in Turkey, recounted with a sense of accomplishment the times that the Turkish community was less established in his part of London and compared that earlier topography of Hackney with what we could call a Muslim topography of the borough today. His account included the mosques that have been built over the years – embellished with stories about the materials used, the importance of their visibility in the urban landscape, their openness to all Muslims, the religious classes and schools, the new halal shops and restaurants and the various Islamic bookshops that can be found in the area nowadays. What was of particular importance in his discourse was a story about the debates of whether the plans for a local mosque should incorporate a minaret or not:

> Those who were against [the minaret] did not understand that the community wanted their mosque not to be hidden away but to let people know that we are here too. This is very important . . . to drive by and see a mosque that people built as a mark of their faith.

Others, too, emphasize the importance of being able to recognize their Muslim identity in the local urban landscape. Azeddine, 33 years old from Belgium, expresses his dismay and anger at the various political, bureaucratic and societal obstacles he and other Muslims in his town have to confront and negotiate in order to get permission to build a 'proper' mosque that, in his opinion, constitutes a need of the Muslim community and a recognition of its presence there.

> It is unbelievable that we had to argue for our right to have a 'proper' mosque in a city where Muslims are so many. We will in the end overcome their objections and even build a minaret! We live here too.

But the geography of locality is not exhausted in the building of mosques; the majority of our informants had stories of gaining 'ownership' or becoming 'stakeholders' in a number of local institutions which eventually became part of the narrative fabric that makes up local European Muslim geographies. Naaz, 29 years old from Belgium, talks about the local struggle to ensure that her local high school would become more flexible as far as acceptable girls' dress was concerned:

> It was a long struggle. I felt at times that this was not my school, it couldn't be because it did not accept me as I was. And when our voice was finally heard we felt that this was our school too, that this was our town as well.

Similar narratives of a collective achievement, from supporting friends in the face of racist violence to campaigning for a mosque or for greater tolerance in a local school, or for providing appropriate care for Muslim elderly people are prevalent in the discourses of our informants. These can, among others, be seen as processes of making space, or of constructing places that feature in the topographies of European Muslims as relevant and familiar. Such talk sometimes takes the form of a rhetoric of 'local patriotism', emphasizing or recounting community achievements, investing local space with emotion and agency.

But as we have already pointed out, locality is not merely a physical space but also a highly symbolic and often mediated domain of social action that, at least at first sight, is characterized by face-to-face interaction and some degree of familiarity that comes with it. In the context of European cities where secularism has not eradicated the visual elements of a long Christian tradition but tends to see with suspicion any further markers of religious identification, this dimension of locality is becoming more important. An eloquent example of this non-physical, mediated character of local Muslim geographies is the case of London's Ramadan Radio, a local, restricted licence station, which used to operate every year during the month of Ramadan in the Borough of Tower Hamlets and which enjoyed widespread appreciation among our local Muslim interviewees. Apart from the non-commercial character of the station and its claim to reflect the local community, our informants' responses to our questions and group discussions introduced another set of revealing reasons for this markedly different attitude towards Ramadan Radio.

Shabina, a 23-year old woman of mixed Pakistani and Bangladeshi origin reflects on how it, in many ways, provided a narrative thread, a sense of intimacy in the construction of a cohesive locality and community.

> Ramadan Radio was much nicer [than other radio stations] to listen to. It offered you the opportunity to feel you are a member of a community. For one, you listened to people you knew personally. You heard their voice on the radio and then when you rang them at home you used to say 'I heard you on the radio you know'.

Zaynab, a devout 43-year-old housewife attending a women's group meeting at the East London mosque adds rather nostalgically to the overall picture the decisive contribution the station made in creating a soundscape that 'populated' the urban landscape.

> Yes and you could listen to programmes from the local hospital, and you know the people who work there too .... And then it was the prayers ... there was something for everyone.

Generally, listeners of Ramadan Radio expressed a sense of intimacy with the people working for the station and the station as a whole and expressed a desire for it to be granted an ordinary licence. As Tsagarousianou has suggested (2008) Ramadan Radio operated at what we could call the 'intimate' level, as it was a very local medium acquainted with the needs related to the intimate realm of religion and rooted in the everyday life of a relatively small local community. In other words, Ramadan Radio had (or perhaps has) become part of the symbolic landscape of the locality, a virtual presence with very tangible impact on community life. What is more, during its operation, it was part of the local urban soundscape, in fact, a welcome addition to what many local Muslims – primarily the more devout ones – considered to be an alien soundscape devoid of the sounds that made it relevant to their daily lives.

But even in the absence of media such as Ramadan Radio, many informants devise strategies that reproduce to some extent sounds that they consider appropriate and relevant to their identities as Muslims. Indeed, several informants resort to various digital and wireless technologies to help them achieve this in various contexts in their daily lives.

Yahya, a 25-year-old student from West London displayed a smartphone application and tried to explain in a group discussion what it could do:

> I can now hear the call to prayers when the time comes...it is not quite like the call from the minaret...but it [London] sort of feels much more friendly.

Sharif, a 30-year-old engineer born in Amsterdam found an answer to the lack of the prayer marking the end of the daily fast and the *iftar* during the month of Ramadan in services provided via mobile telephony:

> I used to always find it difficult to figure out when fasting ended in the evenings during Ramadan. Although I am not that particularly bothered about sticking to other rules – you know prayers and all that – this [breaking the fast] is something nice, something we did since we were little kids. And I want my kids to do it with me and my wife and their other relatives. I was told by a friend about this SMS service that lets me know when fasting ends and it is great.

Whereas various commentators have expressed significant reservations about the impact of wireless communications on everyday life as they see in them the homogenization (Castells et al. 2007) or the devaluation of space and the transformation of their users into 'sedentary voyeurs' (Virilio 1991: 14), the uses of wireless media in these instances seem to be more conducive to reconfiguring local, often 'sterile' space in ways that are enriching the experience of wireless media users.

And beyond wireless media, other aspects of digital technologies such as MP3s and iPods are also actively used in the construction of a Muslim soundscape in people's personal or domestic space. Aisha, a 22-year-old woman from central Paris who was forced to remove her headscarf during her workday at a nursery, intimated during her group discussion that she felt very uncomfortable with the austerity with which the French principle of *laïcité* was imposed but found in her MP3 player a way of enriching her life as a Muslim by listening to digitized religious recitations while travelling to work or during her free time as did Nasreen, a 35-year-old mother from Offenbach near Frankfurt, who was using her own MP3 to listen to recorded *ghazals* (Sufi and more mainstream religious music and recitation celebrating the love of God) as she characteristically said 'anywhere...in the car, at home, while shopping'.

The informants who described their locality as their home demonstrated strong links with and often emotional investments in it. They displayed a sense of belonging to local communities and an interest in local issues, often issues related to their being Muslim as the discourses about registering their presence in the urban landscape indicated. Their local engagement can be described as indicative of their wish to 'make' meaningful and accessible spaces that resonate with them. But such processes are not without obstacles as urban space constitutes a site of contestation, a terrain where various claims and counter-claims tend to compete for its 'definition'. In such processes, local government and local societies seem to have an impact on the everyday lives of their Muslim residents as the latter depend on the former for the provision of crucial services such as schooling, access to spaces for events, licensing and permits. As we have already seen to some extent, and as we are going to see in the next chapter, the nature of the interaction of Muslim residents, local authorities and local societies sets the tone of community relations. Locality seems to be central in Muslim definitions of 'home' and in Muslim mobilizations and the politics of space are increasingly becoming one of the key issues in Muslim cultural politics as European Islam comes of age and emerges from the private to the public sphere.

The production of translocality

In the age of globalization and of 'time–space distantiation' (Giddens 1984) in which things and people become 'disembedded' from concrete space and time (Lash and Urry 1994: 13) localities may no longer be the clear supports of identity, but they still play an important part in the symbolic and physical dimension of our identifications. But in order to integrate localities in such an analytical context, instead of thinking of them as self-contained areas with clearly demarcated boundaries, they can be imagined as articulated movements in networks of social relations and understandings

(Massey 1994: 325). Locality is not static and its boundaries are not impermeable, it is integrated in the global flows making up the complex array of institutions and practices that Appadurai (1996) has called diasporic ethnoscapes, ideoscapes, financescapes, mediascapes and technoscapes.[1] To some extent, due to the diasporic nature of Muslim communities in Europe as well as due to the traditionally universalist character of Islam, the former have developed not only transnational connections but also potent transnational imaginaries which we will now turn to.

In an increasingly globalized world, interaction across distance is crucial in reconfiguring beyond recognition traditional ethnic and local notions of community as the notions of culture and community shift from the more static geography of the locality to the fluid topography of the transnational landscapes Appadurai identifies (1996). These landscapes thus, are the building blocks of what, extending Benedict Anderson's argument (1983), could be seen as imagined worlds, that is, the translocal and transnational bonds which are constituted by the historically situated imaginations of persons and groups spread around the globe (Appadurai 1996: 27). Community, including its translocal variants, is therefore 'imagined', and mediated through the imageries of the 'mediascape', ideologies of the 'ideoscape', and ever-shifting demographics of ethnicity ('ethnoscape') and information.

As we have already seen in the case of the construction of locality in the preceding pages, it goes without saying that this process of 'imagining', of making possible the forging of local and translocal identities and solidarities rests upon the creative engagement of European Muslims, the processes of cultural negotiation and translation which they are involved in and the cognitive and emotional investments they make. In the course of the next few pages we will try to highlight some of the ways in which this creative engagement takes shape during particular instances of cultural production and consumption. If it is possible to summarize the ways in which European Muslims inhabit transnational spaces and engage in the formation of their cultures and identities through processes of initiation, reproduction and cultural change, one could identify two key areas where they play a crucial role.

(a) The construction of translocal/transnational phenomenological geographies:

Clearly, European Muslims actively utilize time/space distantiating technologies to cultivate both local and long-distance relations that are crucial in their identification process. Through these they participate in and mobilize processes of reconfiguration of time, space and place and construct new phenomenological geographies.[2]

(b) The construction and dissemination of shared narratives:
European Muslims draw upon the opportunities provided by the various forms of collective action and cultural creativity available to them in order to engage in practices of meaning creation, drawing upon diverse life-histories and social-historical backgrounds. In doing so, they often arrive at shared interpretations of social reality and narratives of identity.

Translocal and transnational phenomenological geographies

Despite the energy and commitment many of our informants invested in the process of construction of locality and of their local community, it was evident that locality does not generate only positive feelings and attachments. Indeed, many informants, including some of those who chose to participate in community projects and action, saw in the ways their local communities are organized powerful inertia of times gone by. Many among the more religious of our interlocutors were sceptical about the authority of the elders in their community as they considered the Islam they followed corrupted and residual, not a matter of choice but of tedious repetition, marred by selectivity and incomplete adherence to religious imperatives. Others found these very same structures too strict, associated to bygone eras, stifling and suffocating. With very few exceptions, our informants felt that they needed to go beyond the confines of the locality in order to find spiritual guidance, or in order to discover what it means to be a Muslim, and a European Muslim for that matter, or, finally, in order to seek and get to know others 'like them'. Transcending the boundaries of the *local* was seen by most, for a variety of reasons a normal act of engagement with what is beyond, with what Peter Mandaville (2001) and Olivier Roy (2004) called 'reimagining' and 'searching' for the *Ummah* respectively. Both authors have very aptly demonstrated aspects of this process by examining a corpus of texts and resources in cyberspace which reveal a transnational universe of discourse and action. We obviously do not intend to replicate their path-breaking work; instead, in order to explore this process of translocal and transnational social construction, we will adopt a somewhat different approach that focuses on the ways in which our informants transcend the boundaries of the *local* and how they articulate their own experiences and aspirations with those of often remote others who share a common identification as Muslims.

Through observation and our interviews with our informants it became evident that, short of physically moving out of one's local community, a main way of transcending its confines has been utilizing technologies of time/space distantiation through the more traditional but also the various digital, including mobile and locative, media. Similarly, many of those of our informants who chose to move away of localities which they had affinities with, resorted to the very same media in order to seek raw material for making sense of who they are.

Indeed, most of the participants in our research have been extremely interested in trying to articulate their complex position, straddling, so to speak, the boundary between the local and the translocal but also between being *Muslims* and being *European* at the same time. In their attempt to explore this apparent ambiguity they proved to be voracious media users. Regardless of the type of medium they used, our informants expressed their frustration at what they perceived as mainstream media. Their responses largely confirm findings of other minority media users' research that reveals that minority and Muslim audiences are deeply dissatisfied with mainstream media (CENSIS 2002; Millwood Hargrave 2002; Poole 2002). Interviewee responses are unambiguous as to the quality of relationship with mainstream media, public and private alike. In general, there is widespread dissatisfaction and lack of trust towards mainstream media. Only a small minority of interviewees did not express serious reservations about what is on offer. A considerable majority from all five countries believe that mainstream media are more or less untrustworthy and indicate that they feel alienated from them. Their responses articulate, often dramatically, the *aporia* and the intensely felt subaltern position which many of them have experienced or are still experiencing.

When it comes to broadcasting – commercial and Public Service alike – and the national press, European Muslims, regardless of country of residence, tend to express a number of reservations that relate to (a) the misrepresentation of themselves as Muslims but also as residents and citizens of European societies; (b) the accuracy and truthfulness of news and other information relating to the Muslim world; and (c) the values propagated by the media. The overwhelming majority of those who expressed an opinion seem to converge in believing that mainstream media are biased in one way or another. This bias is perceived in various ways, some of which we have discussed in Chapter 1. Overall, it is widely believed that broadcasting institutions and the press misrepresent Muslims in Europe, often associating them with political radicalism and religious fundamentalism. Muslim cultures, according to most respondents, are represented by mainstream media as cultures fostering domestic violence, the oppression of women and of the young, dominated by a misguided sense of honour and a deeply conservative patriarchal ideology. And, although many believe that Muslim communities are facing problems, they find it difficult to comprehend why their 'achievements and hard work', their successes at 'raising good families' and teaching their children to be 'decent people' are misrecognized or ignored by the mainstream media. Such remarks relate also to the perceived invisibility of Muslims from the European social imaginary as this is mediated by mainstream media institutions.

Haroun, a 28-year-old male born in Scotland and living in London characteristically says:

> I sometimes think that, for television, time has stood still. If you look at television, the world of the studios has nothing to do with what happens outside. Muslims but also other people are hard to spot or can sometimes appear as an excuse, just to provide an alibi for those who ignore our presence and contribution [to society].

Ayşe, a 31-year-old female from Frankfurt has a similar experience and comments on her inability to recognize herself on television by drawing links with the dominant political discourse in Germany.

> When I watch television, I see someone else's country. A country without me, without people like me. It is not that surprising then when I hear [politicians] talk about Muslims in Germany as foreigners.

But it is not only the direct representations or the non-representation of Muslims in the mainstream media that come under scrutiny by many interviewees; the accuracy and truthfulness of reports about Muslims at home and abroad is virtually unanimously questioned and feeds a substantial sense of injustice as we will see later on. In response to this inability to draw upon raw material to validate themselves as Europeans and Muslims at the same time, to see themselves as stakeholders in their societies through their use of mainstream media, the overwhelming majority of our informants have devised a number of strategies of media use. These included

a. strategies of scrutinizing the media and
b. an increasing turn towards Information and Communication Technologies (ICTs)[3] and a prevalent transnational orientation.

When it comes to mainstream media, many of our informants intimate that, in view of their lack of trust towards the objectivity and representativeness of mainstream media, they rely on a multitude of media that include mainstream, diasporic and 'Muslim' ones (i.e. media explicitly addressing a Muslim audience). Reading many newspapers, or going through different channels, persistently trying to analyse stories, looking for plots or conspiracies, were some aspects of the repertoire of media usage modes they resort to in order to get a sense of the information that reaches them. This selective and critical attitude is, for many, necessary in order to enable them compare narratives and identify the 'truth' in what is being offered to them. Almost half of those interviewed described what one could call ways of 'reading between the lines' when they encounter local or national stories about Islam and Muslims, or international news involving countries with Muslim majorities or minorities.

However, apart from the deployment of such strategies vis-à-vis the mainstream media available to them, almost all of our informants have been turning their attention to and increasingly using media that they consider more 'appropriate' or more relevant to them as *European Muslims*. These additional media include 'old' print media and radio but also cable and satellite television and, increasingly, new, digital media through the use of Information and Communication Technologies (ICTs). Most of our interviewees could talk confidently and clearly about their uses of ICTs, mobile and wireless

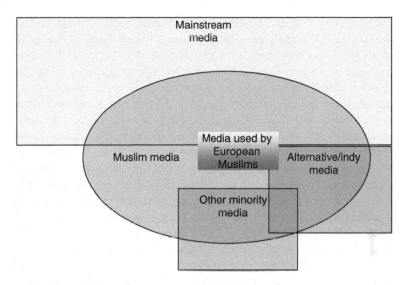

Figure 4.1 Muslim mediascapes

media as well as an array of other media such as satellite television,[4] and their responses to our questions on this topic revealed that, regardless of socio-economic condition, the majority have been early adopters of ICTs and are very skilful navigators of cyberspace, enjoying in this way, access to a host of opportunities to obtain information, news or to be entertained.

This constellation of 'mainstream' and 'alternative' media constitutes what we propose to call *European Muslim Mediascape*. This comprises an array of media that are not necessarily intended for exclusive consumption by Muslims alone; we would argue that its existence relies on continually shifting personal and collective assessments of what is suitable and relevant to, and what is needed by European Muslims. Thus, alongside a critical use of the mainstream media we referred to above, European Muslims increasingly turn to diasporic media that may not address their audience primarily as *Muslims* but as members of an ethnic group – Bangladeshis, Egyptians or Moroccans to mention but a few – although many of our interviewees who use such media justified their choice on the grounds that their output conforms to what they would expect from an Islamic broadcaster (Figure 4.1).

A number of Arabic language news media such as *Al-Jazeera* or *Al-Manar*, are also fairly popular, favoured even by many of our informants who may not speak or understand Arabic. Echoing the views of several of the people who had resorted to such practices, and commenting about his use of *Al-Jazeera Arabic* prior to the launch of an English language counterpart, Aadil, a 30-year-old bank clerk from London suggested that although the language was obviously a barrier to fully comprehending the station's news output, tuning to the channel allowed him to get a glimpse of an alternative, more credible representation of the world, even through his out-of-necessity reliance mainly on the visual dimension of the programmes. This, and a number of similar responses suggest that broadcasters such *Al-Jazeera Arabic* are able to provide a perspective that resonates with many of their Muslim viewers and establish a relationship of trust. This relationship between these media and their audiences relies on their ability to articulate what Hollander and Stappers (1992: 21) call 'structures of relevance' which provide the crucial links that make communication an important means for the forging of community culture and solidarity.[5] Clearly such media appear to 'make sense', speak with a voice they recognize and relate to.

Other alternative media, such as a host of indymedia that, although not necessarily built with the needs of European Muslim audiences in mind, may be relevant to the experiences and information or entertainment needs of Muslims in Europe, and which specialize in issues of advocacy, human rights, provision of independent news and anti-war campaigns regarding various Western military interventions in the broader Middle East have also been quite popular among those who can access them. Again, these were considered to challenge the official version of many events and to provide much needed and more trustworthy counter-narratives according to our informants.

In addition, many of our interviewees involved in community or political activism stressed the importance of these independent media in counterbalancing the bias or indifference of their mainstream counterpart and their usefulness in providing a more sensitive and trustworthy version of social and political realities as well as vital information. Clearly the trust deficit that is obvious in the case of mainstream media is substantially absent here and many of our informants see in such media a much more inclusive regime of representation and narration, despite their 'Western' credentials.

But what is probably quite significant is the emergence over the past couple of decades of a host of media that are addressing Europe's Muslims as precisely that. Rapidly increasing in importance, these comprise what one could call a *Muslim Media Space* (see Figure 4.2). Our findings indicate that this is a highly diverse and polyphonic sector based on a host of different platforms (television, Internet, locative media) that provides considerable choice for Muslims world-wide and European Muslims in particular, serving a host of needs that extend from spirituality, or dealing with discrimination at work, to lifestyle propositions or to finding a spouse, or to practicalities such as information on fasting or prayer times, religious festivals and other occasions in the calendars of the various Muslim communities. Although much of the content is available in Arabic and English,

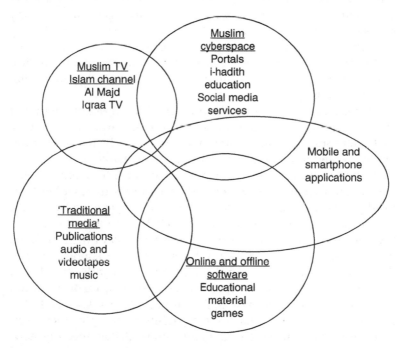

Figure 4.2 Muslim media space

and, to a lesser extent in Turkish and Urdu, the sector is increasingly undergoing a process of 'vernacularization' as it is becoming multilingual in an attempt to become accessible to Muslims in various European countries and other parts of the world.

What is more, an examination of the media available for European Muslims over time reveals the shift in the provenance of what European Muslims consume. For example, the traditional publishing centres of the Muslim world, primarily located in Egypt and Lebanon, and other Middle Eastern newcomers in digital publishing and design Syria and Jordan[6] have seen their share of the Islamic media market squeezed by new media production companies situated in Europe and North America (see Figure 4.3). This, shift, combined with the increased use of European vernaculars spoken by many of the younger generation of Europe's Muslims, partly signifies a response to the needs of European (and North American) Muslims and reflects the transformation this Muslim Media Space has been undergoing towards a polyphonic, multilingual and, in many respects, 'multicultural' space. In it, the diverse experiences of being Muslim, from the point of view of producers and consumers situated in different parts of the globe, contribute to new articulations of Muslim experience and self-identification (and inform European Muslim identities in the process.

It is this, last, feature that is highly significant as this *Muslim Media Space* constitutes, according to our informants, an accessible space that addresses them as Muslims and caters for their various information, entertainment and social needs. For many of the users of such media, cultural consumption and social interaction is often seen as a process of discovery of, and encounter with other Muslims, nearby as well as further afield. In many ways, these media provide the raw material to them to explore their Muslim identities and to become aware of or connect with other Muslims in their or other, more remote localities. As we will see, they give opportunities to their users to empathize and develop solidarities with other fellow Muslims. What is more, the technologies of time–space distantiation employed by satellite television, the various Internet-based and wireless and locative media have the capability to bring to their users that are situated in remote locations almost instantaneously news from other parts of Europe and further afield. Being in a position to enable instantaneous communication, the media that make up this

Figure 4.3 The geography of Muslim media production

Muslim Media Space constitute part of the technologies and infrastructures that give rise to and sustain what Mandaville calls 'translocal space' (2001: 49). In other words, they have the capacity to bring about and sustain a sense of immediacy, contemporaneity and synchronicity to the dispersed populations that they link. This temporal convergence and sense of co-presence is very significant as it brings a qualitative change to the experience of being a European Muslim and the dynamics set in motion by it. Temporal convergence makes possible, and much easier, the convergence of experience: whereas earlier forms of socio-cultural distantiation were inextricably linked with temporal distance, making it very difficult for dispersed populations to share experiences at more or less the same time and form common frames of making sense of these, the sense of contemporaneity and synchronicity made possible through the use of such *Muslim Media* enables new ways of coexistence and experiencing together, of constructing shared experiential frames between hitherto remote and, often unconnected, fellow Muslims.

Drawing on Scannell's discussion of the significance of electronic media in the formation of their audiences' experience, it could be argued that, apart from facilitating the compression of time and space, they bring about new possibilities of being; in particular, 'new possibilities of being in two places at once' (Scannell 1996: 91) – referring to the place where they experience an event and the place where an event 'actually' takes place. Focusing particularly on broadcast public events Scannell argues that '[p]ublic events now occur, simultaneously, in two different places: the place of the event itself and that in which it is watched and heard' (Scannell 1996: 76). We would argue that it is not only media events that have this quality, as their capability of doubling is inextricably linked to 'the liveness of radio and television' (Scannell 172). In other words, although broadcasting – and not only its live variants – revolves around the production of a sense of immediacy, this is by no means exclusive to it but extends to, more or less, most electronic media as they share both the capacity to produce a sense of immediacy and time–space distantiation that broadcasting has. Despite their often notable differences, various contemporary electronic media and information and communication technologies have a profound effect in our sense of space as they produce at least 'two places'. In this sense, the physical remoteness of European Muslims from each other, as well as from other Muslims no longer prevents individuals in remote locations to coexist and interact in ways that we can effectively describe as co-presence.

It is this experience of co-presence that many of our informants singled out as highly significant in the context of their media usage. Rasha, a 23-year-old French hairdresser, who has been trying to distance herself from Islam as a religion, stressing that she is highly secular but chose to participate in our discussion group because of her heritage, admitted that she was fascinated by being able to glimpse into the lives of other Muslims in other parts of Europe through participating in various online discussion on Islamophobia, relationships and culture, especially as she could talk to them almost as she would face-to-face. Similarly, Waqas, a 35-year-old West Londoner recounted his experience of watching live Al-Jazeera Arabic and being at the receiving end of what he called 'the raw truth of the Iraq war'. He pointed out that what radicalized him and his friends who were watching with him was the fact that the television set was like a window that allowed them to stare 'directly' at the misery the West was inflicting, 'to understand the horror of it'. And, finally, Cem, a 40-year-old taxi driver from the Frankfurt area who has been involved in the local Palestine solidarity campaign also uses Internet-based media to learn about his fellow Palestinian Muslims and finds the immediacy of Internet-based news media welcome yet overwhelming.

> I feel I need, we all need to know what is happening over there, the suffering of our Palestinian brothers . . . but I find what is happening very painful. And sometimes, it is unbearable to watch the atrocities almost live; as they happen. You suffer together with the families that lost their children, their loved ones, their homes.

Although considerably different in some respects, these three justifications of the use of Muslim media indicate the importance of the potential of encountering others 'like us', that is, Muslims in similar or different situations. Rasha identified with fellow European Muslims, while Waqas and his friends and Cem identified with fellow Muslims that have been victimized beyond the confines of Europe. Indeed, the sense of 'suffering together', experiencing the pain of other, often distant but fellow-Muslims nevertheless that

can be found in the last two responses is recurrent in our interviews and group discussions and, as we will elaborate on it later on,
in Chapter 5, it is highly pertinent to the process of forging common experiences and solidarities. But what is also significant here
is the fact that such instances of media uses can essentially be seen
as map-making exercises, cognitive attempts to create a translocal
topography of local and remote fellow Muslims. Not unlike the processes of making Muslim space at the local level which we examined
earlier in this chapter, these constitute attempts to 'populate' the
translocal/transnational space, to imbue it with meaning.

The sense of connectedness and simultaneity, and the sharing of
views and narratives across boundaries with everyone who experiences this transnational interaction, provide a unique opportunity
structure for dispersed populations. It enables them to observe and
interact with others, to imagine themselves as people who share
experiences with others who may be living far away to engage in
processes of exchange, translation and hybridization. In this context, processes of mediated interaction across space (such as the ones
unfolding in the course of such encounters) where these parameters
of social experience are reconfigured are of paramount significance.
European Muslims live complex lives situated within locales, in very
specific places – such as the neighbourhood – where aspects of their
experience are grounded, and in national and transnational spaces
that comprise different interconnected localities at the same time.
Actual, physical places coexist with 'virtual' places, or 'non-places'
(Urry 2000).

Tsagarousianou has, in a discussion of diasporas, likened such
processes of translocal encounters to 'the experience of pilgrimage'
(2007). Like pilgrims who 'leave their own space and join with
strangers to whom they have not been connected previously in order
to take part in events that are outside the normal flow of daily life'
(Dubisch 1995: 38), European Muslims embark on somehow similar, albeit mediated journeys. And although these instances are not
sacred as traditional pilgrimages are, their profanity carries with it
the aura of the extraordinary character of discovery that is inherent in these emotional encounters with strangers who are 'so much
like us'. Indeed, pilgrimage as a practice and its meaning-producing
implications have attracted the interest of social anthropologists for
some decades now. A prominent researcher and one of the pioneers

in the field, Victor Turner has described pilgrimage as a *rite de passage* that gives rise to a sense of *Communitas* among those participating in it, that is, the establishment of a community which is (temporarily) marked by a sense of egalitarian brotherhood among its members (Turner 1974). More recently, drawing upon Turner, and echoing work on the integrative and legitimizing functions of such practices, Benedict Anderson focused on other spatial practices such as the travel itineraries of colonial civil servants from their own localities to colonial administrative centres (1983). Anderson argued that, like pilgrimage (and the trajectories formed by pilgrims in their journeys from their own localities to their sacred destinations), over time these practices produce a geographical reality that provides the raw material for the imagining of national communities in the colonies of European colonial empires. Likewise then, we would argue that these practices of mediated encounters among European Muslims, and between them and other Muslims further afield, institute phenomenological geographies and, by extension, support and reinforce processes of construction of European Muslim identities.

5
The Politics of Contestation and the Construction of Injustice

From connectivity to consciousness

As we have seen, the technologies of time–space distantiation employed by the various media used by European Muslims (as well as similar technologies that make physical mobility much easier and faster) have substantially altered the experiences of presence and absence through their capability to overcome distance and boundaries and to bring remote others together. Situated in remote locations, our informants access news from other parts of Europe and further afield almost instantaneously. Being in a position to enable instantaneous communication, the media that make up what we have termed *Muslim Media Space* constitute part of the technologies and infrastructures that give rise to and sustain what Mandaville calls 'translocal space' (2001: 49). In other words, they have the capacity to bring about and sustain a sense of immediacy, contemporaneity and synchronicity to the dispersed populations that they link. This temporal convergence and sense of co-presence is very significant as it brings a qualitative change to the experience of being a European Muslim and the dynamics set in motion by it.

Temporal convergence makes possible, and much easier, the convergence of experience: whereas earlier forms of socio-cultural distantiation were inextricably linked with temporal distance, making it very difficult for dispersed populations (such as Europe's Muslims) to share experiences at more or less the same time and form common frames of making sense of these, the sense of contemporaneity and synchronicity made possible through the use of such *Muslim media* enables new ways of coexistence and experiencing together, of constructing shared experiential frames between hitherto remote and, often unconnected, fellow Muslims.

Having said that, it is important to steer clear of the technological determinism inherent in the assumption that infrastructures and technologies alone are sufficient for the construction of a durable transnational space and, even more so, sustainable transnational identities. It is quite clear that time–space compression and the ensuing sense of immediacy, simultaneity and co-presence are by no means sufficient to provide durability and coherence to a sense of being a *European Muslim* among Europe's Muslim population alone. It is indeed hard to explain how the word *Muslim* could house such disparate populations in terms of culture, language, ethnicity, provenance and socio-economic position, to mention but a few potential resources for identifications by referring to the existence of technological infrastructure alone.

What is then necessary for the transformation of a geographically and culturally dispersed population into a political (in the broadest sense of the term possible) subject as our research findings seem to indicate? Surely, the answer to this question is complex. One of the factors that seems to emerge prominently in our research findings relates to the extensive meaning creating and disseminating processes that European Muslims are engaged in. As we have already seen in the previous chapter, our informants have been engaging in processes of exchanging and accessing information from various local contexts, especially in order to connect with or learn about other Muslims 'like them'. It is important to point out that this process of access and exchange does not constitute an end in itself. Indeed, as we will demonstrate in the next few pages, our informants, like many other European Muslims they learn about and communicate with, are consistently building what we could best describe as a common repository of experience. In other words, they tend to relate the information they acquire about other Muslims to their own experiences. It is this intersection of the complex connectivity that underpins the translocal and transnational field that European Muslims inhabit and of the processes of cultural reinvention and reconstruction that European Muslims are engaged in, that effectively renders communication and the media technologies we have been referring to crucial vehicles for the reproduction and transformation of European Muslim identities.

Central in this production of a common stock of experience, in making possible the crucial spaces where different experiences from remote physical and often alien social contexts become intelligible, translatable and relevant to the dispersed population of Europe's Muslims is what, following Gamson and Ryan, we can term *common experiential* and, even more so, *injustice frames*. The notion of frames is derived from symbolic interactionism; in that theoretical context, frames evolve out of collective efforts to make sense of problems; they help people 'locate, perceive, identify, and label' their experience (Goffman 1974: 21). In social action research, frames are the product of symbolic and cultural production of political actors. According to Gamson (1992), a major proponent of the constructionist approach to framing, political actors actively construct their self-presentations so as to draw support from others. The concept of 'frame' therefore refers to cognitive processes through which people utilize background knowledge to interpret an event or circumstance and to locate it in a larger system of meaning. Framing processes are therefore means through which actors invoke one frame or set of meanings rather than another when they communicate a message, thereby indicating how the message is to be understood.

Articulating and sharing grievances

Turning back to our informants, it is clear that they engage in processes that make intelligible the experience of 'other Muslims', and integrate it into their own stock of knowledge, memory and experience. This process of translation and adoption can, and does, include positive as well as negative experiences; the various narratives of achievement and accomplishment that we recounted in the previous chapter are an example of the former while the experiences of 'being out of place' and under threat we have already discussed are an instance of the latter. During our discussions we found out that such narratives are not confined to the localities they originated in. Through various personal and institutional networks and, more importantly, through the media used by Europe's Muslims these narratives would often become part of a broader common stock of experience. Local stories, having unfolded in remote localities, are integrated into local vernaculars elsewhere. In this context locality and local experience is framed within a broader translocal and, often, transnational network and the latter is, in turn, localized (made sense in terms of its local manifestations/translations).

However, we will focus here on a particular type of frames that is central in the process of defining and framing an injustice and orienting a movement towards its resolution/alleviation, as Ryan and Gamson (2006) describe *injustice frames.*

An interesting way of demonstrating the importance of injustice frames is to focus on the eloquent way in which Médine, a 22-year-old rapper from Le Havre interprets the significance of Islam for him and other Muslims like him in a short text he writes for *Time* magazine.

People like me – the descendants of immigrants, whether Arab, black or Asian – are turning to our roots and embracing our heritage, just the opposite of what our parents did when they arrived. My grandparents, for example, who came to France from Algeria to live, work and build a better life, accepted the role of guest. They did all they could not just to fit in, but to become invisible. Calling attention to themselves usually meant trouble. They tried as much as possible to integrate, and in doing so shut away their customs, language and heritage. I certainly don't belittle their choice. But people of my generation are not shy about embracing their heritage, and far from seeking invisibility we're standing up to denounce the prejudice and injustice we face. In my case, Islam is an enormous part of who I am, just as being French is. The two aren't in opposition, or even mutually exclusive. Yet when you hear the debate in France today, you'd swear they must be.

The people who live in projects like those where last week's riots raged are treated as second-class citizens. We have less access to the rights and services of the republic – schools are run down; job opportunities are remote. What we do have is a supermarket, a mall for low-cost shops, a few fast-food joints and maybe a movie complex. That's it. The idea is to create just enough diversion so we stay where we are. The message is, Don't come in to mix with the people in the city centres. That's what the police tell you when they stop you on a bus coming into town: 'You have no business in the centre? Then you have no reason to be there. Go back where you belong.' Before Sept. 11, I would have said this was a kind of residual racism. The problems people had with us were due to our ethnicity, our skin color. Today, with many young people return-ing to religion as they start searching for their own identities, faith is becoming the difference that's most often pointed out. I'm not just a black guy or an Arab anymore; I'm a Muslim. And that's a code word for alien, someone who's determined not to fit in.

(Médine 2005)

The 'we' Médine is referring to is premised upon perceptions of rejec-tion, of exclusion, prejudice and a sense of invisibility that serve as injustice frames. Although his discourse (and that of many of our informants) is overwhelmingly (although not exclusively) shaped by a desire to be part of the societies in which European Muslims live, this desire is not unconditional as most research participants stressed the need of recognition and visibility of Muslims (however they may have defined the term). On occasion this desire is expressed assertively although quite often it is informed by a profound sense of societal insecurity.

Our interviewee discourses quite often raise grievances that range from issues of visibility and representation to those of exclusion and discrimination. As we suggested when discussing issues pertaining to space and to 'making place' processes, it is clear that practices of investing space with familiar markers of their 'Muslimness' are of high importance to many of them. This importance can be attributed to the comfort and warmth of the 'familiar' but, as some responses indicate, relates to the need for visibility, recognition and validation and, in some way, the affirmation of the permanent character of their residence in Europe. Some of the responses that revolve around the issue of integration of Islam in the urban landscape are very clear in their cynicism. Musa, a 27-year old man from Middlesex is unable to understand why his community is not allowed to have a purpose-built mosque despite the availability of space.

Instead of converting an old characterless building into a mosque why not have a purpose-built one that you can recognize and find easily. But they do not want to have mosques spoiling the view. Not here, not anywhere.

Similarly, Ali, a 21-year-old unemployed man from a working-class suburb in the North of Paris talks about a discussion people from his community had with the local mayor.

Why is there only a couple of invisible mosques in such a big town (cité). Are they ashamed of us? Are they trying to hide us from public view? The same story everywhere. My friend [in Lyon] was telling me that they have to deal with the same stubbornness over there.

Misrecognition and misrepresentation also feature high in their list of grievances. Reflecting on corporate decisions but also on the self-image of French society, 'Jacques', a 20-year-old apprentice from Paris confirms the prevalent view among our French informants:

Normally we do not exist for the bosses of big TV. Their image of France, the one they try to draw through what they show on TV does not have room [for the banlieues]. And if we can be seen, we are seen as criminals, as people without any decency or value. This happens everywhere. The British present us as rapists and wifebeaters, the Germans call us foreigners. They are all telling us we do not belong.

And Rachid, a 37-year-old Parisian, comments on the Mohammed cartoons published in the Danish newspaper *Jyllands-Posten* in 2005 and their subsequent publication in France:

[T]hey [caricaturists] should understand they are forcing people to take sides. I have no choice because their vulgar and simplistic (intervention) is forcing confrontation, not debate...they single us out and target us and that is not acceptable

These discourses contain highly localized grievances that are significant in themselves as they indicate the degree of alienation and displacement experienced by Muslims in Europe. However, what is more interesting and significant is the de-territorialization of these negative experiences and their re-articulation in a broader Europe-wide discourse of injustice. In the examples above, information from further afield – other parts of Britain, of France or of Europe – is integrated into the responses of our interviewees in order to support and generalize their claims.

Similarly, the sense of injustice experienced by French youth residing in the banlieues which Médine encapsulates is by no means exclusively 'theirs' as its various manifestations are accessible to other European Muslims who incorporate them to their own experiences of injustice. A Pew Global Attitudes Survey (2006) has found that awareness of the 2005 riots in France was relatively high among other European Muslims. But what is more interesting is that European Muslims 'irrespective of their views about the riots per se – say they are sympathetic to the youths from immigrant and working class suburbs in France'. Our own findings corroborate this but go a step further as they provide insights into how this sympathy is articulated in the discourse of our informants. Over half of our non-French interviewees, when they were prompted to discuss issues of societal fairness and injustice that affect them, mentioned in their lists of injustice directly experienced by them the inequalities and prejudice that prompted their French counterparts to riot, even when they did not actually share the living through the social and spatial segregation the French youth involved in the riots have been experiencing. Again, many mentioned in the same context the Mohammed cartoons published in the Danish newspaper *Jyllands-Posten* on 30 September 2005 as well as earlier debates on employment or school bans of Muslim women wearing the headscarf which they interpreted as proof of discrimination even though many had not experienced such bans in their own societies. Similarly, discussions about local acceptance or rejection of plans to build mosques or community centres almost invariably revealed that our interviewees were quite aware of debates and conflicts in other parts of Europe. Despite the fact that our interviewees' nationalities and countries of residence, their ethnic or cultural differences, diverse occupational patterns, educational attainment and age may have given rise to markedly different experiences and diverse perceptions of discrimination and exclusion, this diversity has not affected their ability to empathize and identify with other European Muslims. Indeed, the spatial and social segregation and unemployment experienced by French Muslims, the intense racism felt by many of our Belgian and Dutch informants were often subsumed to an overarching perception of injustice – our informants perceived these different experiences as part and parcel of a general feeling of injustice, in other words, through a translocal lens (and here the media they use played an important role), they perceived their distinct local negative experiences as part of a broader injustice that was pertinent to their own everyday lives.

In these instances, it is clear that European Muslims adopt a *European* perspective, not only developing an interest for developments in other parts of Europe that, they feel, affect them, but also integrating this knowledge to their own experiences and worldviews. But the raw material for the construction of injustice is by no means derived from Europe alone. Discussions and interviews with our informants revealed a quite widespread sensitivity to suffering in countries where Islam is practiced by the majority or large minorities of the population. Some of the most notable cases are Palestine which has been mentioned in highly emotional terms by the overwhelming majority of the people we talked to, closely followed by Iraq and Afghanistan where Western countries have intervened militarily, Chechnya which has been subjected to several Russian military campaigns, Kashmir which is bitterly disputed by both Pakistan and India, and Bosnia, the stage of a bitter military confrontation between Serbs, Croats and Muslims as Yugoslavia disintegrated in the 1990s and whose Muslim population was subjected to a campaign of ruthless ethnic cleansing. Indeed, the plight of the Bosnian Muslims has been a seminal moment that set in motion the process of identifying as Muslims for many of our older interviewees. Magdi, a 37-year-old paramedic from Belgium has vivid memories of the news coming from Bosnia through his television screen.

> It is hard to forget the suffering of those people. I remember not bearing to watch the news. And I will never forgive the inaction of the world as a whole people was being subjected to genocide just because they were Muslim. Just because they [their Christian neighbours] decided they did not have the right to be there. I was not, until then, particularly concerned about religion – my father was not that religious anyway – but I thought that this was the moment. That this is some sort of revelation, telling me that others are ready to die and they pay the price for being Muslim.

Asad, a 48-year-old West Londoner, an Islamic charity campaigner who had previously been a left-wing activist prior to the Bosnian

conflict also recounts the war and how he abandoned his engagement
with left politics:

> How could they [western governments] turn a blind eye to what
> was happening. And how could the media present their [Muslims]
> slaughter day in and day out. We would wait for the news, we
> would try to find a channel that would say it – that this was a
> genocide. As we could not stand the apathy around us, we decided
> to link up with others and start collections for our brothers and
> sisters. Cash, blankets, medicines, food.... A friend volunteered to
> drive the stuff but at the end the mosque was better networked
> and arranged its transportation. Bosnia had a profound effect on
> me, on my priorities.

Empathy with other fellow Muslims in such cases has a transfor-
mative effect, sometimes as dramatic as that described in Magdi's
and Asad's accounts, sometimes subtler and more incremental. It
is equally interesting to observe how identification with the suffering of 'fellow Muslims' eliminates the reservations of some of our
interviewees to identify themselves as Muslims.

In a group discussion with members of an Afghan association in
London, Naima, a well-dressed woman in her late forties, insisted
that she and her Afghan friends were highly secular and doubted
if our discussion would provide us with any useful information.
Although in the course of the discussion, some members of the group
acknowledged the importance of Islam in their identity, she remained
adamant that this was not the case as far as she was concerned.
As the discussion focused on international issues, the group started
to discuss the plight of ordinary Palestinians under Israeli occupation. Naima followed silently the discussion and finally decided to
intervene.

> I am really sad. When I hear that a child has died, shot by Israeli
> soldiers or blown by American mines, I realize how little our lives
> matter. If it is Muslim lives no one cares, no one thinks about them
> as human beings.

In her intervention, Naima switched from the lives of Palestinian,
Iraqi or Afghan children ('they', 'them') to a more inclusive 'we'

and, moving on, defined this 'we' as 'Muslims' despite her earlier statement that Islam does not mean anything to her. Whereas she dissociated herself from a religious identity which she seems to reject, she was much more comfortable with a definition of Muslims (including her) as the victims of a profound injustice and disregard. Although she articulated this in very clear terms, she was not the only one. Many 'secular Muslims' we encountered during our research, identified themselves as Muslims by using what we could call political criteria such as solidarity with Muslims whose lives are ravaged by war and violence or those who encounter in their daily lives racism and islamophobia.

Yasmin, a 22-year-old student expresses this eloquently as she describes the way she experiences racism.

> I do not have time for mosques and prayers. I do not even know if I believe in anything. But I experience the prejudice. It is how people stare at us, it is the police stopping you in the street, it is the comments that people make. We are Muslims because that's what we are. We cannot escape it.

In Yasmin's discourse 'us' refers to European Muslims, not as a religious group, but as a minority that is subjected to prejudice and racism. And Rupa, a 26-year-old college tutor from West London echoes Yasmin's definition by suggesting that 'being Muslim' constitutes a meaningful and, at the same time pragmatic, political act that enables her to cope with an adverse political and social environment.

> My parents wanted us to go to [a white school]. We had to cross the town every morning. They wanted us to fit in. But you pay the price as at the end of the day people still call you Paki this and Paki that. I understand their choices but at the end of the day, I am Muslim and only by embracing this I can resist [racial harassment].

While, finally Hassan, a 35-year-old Parisian of Algerian origin distinguishes between Islam as a religion and Islam as a political identity that can sustain forms of political action and protest against discrimination.

They teach people superstition and passivity. For me Muslims should not flock to the mosque...they [should] mobilize against bigotry and fight for their rights. This is our heritage and our tradition.

In all these instances, the various forms of discrimination experienced by Muslims elsewhere, the suffering of Muslims in war zones and occupied territories as well as the immediate experience of racist violence described when discussing the topographies of fear sketched by our informants in Chapter 4, or more mundane experiences of being made to feel out of place, amount to what Glenn Bowman calls constitutive violence (Bowman 2003: 319–320). Examining the emergence of Palestinian and Yugoslav nationalisms and trying to make sense of how national identities emerge and are crystallized in the context of conflicts such as the Israeli-Palestinian and the Bosnian one, Bowman argues that

> violence is not simply a device nationalists of certain persuasions take up strategically in pursuit of ends...but something that plays a constitutive role in the formation of all nationalisms. The violence which engenders nationalism is not the violence the imagined community of the future nation turns against its 'enemies', but the violence members of that not-yet-existent nation perceive as inflicted upon them by others.... An antagonism, rather than threatening a pre-existing and self-conscious entity, brings the community it threatens into being through that threat, and gives shape and identity to what it threatens through placing it at risk. Perceptions of a violence afflicting a diverse range of persons give rise to a concept of a 'national enemy' and, through that concept, to the idea of solidarity with those whom that enemy opposes. (320)

Despite the explicit link Bowman's definition of 'constitutive violence' introduces to nationalism and the equally explicit reference to an 'enemy', his argument remains quite a potent and pertinent one even if the processes we are exploring do not culminate in the development of a nationalist movement or do not necessarily entail an 'enemy' in the sense that Bowman defines the term. In the case of European Muslims, what is clear is that through the translation and domestication of narratives produced in remote locations and through diverse experiences, a common stock of experiences of injustice, even of constitutive violence becomes intelligible, accessible, meaningful and, more importantly, relevant to many. This sense of injustice and the narratives that underpin it make possible the imagination of a 'we', of all those who suffer 'the same' injustice. This collective sense of injustice and the 'cultural trauma' that it entails draw together the 'multiplex strands of violence, risk and threat afflicting people's everyday lives' (Bowman 2003: 320), to mobilize those who perceive themselves as affected. This mobilization is crucial to setting in motion processes of 'reinterpreting the past, narrating new foundations' (Hale 1998: 6), effectively instituting, reconstituting or reconfiguring a collective identity through collective representation, as a way of repairing the tear in the social fabric caused by 'injustice' and 'inequity'. Associating their identities as Muslims in Europe with the traumatic experiences of others entails therefore adopting a perspective derived, as we have already suggested in Chapter 4, from mediated experience. To be more clear, the suffering of young Afghans due to the war in Afghanistan's Helmand province and the repercussions of a headscarf ban in some municipality in Spain, which are experienced through various media by a young Muslim woman in Britain, combined with the immediate and direct experience of racism in her school, neighbourhood or workplace, are some of the possible ingredients of how she experiences herself being a Muslim in Europe today.

Injustice, identity and agency: Muslim charities, Jihadi websites and their audiences

It is not accidental that the expanding Islamic charity sector comprising some very active organizations such as *Islamic Relief/Secours Islamique, Muslimehelfen, Muslim Aid or Muslim Hands*, has been central in the discourse of many of our informants and recognizable by almost all. Although most Western Muslim charities do not distinguish between Muslim and non-Muslim aid recipients and strive to reconcile the culture of Muslim solidarity inherent in Islamic aid discourse on the one hand and the universalism inherent in development aid discourse (Juul Petersen 2011: 84), they nevertheless play a very significant role in focusing the attention of their audiences to the plight of Muslim victims of warfare, violence and natural disasters. *Islamic Relief*, for example, has very successfully managed to mobilize communities in support of victims of earthquakes in Kashmir and Pakistan, of victims of war and neglect in other parts of the Muslim world. Those of our respondents who have defined themselves as part of the audience of Western Muslim aid charities have confirmed that they have been instrumental in spreading awareness of the plight of other Muslims and, perhaps indirectly and unwittingly, providing raw material for the construction of a structure of empathy and, potentially, of injustice frames.

Interestingly, Ahmad, a 41-year-old shopkeeper from London, very astutely pointed out the dual impact of Muslim aid charities referring to his involvement in *Islamic Relief* work and to how the charity has adapted fundraising methods widely used by other development aid charities.

> It is not like in the old days. When we would just go and put some coins in the box. The simplicity of *Zakat*[1] ... it was a private thing. Now we have fundraising galas.... I have helped set up a couple. These are always dedicated to specific causes. The Kashmir earthquakes in 2005, the floods in Pakistan next year.... And then, now that everything is networked you learn how much the Leicester gala raised, and how well the Bradford do did. And you are no longer the little boy putting the coins in the box, you are one of many caring for the same people. Mind you, there is competition between different dos, but it's good spirited, it's for the brothers and sisters who are in need.

Ahmad raises several issues that are very pertinent to our discussion. He stresses the dimension of empathy that links European Muslims with their 'brothers and sisters in need'. But he also identifies another important development. The transformation of the private act of *zakat* (what Juul Petersen has associated with the culture of Islamic aid (2011)), more often associated with the notions of charity informing the work of the *Muslim Brotherhood* and the *Jama'at-e Islami*, to the high-profile, cause-specific, mediated and networked fundraising events that bear more relationship to the fundraising methods employed by Western development aid NGOs introduces new elements in the act of giving. It introduces a sense of competition, but also a sense of community among the different local charity audiences that compete but also share a common cause. The common endeavour creates a space of encounter with other Muslims, becomes part of the stock of collective experience, generates shared narratives of working together with others who may be located far away or may be different in terms of ethnicity, language or occupation. More importantly, this bond is formed not only through the realization of a common predicament, a shared perception of injustice, but through the positive action that is collectively undertaken.

Muslims in Europe today find themselves present, even active, in several places at once. Broadcasting and electronic media share the capacity to produce a sense of immediacy and time–space distantiation and facilitate the construction of a common space where Muslims, who may not coexist in terms of physical co-presence, encounter each other and quite often, exchange and reconstruct narratives, grievances and aspirations. This space of co-presence, the physical remoteness of European Muslims from each other, as well as from other Muslims no longer prevents individuals in remote locations to coexist and interact and, even, be virtual witnesses of the injustice endured by other Muslims.

Some, like Waqas, a 35-year-old website designer from West London, would actively pursue information that confirmed and reinforced their own self-identification as 'the underdog' at home and abroad. He described in some detail how he and his friends would seek on the Internet information about the treatment of Palestinian civilians by Israeli occupation forces and how this search radicalized them as it brought them in touch with Hamas. He remembers vividly accessing the Hamas-run Palestinian Information Centre website (www.palestine-info.com) and other more radical and sometimes 'clandestine' websites giving graphic information on the plight of the Palestinians in Gaza and what Bunt calls 'martyrdom' sites (2009: 266–274) that contained videos of 'martyrs' getting ready to die. These presented a romanticized version of various armed resistance actions as well as of the practice of suicide bombing through a series of videos of deceased 'heroes'. Despite their distance from Gaza, Waqas and his friends found the content of the websites and videos very pertinent to their own lives as they provided an 'honourable' response to the violence that was exercised upon the Palestinians. In a highly nuanced discussion, Waqas tried to explain that his appreciation of martyrdom had nothing to do with condoning violence. What really appealed to Waqas and was seen as relevant to his own experience was the attempt inherent in the act to gain voice and visibility in a very unequal situation. Waqas suggested that Palestinian 'martyrs' had to resort to an extreme act as they had been denied any other choice. He considers them indicative of Palestinian exceptionalism as Palestinians are, in his opinion, subjected to a brutal and dehumanizing occupation. Here we can clearly see processes of translation and domestication of meaning taking place as Waqas effectively 'distills' the meaning of a particular act from the means and the form this act takes. For him what is important is the struggle for voice and visibility, not necessarily the extreme violent desperation of the 'martyrs'.

A similar interest in 'martyrdom' and jihadi websites was shared by a small number of younger, mainly male, informants, primarily from Britain, France and the Netherlands. Among them, a very small minority talked about these with fascination and excitement, often idolizing the extremity of suicide bombing or other forms of indiscriminate violence.

Samir, a 21-year-old vehicle repair apprentice from outside Amsterdam, talking about web videos showcasing the use of booby traps and mines by the Afghan Taliban, explained his fascination in no uncertain terms:

> The Americans understand only naked, brutal violence. This is the language they talk and this is the way they [the Taliban] talk back to them. You cannot help being fascinated by the shock and panic they [the attacks of the Taliban] cause.

Similarly, Fuad, a 25-year-old West Londoner, originally from the Midlands has been sharing his interest in jihad videos with a group of close friends he met from his years of involvement in the *Hizb-ut-Tahrir*.[2] Fuad finds jihad videos 'awesome displays of power'. Fuad explains that he believes that jihad is 'the ultimate confrontation with the infidel' and that 'terrorizing civilians is acceptable as it prepares them to submit to the true God'. Finally, in another group interview, two male participants of Somali origin – Ismail and Mussa – who had meticulously tried to distance themselves from violent forms of jihad, eventually suggested that they and their friends derive gratification from descriptions and depictions of such acts.

> [we and our friends] have had enough with the 'legit' scholars who condemn the use of violence against the Israelis or the Western occupying forces. Resistance is part and parcel of Islam and, if needed, it can be gruesome. Spreading fear, shocking the enemy is not a problem. It should not be taboo and we don't shy away from it.

Although Samir, Fuad or Ismail and Mussa are not the only ones who express such an attitude towards jihadi narratives and videos, it is important to point out that not everybody who accesses them accepts the rigid, bipolar and antagonistic understandings of violence inherent in the above excerpts. Instead of generalizing out of a handful of such instances and interpreting this fascination as a generalized obsession with terrorism, as some commentators seem to argue, one should consider the importance of 'martyrdom' and self-sacrifice as a framing mechanism, as a way of accentuating the injustice inherent in the daily lives of Muslims in parts of the Middle East and its repercussions in the way Muslims perceive their position in the West.

Indeed, the majority of those of our interviewees who told us they were interested in these websites drew upon the symbolism of 'martyrdom' in order to reinforce the sense of injustice and trauma that Muslims in Palestine and elsewhere are subjected to, saw it as a cornerstone upon which they could develop their empathy, their appreciation of the suffering of their fellow Muslims in Palestine and elsewhere, but certainly made it very clear that they did not condone 'martyrdom' or consider it an act to be emulated.[3]

Rawaan, a 26-year old woman born in Antwerp, very eloquently provided a nuanced interpretation of the acts of suicide bombing featured in 'martyrdom' websites:

> I do not find the violent message intriguing. I do not think that killing people is acceptable. But I must admit, in the few times I have watched these videos I could not take my eyes away from the eyes of the women. Behind their cold look I could see desperation. The need to say something and be heard.

Rawaan goes even beyond the symbolic character that others see in martyrdom. It is interesting to note Nadia Taysir Dabbagh's interpretation of suicide as an act of communication (2005), referring, not to suicides for a 'holy' or a 'political' cause, but to the private acts of those who attempt to take their own lives in the occupied Palestinian territories, her assessment is still significant as it throws light on the way many of our respondents seem to make sense of suicide bombers.

> The suicidal actions of these particular men and women can be seen as a means of communication when words fail, an act of protest or rebellion, a cry for help and attention ... or an act of desperation when an individual's will to go on living in particularly difficult social circumstances has been lost.
>
> (Taysir Dabbagh 2005: 233)

> While the majority of our interviewees consider the loss of life that suicide bombing or other forms of inflicting mass civilian casualties entail unacceptable, it is also clear that they make sense of it as understandable. Most of those who have not outright condemned such acts or who have remained ambivalent towards them have been pointing out, not so much the violence and the terror of the act of 'martyrdom', but the communicative quality of the act, the attempt of those subjected to a brutalizing occupation to gain voice when no one is there to hear them.

It is important to note here that mass-mediated experience such as the ones we have largely been encountering in the accounts of our informants, always involves selective construction. The construction of what Alexander, in his discussion of the notion of cultural trauma, calls the 'trauma process', a crisis of meaning and identity that prompts the (re)articulation of a group's self-definition (Alexander et al. 2004). This process, Alexander suggests, always engages a 'meaning struggle', a grappling with events that involve identifying the 'nature of the pain, the nature of the victim and the attribution of responsibility' (ibid.). Whereas Eyerman (1994) argues that, in such situations, the interests and desires of the affected are articulated and represented by intellectuals, in the term's widest sense, in the case of the construction of cultural trauma by European

Muslims we would argue that, although a sense of profound injustice is often propagated by 'intellectuals', either drawing their authority from institutional association or public following, 'ordinary' Muslims are increasingly playing a more active role in such processes. This is largely due to the 'democratizing' impact of the technologies they utilize in their search of news and information about 'others like them'. As we have already seen, the use of the Internet and of other media of time–space distantiation are seamlessly integrated into the lives of most of our informants; they have for the most part demonstrated not only familiarity with media technologies but also the ability to skilfully navigate the rich mediascape available to them.

There are ample indications that the construction of a Muslim identity drawing on a sense of injustice and trauma is well underway and is proving to be enduring. Clues to its durability are provided by Neal's analysis of 'national trauma' (1998) – a concept closely related to that of 'cultural trauma'. Neal refers to its 'enduring effects', as it relates to events 'which cannot be easily dismissed, which will be played over again and again in individual consciousness', and which, with the passage of time will become 'ingrained in collective memory'. In the case of our informants, the mediated experience of suffering and discrimination becomes the subject of reflection, discussion and emotional investment. Our informants described how such news becomes the focus of collective endeavours of search, of discovery, of anxiety and, eventually of exchange and discussion. Peer groups in the context of face-to-face daily interaction, but also in virtual space, often constitute a space for such exchanges, as do more formal settings such as the mosque, the community associations, the university or college. It is in these spaces that the notion of injustice but also those of agency and identity (Gamson 1992) are understood, explained and made coherent through the means of public reflection and discourse. As Smelser (in Alexander et al. 2001) suggests, 'cultural trauma' constitutes 'a memory accepted and publicly given credence by a relevant membership group and evoking an event or situation which is (a) laden with negative affect, (b) represented as indelible, and (c) regarded as threatening a society's existence or violating one or more of its fundamental cultural presuppositions'. It is also clear that the impact of the experience of trauma is not exhausted in the articulation of notions of injustice and harm, or the (re)articulation of identity as Alexander suggests. Agency springs out of the realization that something needs to be done, that 'brothers and sisters' need to be supported, or that voice needs to be gained.

Over the past few pages we have explored the ways in which the experiences of remote others become part of the complex narrative fabric that constitutes the experiential and, in particular, injustice frames through which European Muslims situate themselves in European societies. This weaving of narratives that integrate various localities in a complex translocal and transnational web of relationships, encounters and exchanges is the product of the collective action of Europeans who identify themselves as Muslims in a variety of ways and engage in the construction of cultural and political networks. This is a fluid and continuously evolving terrain whose contours and morphology are constantly redefined through complex processes of negotiation, interaction and contestation. In this space, as we have seen, locality and local experience are interweaved and framed within a broader transnational network of flows of people, information, ideas and action. At the same time, the experiences of remote others and the translocal sites of narrating Muslim identity are localized and domesticated and made sense of in terms of their local manifestations and translations. This is a space where participants are agonizingly seeking ways of overcoming what they perceive to be under- and mis-representation and, ultimately, marginalization. It provides the means for 'inhabiting' local and translocal/transnational domains by rendering these familiar in terms of sounds, images, negating and overcoming absences and silences.

We are clearly talking about a locus of encounters, exchange and imagination: a public space that hosts multiple voices and multiple narratives and provides the raw materials for new articulations of identity, for testing boundaries and providing frameworks of experience and memory. Interviewee responses to relevant questions provide clear evidence that the solidarity felt towards other Muslims is reminiscent of what Mandaville has very aptly termed *reimagining the Umma* (2001). Apart from the various controversies that have developed in the domestic sphere of the various European societies, we have seen that the perennial issue of the fate of the Palestinian Muslims and the two intifadas, the Russian treatment of the Chechen people and the plight of the Bosnian Muslims during the war in Bosnia, have functioned as what we have termed following Bowman, instances of *constitutive violence*, moments of profound injustice not only towards the Palestinian, Chechen or Bosnian Muslims but towards all Muslims according to just under eight out of ten of our informants, including those residing in Europe. What is more, this narrative is reproduced in the various public spaces that European Muslims have established such as the Muslim media, offline and online, the international charities that have been founded primarily during the Bosnian War, and everyday discourses and practices of European Muslims. This re-imagined *Ummah*, coexists with a sense of European Muslim particularity that assumes the form of challenges as well as opportunities arising from residing in the socio-political and cultural space that is called Europe, by interacting with European societies and institutions and having to develop appropriate strategies of discourse and action. In this context, we can therefore argue that the sense of a European Muslim identity is very much a project in progress, one that is largely premised on empathy and the mediated *witnessing* and *remembrance* of the suffering of fellow Muslims throughout the world.

6
Spaces of Identity and Agency and the Reconfiguration of Islam

From injustice to identity and agency

The complex narrative fabric that constitutes the experiential frames through which European Muslims situate themselves in European societies is not, however, exclusively premised on the construction of injustice frames and is by no means singularly derived from the experience of collective trauma. Although our research findings indicate that this sense of injustice constitutes a significant element in the construction of a sense of a European Muslim identity, they have also indicated that processes of production of 'positive' narratives, looking towards the future, searching of ways to build a sense of agency and creativity are very much in evidence. This is indeed in line with the distinction between three principal components of collective action frames that Gamson proposes, namely, between justice, identity and agency frames (1992).

As we have already seen, by injustice frames Gamson refers to the sense of 'moral indignation' that does not exhaust itself in 'merely a cognitive or intellectual judgment about what is equitable ... [because it] requires a consciousness of motivated human actors who carry some of the onus for bringing about harm and suffering' (pp. 6–7). Our discussion over the past few pages has focused on this sense of injustice, the perception of the West either tolerating or inflicting this suffering on Muslims in Europe and worldwide and, equally importantly, we touched upon on the impact of this framing process in the formation of a space where notions of agency and identity are discussed and elaborated. Identity frames refer precisely to the definition of the 'we' that is subjected to suffering and harm (p. 7). Gamson also argues that this 'we' is typically posited in opposition to some 'they' who? have 'different interests or values' (p. 7). Although it is obvious that the very notion of injustice frame incorporates logically an assumption that someone perpetrates this injustice, we would argue that adversity is not always personalized and does not always take the form of an actor who inflicts damage. And, although 'personalization' and 'antagonism' strategies may prove more effective in mobilizing a particular group, a sense of collective injustice where the 'other' is diffuse may also provide the necessary connective material, so to speak, that can bind a group. Agency frames, according to Gamson, refer to 'the consciousness that it is possible to alter conditions or policies through collective action' (p. 7), that is, relate to the transition from the articulation of a common identity to the empowerment of a group to engage in collective action. It is obvious that the distinctions introduced by Gamson are analytical as, as we have already seen, injustice, identity and agency are interweaved and inextricably linked in the ways in which our informants produce their social reality.

Having said that, our research findings that this 'we' that European Muslims construct is not homogeneous or monolithic. Indeed, even the processes of construction of injustice that we have examined in Chapter 5 are not necessarily bringing about monolithic identities and closed definitions of the situation. Instead, they retain a considerable degree of openness and variation, of different emphasis and types of raw material for the construction of Muslim identities.

Bearing this element of diversity, inherent in the project of European Muslim identity construction in mind, over the next few pages, we are going to cast a closer look at the complex public spaces where European Muslims 'encounter' each other and other Muslims and engage in processes of exchange and imagination focusing primarily in processes of articulation of identity and agency with particular emphasis on the diversity of the conceptualizations of Islam and Muslim identity that are hosted and elaborated in them. We propose to do this by focusing on a number of areas of action and exchange that involve the negotiation of the meaning of Islam, authority and authenticity.

Veils, fashion, agony aunts and finding Mr Right: Reconfiguring Islam

As we have already pointed out in Chapter 1, as migrants of Muslim backgrounds became more settled in Europe and as the predominant pattern of settlement shifted from that of single guestworkers to families, the latter brought to the foreground a number of issues, concerns and aspirations linked to their social and cultural reproduction. Interaction between European Muslims and the broader societies which they formed part of, eventually revolved around symbolic issues such as blasphemy and the limits of free speech, the visibility of Islam as an element of European societies and cultures, as well as more practical matters such as the right to religious schooling or to sharia governing personal status law. Whereas conflict between 'the mainstream' of European societies and European Muslim communities has traditionally been latent or of low intensity, only occasionally disrupted by more manifest and widespread disputes, during the past couple of decades or so it became much more visible and pervasive.

In France, the *affaire du foulard* gave rise to an intense debate that has framed public perceptions of Islam and Muslims since the late eighties over the alleged threat headscarves posed to the principle of secularity (*laïcité*) in French schools and public institutions. The debate that focused on a visible item of clothing and transformed it into a symbol of cultural alterity and of a cultural clash lasted several years and, more importantly, informed public debate throughout Europe. Indeed, the dress codes observed by some Muslim women in Europe have continued to provide fertile ground for the mobilization of critics of Islam in general and of the treatment of Muslim women in Muslim cultures. As we have already seen, during the past decade, a relatively small minority of Muslim women using variations of the *burqa* or *niqab* has become the focus of public, often inimicable, scrutiny., The full veil, a visible and quite alien item of clothing for the majority of the Western European population, has acquired a symbolic significance far exceeding a mere preference of attire. The arguments and, later on, bans of the *niqab* revolved around security reasons, 'the dignity and freedom of [Muslim] women' (Sofos and Tsagarousianou 2010) or their potential to being barriers to intercultural communication and social cohesion.

The debate about the face veil, and more generally the acceptability of other forms of female Muslim attire in the West, is not a novel one. Muslim notions of modesty have often been subverted and colonized by patriarchal practices seeking to restrict women's autonomy and have caused genuine concerns.[1] As such, the veil issue has mobilized social forces inspired by liberalism and feminism and generated valuable criticisms of patriarchy in Muslim communities. On the other hand, the highly symbolic value of the topic transformed the veil issue into a potent mobilizing symbol for xenophobic, right-wing forces.

What is remarkable however, and should be noted, is that this debate is also one conducted over the absence of the women in question, as it largely leaves the affected women in a position of aporia, voiceless and powerless in the midst of a cacophony of opinions offered by Western politicians, human rights activists and feminists on the one hand, and Muslim community leaders on the other: veiled women constitute the battlefield between abstract discourses of emancipation and discourses of cultural autonomy that emphasize the lack of competence on the part of liberals and feminists to criticize an essentially reified 'Muslim' culture and tradition. It is true that behind the veil one can find women that are isolated, lonely, abused and oppressed. In such cases the veil can dissimulate suffering and silence a cry for help. In such cases it is clear that we need to devise ways of listening, of intervening and of empowering the women affected. On the other hand, considering the veil simply as a means and symbol of oppression may be misguided as it decouples it from its social–historical context.

Muslim women are seen as inherently oppressed through an excessively patriarchal religion and culture that restricts women's participation in social life. Such 'regimes of representation', Ahmad suggests,

> falsely construct Muslim women's experiences and identities as confined within artificial binaries such as 'modern', referring to women as Western, educated, secular, free and 'traditional', with images of Muslim women as uneducated, 'backward' and

religiously oppressed. They also homogenize both men and women's narratives and experiences and mask sites of complexity, social change and agency.

(Ahmad 2012: 194)

Indeed, a growing body of literature has questioned the assumption that women's participation in Islam invariably supports social norms that assign them secondary status as servants of Allah and as social subjects. Scholars, such as Saba Mahmood (2005) and Lila Abu-Lughod (1991), have argued against facile assumptions that 'Muslim women need saving' and suggested that our approach towards women embracing Islam and the practices that underlie it should be informed by an appreciation of their agency.

In the course of our research we have encountered numerous young women who defy the starkness of such categorizations and provide interesting insights on the practice of covering; these informants experiment with covering their hair or a much smaller number of women who even choose to cover their face have stressed in very articulate ways that this was a matter of choice and not coercion. Our informants have, on most occasions – with exception of one of our British interviewees who chose not to comment – provided articulate responses to our questions and mentioned numerous reasons for covering or veiling themselves. These included the affirmation of their identities as young Muslims, protesting against assimilationist ideologies and practices, or expressing their religiosity and protecting themselves from the objectification of the male predatory gaze.

Hayfa, a 27-year-old student from Germany recounted the difficulties she faced when she decided to wear the *niqab* and then emphasized the fact that, for her, this was the product of a conscious and free decision.

It [the *Niqab*] is a choice, a decision [of] whether it is required or not but, in the civilized world, the right to exercise personal choice ought to be protected. This is something called civil rights that we enjoy in civilized societies.

Aminah, a 29-year-old from Britain living in France, is not covering her head or face but nevertheless is passionate about the issue which she explicitly links to 'choice' when she refers to the then ongoing debate in France on whether face veiling should be banned:

> Although I consider myself a feminist Muslim who usually does not cover, [nonetheless I think] ... freedom is peculiar when it only allows you to make whatever choice the state wants.

The very same idiom of choice is utilized by Nadifa, a 28-year-old British nursery worker who had made the choice to cover her face against the wishes of some members of her family; 'I started covering as a matter of choice... I do not want others to tell me how they want me to be', as did Amina, a 21-year-old French student in the Netherlands, who considers the veil an indispensable part of who she is.

> I choose to wear it. Not every day, just now and again. But when I do wear it, it is entirely of my own will. No one is forcing me. If they make me take it off, they'll be taking a part of me.

Although the issue of assertiveness is implicit in our respondents' responses, we found that the latter, in their majority, echoed the underlying reasoning of a comment posted by a visitor in *Al-Muhajabah's Islamic Pages* (www.muhajabah.com) which was pointed out to us by one of interviewees.

> *Niqaab* has given me a feeling of power over myself, not just my outer, physical being but my inner mind also... I can now say I'm a woman of honour and dignity that no one should dare to mess with.

As this comment and the interview excerpts above indicate, these young women have no difficulty in bringing together Islamic discourses about modesty and the language of choice, needs and human rights which originates in the discourse of the enlightenment that Europeans usually juxtapose to Islam as belonging to a totally distinct intellectual and cultural tradition. Of course, one can always question and disagree with some of these rationalizations of veiling but the fact remains that veiling in these instances is understood as a positive assertion of rights and affirmation of identities.

In addition to this development of a discourse of reclaiming the *niqab* as a choice and right, this onslaught against women wearing the veil has been met with other, alternative, responses not only by the affected women but also by Muslim women in general that attempt to create enunciation spaces that enable them to offer alternative definitions and perspectives about themselves and their relationship with Islam and European or Western modernity. One of the strategies employed can be described as what we call 'normalization'. Over the past few years, a Muslim lifestyle and fashion industry has developed in Europe and, more broadly, in the West and has contributed to attempts to redefine and reclaim the face veil and other aspects of Muslim attire and femininity from the Western discursive association with oppression and subordination.

A number of glossy colourful lifestyle magazines with articles on love, on what it means to be a woman, marriage, having kids, marital discord, house decoration, food and, of course, fashion, cautiously bring to the public discussion a host of issues that have, in their majority, traditionally been confined to the private or more intimate domain. These include *Sisters Magazine*, which defines itself as the magazine for 'fabulous Muslim women', that comes out in both digital and print form, *EmEl* magazine, describing itself as the 'Muslim lifestyle magazine', the Turkish Âlâ magazine that has several Turkish-speaking readers in Europe and the United States-based, but quite popular among English-speaking Muslims in Europe, *Illume* magazine. Emulating the format and style of *Sisters Magazine*, the United States-based *Muslim Quarterly*, is a lifestyle magazine for men that some of our male informants referred to in more recent correspondence. These magazines as well as an increasing number of lifestyle web portals, sites, discussion groups and email lists explore issues such as 'Halal Sexuality', sex, sexual health and sexual etiquette, marriage and relationships, domestic violence, but also fashion and beauty from an 'Islamic perspective'.

Twenty-six-year-old Iraqi-born Zaynab from London reflects on her use of cybermagazines

> 'It is so important to have a place to read other sisters' views on these issues [love and relationships] and to discuss'.

Whereas 22-year-old Yasmin from Paris compares the Internet and the mosque: 'We often discuss with my friends stuff about marriage you find on the internet. You can often find much more wisdom about love and relationships in Muslim [internet] sites than in many of our mosques.'

Shireen, a 22-year old student from South London, talking about the diversity of such Internet resources and, at the time, of the first lifestyle magazines, explained their appeal to her age group:

> We can talk about relationships or other sensitive issues without having to be preached by family or horrible ladies like the one in our mosque. Sometimes, people who advise young people in the mosque are so out of touch. They do not understand we are Muslim but live in a complicated world.

Nushmia and Maryam, 26 and 27 years old respectively discussed the story of a friend who was in need of advice from a peer support website about her difficulties in having a relationship with men.

> Nushmia: She had been told time and again that meeting a man before marriage was forbidden in Islam but she felt she was pretty isolated. Her family were totally negative, she didn't get any support from friends who had moved on ... you know, she could not face the dating agencies.
>
> Maryam: Yeah. She got so many responses by well meaning people ... She was told that the world today is quite tough and that she was not the only one facing such problems. ... [people] advised her to develop networks of Muslim friends by joining activities, taking classes and the like ... She was also told it was not forbidden to initiate conversation or to seek relationships with men but the only thing that she should not do was to be alone with a man. ... She was told that Allah chooses a person for everyone. She just needed to get out there and find her own mate!

Clearly, here we can see an elastic interpretation of how two persons of the opposite sex can relate to each other. The various responses condoned dating, albeit with a number of restrictions that rendered dating more compatible with Islamic values. Still, although the girl's interlocutors adopt an Islamic standpoint, they do so selectively as they suggest behaviours, such as actively seeking a prospective mate or initiating conversation, that many traditionalists would consider unislamic. In a number of several similar discussions our respondents described this ability 'to find someone who understands', 'to discuss intimate concerns without being preached' or to 'get advice that is in line with the times' as the main appealing point of the relevant web resources and lifestyle magazines. Even in cases where the advice provided or the discussion was not as controversial as the examples above, it was quite clear that our respondents were more appreciative of the positive ways in which messages were articulated and contrasted them with the more negative, prohibitive messages coming out of the mosques and other loci of traditional authority.

While, therefore, such Internet resources and magazines affirm Islam as the *leit motif* of these discussions, they have a potentially 'desacralizing' effect on an array of topics that had hitherto been part of the domain of the jurisdiction of Islamic scholars or of male or female elders who derived their authority from 'Islamic' experience. Through the transformation of these issues from issues subjected to absolute religious or quasi-religious authority to issues that are now subject to discussion, exchange, evaluation and, ultimately, contestation, new public spaces where a new Muslim public can form their own opinions and interpretations not only on issues such as relationships or lifestyles, but also on Islam itself, have opened up.

In these new contexts too, one could locate the growing interest in Islamic fashion. Over the past few years, a Muslim lifestyle and fashion industry has developed in Europe and, more broadly, in the West and has contributed to attempts to redefine and reclaim the headscarf, the face veil and other aspects of Muslim attire and femininity from the Western discursive association with oppression and subordination There is nowadays a considerable number of Islamic designers who offer fashion products that adhere to 'Muslim tradition' but still provide women with choice and the possibility to express aspects of their own selves through it. It is interesting to see how women discuss fashion trends and styles, the use of accessories and clothes for different occasions such as parties, formal events, casual settings and so on in social media such as Facebook or MySpace, personal blogs and in everyday conversations, or how they customize their attire, be that a *niqab* or a *hijab* or *abaya* as a process of making 'dull' Islamic attire more lively and more individual. Also, most magazines or advertising adhere to the principle of non-depiction of human likeness and avoid showing faces, opting for photographs where faces are barely visible or the use of mannequins; then again, material developed for younger women might show human faces but it is still done with respect for the principle of modesty. And even the very notions of modesty are reconfigured and reconciled with those of beauty and choice as a host of colours, styles and accessories to liven up and personalize women's attire are on offer. To be sure, these developments constitute modest, mundane, everyday attempts to decouple 'Islamic' notions of femininity from assumptions of subordination, oppression and lack of dignity. They also destabilize and reconfigure the very notions of the *Islamic* and the *Western*, or rather, the positing of women within the antithetical scheme structured around these two apparently contradictory poles. Khan (2000), reflecting on such practices that navigate through this difficult terrain, called the space that Muslim women construct through their complex negotiation between Islamic and Orientalist demands and claims as the Muslim 'third space' – a space *in between* the two.

By acquiring a central position in these new enunciation spaces, Islam is progressively 'routinized' and reinterpreted in a variety of ways. Similarly, the articulation of 'being Islamic' in terms of human rights and citizenship (as we have seen in the case of our respondents talking about the *niqab*) and through the reinterpretation of key Islamic notions such as that of modesty through their coupling with beauty and choice (in the cases of lifestyle and fashion), the assumed rigid boundaries between the *Islamic* and the *Western* are relativized and blurred and the binary logic of their juxtaposition is challenged and destabilized. In addition to this development of a discourse of reclaiming the *niqab* as a choice and right, this onslaught against women wearing the veil has been met with other, alternative, responses not only by the affected women but also by Muslim women in general that attempt to create enunciation spaces that enable women to offer alternative definitions and perspectives about themselves and their relationship with Islam.

Linked to the issue of modesty is also that of marriage and premarital relationships that many of our informants talked about in the course of our discussions. This is obviously a subject of considerable complexity that could not be discussed extensively in the context of this chapter; however, of particular relevance to our discussion of notions of modesty here are the discussions we had about the relevance or not of parental say in the choice of one's partner, the notion of dating and the existence of matrimonial websites and agencies that are catering for the needs of a small but expanding Muslim professional middle class that is emerging in various European cities.

Referring to the issue of choosing a partner, almost all of our female informants and over half of our male interviewees argued that they do not expect parents to determine the choice of a partner for their children. Just under half of those who expressed an opinion suggested that parents should be involved in some way – primarily by providing their approval. Younger women questioned the ability of their parents to make 'safe' choices for them in an environment markedly different from environments in which they grew up and argued that the principle of a woman and a man behaving 'modestly' (by not dating or engaging in premarital relationships) was not pragmatic.

> My parents cannot have the necessary information to know if I and a potential partner are compatible. They have not got experience [of western society] and they cannot advice me on what is best for me.
>
> (Sabah, 22 years old from Amsterdam)

> Our parents' expectations are based on them growing up in India or Somalia, or what have you. Many start to understand that we are not growing up back there.
>
> (Mussadika, 25 years old from South London)

Several of our older informants who have children of their own seem to share this point of view and to reject the argument that arranged marriages ensure that partnerships are not based on 'inappropriate' motives and that prospective partners behave modestly. Arguments such as 'it is a matter of upbringing' (Ayhan, 45), or 'good children know what is best for them' are indicative of how tradition is being questioned or modified by both younger and older people alike.

It is at this point that the issue of matrimonial agencies becomes quite illuminating in the transformation of European Muslims' understanding of *Islam*. Although only four of our informants had used an agency – and they all declared they were 'happily married' – many more readily expressed an opinion of whether they consider Muslim matrimonial agencies to be appropriate for European Muslims. Their responses largely confirm findings of research that has demonstrated that second-generation Muslim women are able to negotiate issues such as marriage and education choices by recourse to women's rights within Islamic discourses (Bhachu 1996; Bradby 1999; Dwyer 1999) and that matrimonial practices have been adapting in order to accommodate changing social realities (Ahmad 2001; Ahmad, Modood, and Lissenburgh 2003; Basit 1996, 1997; Dale et al. 2002a, 2002b). Indeed almost three-quarters of our interviewees considered that online matrimonial services for Muslims are a means of reproduction traditions crucial to one's Islamic faith and the values that underpin it. At the same time, they also recognized that these practices constitute modifications necessitated by contemporary localized situations and experiences. The recognition of this symbiotic relationship of elements of change within an overall sense of continuity is not seen by most as a departure from Islamic traditions but as an extension or adaptation of existing practice despite the impact such an adaptation has on definitions of modesty, propriety and decency. Whereas, most of our respondents reject Eurocentric terminologies such as 'dating', their responses indicate that they are actively seeking to redefine both *Islamic* and *Western* practices in a way that would both be practical but also not deviate from principles they consider central to their faith.

Another significant and controversial area where Islam is reappraised and redefined relates again to issues of sexuality, in particular the increasingly noticeable debates regarding the compatibility of homosexuality and membership of the *Ummah*. Issues pertaining to this topic have been raised by our informants both in the initial interviews and follow-up discussions. Although our sample did not include a large number of openly gay and lesbian informants, discussions on sexuality also opened up the issue of homosexuality and its acceptability within Islam. Although approximately three-quarters of our interviewees were dismissive of any connection between the two, just over a quarter of our informants were more open to the possibility of a practicing Muslim being gay or lesbian.

Fuat, a 30-year-old office worker from Frankfurt illustrates the way in which he and various other Muslim young gays and lesbians of different ethnic backgrounds are trying to challenge their exclusion from their Muslim communities. Talking about a local support network, he identified the ways in which this operates.

> We have been having meetings where we discuss issues that affect us as gay and lesbian Muslims. We talk about our experiences and the way we deal with prejudice at home, at work, in the community.... [Our meetings] are about getting to know people who are like us and who are prepared to challenge homophobia within our communities. We talk about how we can claim the right to be seen as every other Muslim person. We cannot turn our back to our faith but we cannot pretend that we are not are the way God made us.

Musa, a 23-year-old student from central Paris, while being equally adamant that neither his faith nor his sexuality are negotiable, prefers to explore such issues in a different way. He talks about how crucial the Internet has been as it allowed him to explore and discuss more issues that he could not discuss with people in his family or community.

> There were times where I felt so lonely, so frustrated...I had no one to talk to, no one to listen to me. I thought I was abnormal, that I had feelings that condemned me turn my back to God.... This affects your sense of self-worth....I often thought about ending my life but I could not bear to commit such a sin. Looking through the internet I found the organization [Musulmans Progressistes de France (http://www.musulmans-progressistes-france. org)]....It changed my life, it brought me in touch with other people like me – not only homosexuals – who felt excluded and suffocated by a narrow-minded, vindictive Islamic establishment.[2]

Virtually unthinkable a decade ago, such voices are increasing and are behind various local and translocal initiatives to redefine Islam in ways that are accommodating to what established orthodoxy considers deviant sexuality. As Mohamed Omar, the initiator of a gay-friendly mosque in Uppsala, Sweden says, such initiatives are challenging not so much the Muslim communities but the Muslim leaderships that have deeply conservative and homophobic agendas. And although the majority of our informants were not positive towards such initiatives, it is interesting that just over a quarter were sympathetic to a more open approach towards issues of sexuality and sexual preference. The following exchange between a group of interviewees in Amsterdam is illustrative of the controversy this issue stirs up and the diversity of opinion it gives rise to:

> Fatima: I do not see why Islam should not welcome people that are different... you know...
>
> Hakim: If mosques open their doors to homosexuals they will not be mosques any more. It would not be different than going to the circus.
>
> Fatima: I know this is difficult. I am not very comfortable... but I know decent people who are homosexual. I know they believe in God and they are really decent. Why allowing them to the mosque would be a problem? More than allowing someone who beats his wife?
>
> Elif: And if homosexuality is a weakness or a sin, should not mosques accept sinners who are more in need of divine guidance?
>
> Ibrahim: If God says in his blessed book that something is prohibited, then it is prohibited. Modernising interpretations may try to twist His word but...
>
> Selma: but Islam is based on interpretation. That's why there are scholars and different schools of thought. There is a place in Islam for all of us, women, men, tall, short... why not lesbians and homosexuals?

Apart from an obvious gender divide which largely reflects a slightly greater openness towards rethinking Islam and the boundaries of what is acceptable and not on the part of our younger female interviewees – although we also encountered several young women that uncompromisingly supported deeply conservative positions – it is clear that a not negligible minority is prepared to accept more open interpretations of what is *haram* (not permitted) and more inclusive definitions of the *Ummah*. Fatima's case is typical of many like her who, although finding it hard to talk about such issues, are prepared to embrace a more inclusive approach premised, not on the letter of the Qur'an, but on what they consider morality derived from the spirit of the text. Obviously, this is a highly contentious area and the controversy that attempts to push the boundaries of acceptability and inclusiveness is not pertaining to Islam only, as similar debates are taking place within Christian churches and, even, within the context of secular European states.

Who does Allah listen to?

Such boundary-challenging practices can be found in everyday, private and public, profane and sacred contexts. One other particular instance where women are actively exploring the boundaries of the acceptable involves the gendered character of dailiness – in particular, the questioning of the primacy of men in various domains of social and religious life. In a group discussion among young Muslim women and men from Amsterdam, a heated yet highly nuanced debate broke out as to whether and when women should be allowed to lead prayers. In the course of the debate, apart from the extreme positions that either denied, or emphatically asserted the right of women to do so, it became clear that several different negotiating positions were articulated, each probing the rigidity of other opinions and seeking a broader consensus that went beyond the more dominant conservative positions.

'Enlightened' males such as 30-year-old school teacher Vedat suggested that women were in no way inferior to men but quickly qualified his argument:

> Men and women are equal... Women should definitely have the right to lead prayers. It might be appropriate, however, to lead when those praying are female.

Whereas he accepted the equality of men and women in terms of their capacity to perform a sacred duty, he nevertheless considered that distinctions should be made at the realm of the performance of that duty. In other words, his recognition of equality of women and men does not go as far as to challenge the established and highly gendered division of labour as far as the performance of sacred tasks is concerned. Not unexpectedly, his position was challenged by 25-year old hairdresser Nadia who accused him of double standards.

> You talk about equality but you have no problem with men being more equal than women. Does it not make you wonder why you do not question the right of any man to lead the prayers but you so easily accept the same right for women only behind closed doors?

Hassan and Zaynab, both 35 years old, suggested that this equality could be best expressed within the domestic sphere where experienced elder women could lead younger and less experienced members of their family. Hassan added:

> [O]f course, this could not happen all the time but only when a more senior male member of the family cannot be available.

Again, here we see a position that confines the exercise of female authority within the boundaries of the domestic sphere and effectively treats it as a last resort.

Forty-year-old housewife Naima agreed that women should not be segregated and their claim to equality should not be negotiated but tried to introduce criteria that would make the equality argument more acceptable to sceptics:

> I think everybody would agree that it does not matter if one is a man or a woman as long as they have the qualities necessary for leading prayers. If an older woman possesses the same knowledge as a man and finds herself in a situation where she is the most qualified to lead prayers no one should stop her.

Here we see a slightly modified position that is premised on a statement about the equality of men and women but attempts to frame this in terms of possessing the necessary qualities and ritual know-how. In this way not every woman can lead prayers as not every man should.

Such discussions are testing the boundaries of the *possible* and of the *appropriate* in Islam and, although they are not taking place among European Muslims but among Muslims in general, in the case of our respondents they appear to be related to the need to adapt to life in Europe or respond to challenges they face as Muslims in Europe. The discussions summarized above were typical of similar concerns expressed by the majority of interviewees and demonstrating the centrality of gender relations in processes of redefining Islam by European Muslims. These were, in most cases, highly nuanced discussions with expressed opinions often being antagonistic to established practice or attempting to avoid a direct collision with existing authority structures opting for a piecemeal modification of the hegemonic discourse within European Islam.

The discussion that has preceded indicates that the spaces that European Muslims, construct through their collective efforts, constitute loci that host multiple voices, multiple narratives which provide the raw materials for new articulations of identity, for testing boundaries and providing frameworks of experience and memory. These are spaces where authority structures within European Muslim communities are negotiated and transformed. We are essentially dealing with a fluid and continuously evolving terrain, whose contours and morphology are constantly redefined through complex processes of negotiation, interaction and contestation. It is a new landscape where participants are agonizingly seeking ways of devising the means for 'inhabiting' Europe, to overcome historically conditioned and culturally sanctioned binary juxtapositions between Islam and Europe, Islam and the West, and to 'normalize' Islam, in the sense of countering ways of representing it as 'exceptional', 'different' and 'alien'.

The quest for authenticity and the idiom of 'choice'

Tam is a 37-year-old parent of one young child living in Zaanstad, a primarily working-class town just outside Amsterdam. He and his wife describe themselves as religious. They are known among the local Muslin (mainly Turkish) community and they frequent the local Sultan Ahmet mosque. Although Tam and his wife are of South Asian origin, they, nevertheless, have blended very well in the community as, Tam suggests, 'Islam does not know boundaries of language or ethnicity'. However, he occasionally drives to another mosque in Amsterdam, not to pray, but to listen to and discuss with a local scholar. As he points out, when asked, the majority of those frequenting the mosque are of North African origin, so the appeal of his chosen mosque has nothing to do with ethnicity. He points out that although any mosque is a 'home' for a Muslim, he chooses to visit Amsterdam as the discussions there are stimulating and enable him to explore more his beliefs and values.

A somewhat similar case is that of Zia, a 40-year-old from East London. Zia also describes himself as a religious person. He and his family attend the East London Mosque in Whitechapel regularly for prayers bur Zia says that his Internet network where he explores and discusses issues pertaining to his faith is an equally stimulating 'place'. When prompted he points out that the physically remote interlocutors and scholars share with him the passion of exploring his faith. He spends quite a lot of his spare time discussing the Qur'an and Hadith online as well as reading texts of his favourite scholars. He considers the Internet a valuable resource and he is concerned at the transformation of many mosques into 'Disneylands' as he characteristically calls them. As mosques are no longer, in his opinion, places of learning, the Internet provides a way of bypassing the constraints of physical space and getting close to scholars and interlocutors.

Although 22-year-old bank clerk Anser and 25-year-old Bushra both came from Muslim backgrounds, they considered the Islam practiced by their parents 'residual' and 'inauthentic', tainted by practices and beliefs that were not Islamic. Their own notion of Islam is marked by what one can describe as a move from a 'lived' Islam (i.e. the one of their parents) to a 'constructed' one to borrow the terminology deployed by Babès (2004) to describe similar transformations taking place among French Muslim youth.

Anser, reflecting on how Islam is lived and practiced by his extended family and on his 'discovery' of Islam says,

> Islam is not handed down, it is not family property...It has to be discovered and embraced. Prophet Muhammad had, himself encouraged Muslims, to follow the path in the pursuit of knowledge.

Bushra is similarly seeing becoming Muslim as something different from just following rituals without really reflecting on one's faith.

Just because you are told how to pray and how to behave does not mean you are a Muslim. You have to seek knowledge, to strengthen your faith with it.

Together with Tam and Zia, Anser and Bushra are representative of a not negligible portion of our respondents who have been looking beyond the 'residual' practice of Islam for a more 'authentic' experience. In his quest for authenticity, Tam has resorted to physically moving between Zaanstad and Amsterdam as he felt that the more remote Amsterdam mosque provided him with a more rewarding religious experience. For Zia, Anser and Bushra the rich debate that can be found on Internet has provided a space where they could seek and discover Islamic knowledge and a means of 'discovering' Islam, of seeking authenticity. We have already referred to the use of the Internet and of other media of time–space distantiation and noted how they are seamlessly integrated into the lives of most of our informants. Not only have the latter, for the most part, demonstrated familiarity with media technologies but also the ability to skilfully navigate the rich mediascape available to them. This is a space where notions of Islam and the Islamic are explored and articulated but also, as Anderson notes referring to the public sphere of Islam,

> an arena of contest in which activists and militants brought forth challenges to traditional interpretative practices and authority to speak for Islam, especially to articulate its social interests and political agendas. Patrick Gaffney (1994) has astutely noted that their claims draw on social and political experience as alternatives both to expertise in textual hermeneutics associated with the learned men of Islam (ulema) and to more illuminationist priorities exemplified in Sufi and generally mystical ways.
>
> (2003: 887–888)

Indeed, this is not something entirely new. Islamic public space has always been diverse and open to various degrees of challenge and contestation. Examples of this are the 'small media' studied by Sreberny-Mohammadi and Mohammadi (1994) and the audiocassettes that carried sermons of then-exiled Ayatollah Ruhollah Khomeini into pre-revolutionary Iran that contested the process of secularization of the country by the Shah, and which were copied and further disseminated from household to household. Or similarly, what Hirschkind calls the 'ethical soundscape', the space opened up by the replaying of recorded sermons by popular preachers into neighbourhoods, public spaces, shops and taxis that culminated in the formation of Muslim counterpublics in Cairo (2006). These are instances of a highly diverse terrain comprising a multiplicity of 'moral' and 'political' centres that compete in the interpretation of what is Islamic and what is not.

What is probably new is the elimination of the constraints that spatial and temporal distance placed to the development of these public spaces. Technological advances have made possible the further multiplication of spaces of enunciation and spaces of 'belonging' for Europe's Muslims. As we pointed out earlier, media technologies today enable a sense of simultaneity and co-presence, of immediacy. This is significant as, in many ways, it brings ease of access to various enunciators, be they scholars or 'lay', and blurs the boundaries between more traditional and established scholars on the one hand, and relatively newer 'outsider' scholars, such as the phenomenon of the ascendance to prominence of the hitherto relative outsider in Islamic jurisprudence, Yusuf al-Qaradawi, seems to indicate (Skovgaard-Petersen and Graf 2009). Equally significant is the blurring of the boundaries between ulema and lay people as this new public sphere opens up the possibility 'for new discursive practices to develop . . . and fosters new habits of production and consumption' (Anderson 2003: 888) and for spaces of discussion, scrutiny and interrogation.

Interestingly, this space of authenticity that our informants yearn for and pursue is not located in some remote past close to the genesis of Islam and should not thus be perceived as an instance of persistently 'looking back' and trying to recover an irretrievable past. Rather, it constitutes

> a peculiar longing, at once modern and anti-modern. It is oriented toward the recovery of an essence whose loss has been realized only through modernity, and whose recovery is feasible only through the methods and sentiments created in modernity.
>
> (Bendix 1997)

The Islam that many European Muslims are trying to retrieve through the exercise of 'choice' is one yet to be discovered, or even to be constructed. It is precisely a work in progress, drawing upon the individual and collective efforts of European Muslims. It is a work of contesting authority and established norms, testing boundaries and expanding them. Whether it is piety, authenticity or a way of reconciling the various worlds that European Muslims inhabit at the same time, these public spaces and the networks that link them represent veritable laboratories of social imagination.

7
Is There a Space for European Muslims?

This study has attempted to shed some light in a subject that, although central in European public debate, has customarily been approached in a rather emotionally charged way. Muslim lives in Europe have become the object of public concern and scrutiny, Muslim cultures have been shunned upon and most attempts to articulate a legitimate and audible Muslim voice have been frustrated. Living in a continent whose self-definition has, for just under a millennium, been constructed in opposition to Islam (Delanty 1995; Neumann 1999; Said 1978), in the midst of societies that have painstakingly strived to expunge the memory of their encounters and cultural exchanges with the world of Islam, having to navigate through a treacherous landscape shaped, not only by a long and overwhelming Orientalist tradition that has traditionally viewed Muslims as bearers of an impossible cultural baggage of belatedness and barbarism but also by more recent processes of securitization and criminalization, European Muslims have found themselves in an unenviable position.

Already by the late 1980s immigration had become a potent element of the public debate with particular political forces mobilizing it as a means of gaining legitimacy and political capital (Mény and Surel 2002), especially as they targeted Muslim migrants and stressed the alleged incompatibility of Islam with European culture. This fusion of far right populism and islamophobia was so successful that it has informed public debate since then and has rendered discussions of immigration and the failure of multiculturalism inseparable from questioning the place of Islam and Muslims in Europe. As the debate was cast in highly polarized terms, European Muslims found themselves in the unenviable position of having to confront an onslaught against them. The September 11 attacks against the United States rendered Islam and European Muslim communities 'acceptable' targets of scrutiny, criticism and often aggression and violence.

As we have tried to demonstrate, European Muslims have had to come to terms with this increasingly inimical environment and develop appropriate responses to their perceived, symbolic and often physical, marginalization. We have stressed that although there is evidence pointing to European Muslims experiencing increasing discrimination and prejudice (Open Society Institute 2010), this has been uneven throughout Europe. In this book we have focused on the *perception* of rather the actual and often quantifiable marginalization of European Muslims as it is the latter rather that provides the background which identity and social action are built upon. Within a highly polarized sociocultural context, Muslims in Europe have formed over time particular perceptions of themselves and of their place in European societies.

As Cesari (2008) points out, this perception of marginalization and of *aporia* has a number of potential consequences. Although her classification of the options available to European Muslims constitutes an analytical tool as reality on the ground is much more complex and nuanced, it can, nevertheless, serve as a useful starting point for the examination of the politics of identity underlying the formation of what we have called a European Muslim identity:

> [I]n such a situation, in which the relationship between dominator and dominated has had such vast consequences, three modes of integration are possible for Muslims: acceptance, avoidance, or resistance.... These three modes underlie all the possible types of Islamic discourse and activity, both within the Muslim community and in relation to the non-Muslim world 2008: 156.

Acceptance entails the adoption of the dominant discourse of the 'host' cultures, combined with a process of forgetting or repressing any markers of difference. Many of our interviewees, especially those from France, recognize elements of this strategy in the way older generations tried to 'fit in', to 'become invisible' or to 'leave who they are behind'. This seems to be understandable yet a no longer preferable option for most of the people we talked to as it is deemed as tantamount to cultural annihilation.

Avoidance, according to Cesari, 'refers to types of behavior or language that attempt to separate Muslims from the non-Muslim environment as much as possible: for example, by developing a sectarian form of Islamic religious belief' (Cesari 2008). This is a relatively marginal strategy encountered among our sample in a variety of permutations from instances of withdrawal from aspects of mainstream culture, such as the rejection of television or other media and the recourse to 'purer' alternatives, or various instances of mental or physical withdrawal from 'Western society' or movements towards home schooling of Muslim children or some strands of the broader movement for the establishment of Islamic schools.

Resistance, according to Cesari (2008), means developing strategies of rejecting the dominant definitions of Islam and of Muslims. This is what we termed *assertive modes of identification* mainly because we believe that *assertion* lies at the centre of such practices and, partly because we would argue that *resistance* emphasizes too much on the reactive and not the creative dimension of these. Assertion can be formal or informal. It assumes forms that are exceptional, spectacular or violent. It can also be located in banal and mundane daily practices at the interstices of the private, the intimate and the public. Although it can involve action revolving around what Fraser (1995) would call politics of redistribution, we have seen that assertive practices revolve around a politics of identity, or of recognition. They are highly symbolic and challenge established boundaries of visibility and audibility – they range from investing intimate and private spaces with familiar markers of what being a Muslim means to individuals, to adopting dress codes and behaviours that challenge dominant or official expectations,[1] to the more high-profile politics of protest. This is indeed the context in which we situated our discussion of the various disputes over the erection of mosques and other buildings associated with European Muslim communities, the veil and burqa controversies and most other mobilizations of the past two decades.

Injustice frames and European Muslim identities

Through the complexity and considerable diversity of the responses of our interviewees, we saw emerging, earlier in this volume, an overarching theme in their own self-representations: Our data suggest that Muslims in Europe have been constructing representations of themselves as victims of processes of systematic marginalization and discrimination. We have also pointed out that complementing this widespread view among them is the overwhelming sense of Muslims beyond Europe itself, in more or less remote locations in the world, being subjected to various forms of political and economic injustice by Western states including the European countries they reside in or whose citizenship they have. Thus, although discrimination is more directly experienced *at home*, it is complemented, reinforced and confirmed by the visibility, in European Muslim eyes, of the suffering of Muslims worldwide. Such perceptions are also compounded by the perceived culpability, again in European Muslim eyes, of the West, including Europe, who are seen to inflict, or tolerate others inflicting, hardship and suffering to *people like them*. In this context, empathy and identification with the suffering of *other Muslims* becomes a key element in the formation of a European Muslim identity.

More precisely, this self-perception is particularly important as it introduces an explicit link between experiencing, or rather, forming perceptions of marginalization on the one hand and identification as a 'Muslim' as opposed (or often in addition) to particular class or ethnic identities, educational or other socio-economic characteristics on the other. This prevalent sense of injustice provides the raw material for the construction of what, following Gamson (1995), we call *injustice frames*, that is, a particular lens through which the diverse category we can descriptively call 'European Muslims' view the public debates and practices that relate to them and affect them as such. In other words, injustice and, more broadly, experiential frames constitute a threshold beyond which the term *European Muslims* is no longer merely descriptive but acquires a more concrete meaning and significance for those it has been used to describe. In this process of construction and convergence of these frames, four important facets seemed to be significant:

1. Local experience: the majority of our informants demonstrated strong links with their localities (cities or regions). They displayed a sense of belonging to local communities and an interest in local issues. Local government and local societies seem to have an impact on their everyday life as they depend on the former

for the provision of crucial services such as schooling, access to spaces for events, licencing and permits, and the nature of their interaction with the latter sets the tone for community relations. Interestingly, many recounted particular instances such as local events, debates or disputes, which they, personally, or their local Muslim community, made sense of as instances of injustice exercised against them because they were Muslim. The local society also appears to be an important locus where they 'experience' broader instances of prejudice or discrimination, in the sense that they make sense of them in the course of interaction with their peers (Muslims and non-Muslims alike), and of the articulation of relevant responses where appropriate.

2. Experience at national level: the responses of the majority of our interviewees provide evidence that the country of residence, the national administration, political culture and society constitute important points of reference for them and meaningful contexts for social action and identification of themselves as Muslims. Again, a majority claimed in no uncertain terms that Muslims in their own country of residence were subjected to discrimination and encountered prejudice. Interestingly, their expectations and aspirations as well as the nature of challenges they claimed they encountered were inflected with the idiom of the nation state, that is, they were informed by the opportunity structures and constraints posed by the prevalent political culture, political system and administrative apparata of the nation state in which they find themselves situated.

3. *Europe-wide experience*: the sense that Muslims in Europe are confronting particular challenges that can primarily be defined as 'European' is prevalent. Despite their undeniably strong attachments to locality and their increasing awareness of the importance of the national level in terms of it constituting a privileged framework for interaction and social action, 'Europe' looms large in the narratives of our informants. Instances of 'injustice', campaigns, forms of community organization in other parts of Europe are important in the process of formation of European Muslim experience and identity. Not surprisingly, this 'tuning in' into what affects Muslims in other European societies requires considerable effort, the formation of information networks and spaces and engagement in processes of cultural translation and

'domestication' of experiences of 'others', sometimes quite different from their own. In other words, the implementation of the
burqa ban in France (affecting primarily some French Muslims)
was integrated into the injustice frames constructed by many of
the British Muslim informants who have not faced such restrictions in the United Kingdom as it was deemed to be a problem
faced by European Muslims *tout court*. It should, of course, be
pointed out that *Europe* has often been used interchangeably with
other related terms such as *the West* which obviously alludes
to broader experiences that transcend the confines of Europe
and affinities to North American and other Muslims worldwide.
Although it cannot be denied that European Muslims not only
perceive themselves as part of the broader Muslim community of
the 'Western world' but also confirm this through their cultural
and material consumption strategies and practices and the networks of rows of people, funds and organizational 'know-how' as
discussed earlier, we would argue that this by no means negates
the fact that a substantial part of their experiential horizons
remains focused on Europe and on their presence in it.

4. *Being Muslim in a broader transnational context*: as the very essence
of being Muslim is informed by the universalism inherent in
Islam, it was not surprising to come across overwhelming confirmation of the awareness of and sensitivity to events that have
been unfolding in the various parts of the globe where fellow Muslims live, including the broader West and also the Middle East,
Central and Southeast Asia which are home to the bulk of the
world's Muslim population and other areas beyond these where
Muslim communities are established. Although part of this interest may relate to what we have termed *politics back home*, that
is the social and political developments in the countries of origin of those European Muslims who have migrated to Europe, it
would be misleading to fall to the rather easy pitfall of not looking
beyond that. As a matter of fact, European Muslims are inspired
by a more encompassing solidarity towards Muslims who are situated in remote and unfamiliar locations. Interviewee responses to
relevant questions provide clear evidence that the solidarity felt
towards other Muslims is more in line with what Mandaville has
very aptly termed *reimagining the Umma* (2001). Both interviewee
responses and other research findings related to the cultural and

material practices of European Muslims provide ample evidence of the complexity and intensity of such relationships, affinities and solidarities. This transnational and universal dimension of European Muslim identities has played a significant role in the formation of the latter. Apart from the various controversies that have developed in the domestic sphere of the various European societies, we have seen that the perennial issue of the fate of the Palestinian Muslims and the two intifadas, the Russian treatment of the Chechen people and the plight of the Bosnian Muslims during the war in Bosnia have functioned as what we have termed following Bowman, instances of *constitutive violence*, moments of profound injustice not only towards the Palestinian, Chechen or Bosnian Muslims but towards all Muslims according to just under eight out of ten of our informants. What is more, this narrative is reproduced in the various public spaces that European Muslims have established such as the Muslim media, offline and online, the international charities that have been founded primarily during the Bosnian War and everyday discourses and practices of European Muslims. This re-imagined *Ummah*, as well as a sense of a European Muslim identity, is therefore one that is largely premised on empathy and the mediated *witnessing* and *remembrance* of the suffering of fellow Muslims throughout the world.

It is important to point out here that this sense of 'moral indignation', although a crucial means for constructing spaces of cognitive and emotional convergence, of empathy and solidarity, is not the only one at play. Injustice, trauma, a sense of being subjected to physical or symbolic violence are part of the complex processes of identity formation and its activation, of turning European Muslims from a mere demographic fact into a social reality, into bringing about the realization that it is possible to alter conditions or policies through collective action. Needless to say that such processes are inextricably linked and largely simultaneous. We have examined in this context the processes of construction of narratives of belonging and their activation in various contexts of collective action, such as local action for the erection of mosques, for making schools welcoming for Muslim pupils, as well charity engagement, rethinking and reinterpreting the concepts of Jihad and martyrdom.

We have seen through our empirical research findings that this 'we' that European Muslims construct is not homogeneous or monolithic. Indeed, even the processes of construction of injustice that one could think have the unique capacity to focus energies and minds to one goal and, therefore, the potential to reinforce tendencies towards homogenization, do not seem to affect the polyphonic and polysemic universe we call European Islam.

Our analysis suggests that the public spaces where European Muslims 'encounter' each other and other Muslims, and engage in processes of exchange and imagination are diverse and give rise to various and diverse conceptualizations of Islam and Muslim identity. Discussions as diverse as those we examined on dress and fashion, on intimate issues such as love, courtship and the selection of one's partner, or the exchanges that we examined, pertaining to issues of parental and communal authority in this respect unequivocally reveal the creation of spaces where plurality and diversity are actively and continually constructed. These are spaces of experimentation and contestation, of complex and intricate negotiations, of perilous navigation between the claims of both traditionalism and Western modernity. These are places where voice is articulated and Islam is reconfigured and modified, reinterpreted and routinized, while forms of authority are scrutinized and challenged.

What kind of Islam?

If we are then to speak of a European Muslim identity, we have suggested, we have to visualize this as inherently diverse and polyphonic, as characterized by multiple intersections of diverse experiences. Not only is the Muslim population of Europe diverse in terms of languages, ethnicities, sects or schools of thought, orthodoxies and heterodoxies, it is permeated by the distinctive outlooks that gender and generation bring to daily life and longer-term orientations and it is coloured by the inflections of locality of settlement and dailiness. What is more, the different challenges and opportunities that distinct national frameworks present to Europe's Muslims as well as the diverse claims that countries of putative origin are making over 'their diasporas' complicate the picture even more. To this, one should add the increasing numbers of converts, a younger generation that, as we pointed out earlier, 'rediscovered' an Islam 'untainted' by the 'backwardness' of their parents' cultures and, of course, the many other facets and degrees of Muslim affiliation and religiosity. Radical and fundamentalist Muslims share this polyphonic universe with more moderate voices, the devout meet the less religious or even secular Muslims (the cultural Muslims according to Dasseto)[2] in a variety of contexts. Faith finds itself alongside a sense of cultural heritage or of political exigency or ideology in the face of adversity and prejudice, and all these factors give rise to a complex constellation of attitudes, motivations and practices that make up what we call European Islam and European Muslims.

As Europe comprises a rich array of different polities and civil societies, each one of which has developed over time distinct institutional and cultural responses to diversity, minorities and religion, it is not surprising to encounter a complex mosaic of Muslim responses and attitudes towards different European policy frameworks. Corporatist or statist or more liberal political cultures and policies often shape the ways in which Muslims will engage in associational life and processes of representation. The vast array of responses to difference ranging from the assimilationism, traditionally though not entirely accurately linked to the French republic, to the different multiculturalisms of countries such as the United Kingdom or Sweden, or consociationalism as practiced in the Netherlands, Belgium or Northern Ireland, have also informed the ways in which European Muslims have been responding to the institutional and cultural frameworks that they encounter in their everyday lives.

Furthermore, the gendering of Muslim experience in Europe, as well as the smaller or even considerable generational rifts that often mark European Muslim lives make an important contribution in shaping distinct outlooks towards life, coexistence or interpretations of religion and authority. Different perspectives on social hierarchies, authority structures, ingroup and outgroup relationships as well on the meaning and importance of Islam are coloured by gender and the different generational experiences of Muslims in Europe. As Werbner points out in her study of Manchester Muslims, gender and generation activate different perfomative spaces and contribute to differential empowerment and identification processes (2002: 217–230).

But performative spaces are activated by a variety of experiences beyond gender and generation and set in motion processes of translation, invention and social construction. As we have seen when examining the cultural practices of European Muslims, the multitude of Muslim television channels and the extensive and diverse Muslim cyberspace, apart from being used as sources of news, consumer, lifestyle, religious and political information, provide spaces for encountering remote others and exploring Islam and Muslimness. European Muslim women, for example, actively utilize them to locate interpretations of domesticity and domestic hierarchy and to explore intimate and domestic issues, effectively bypassing traditional authorities often in the name of authenticity. Others, in search of an 'untainted' Islam resort to similar selective tactics of construction of their 'own' Islam, while queer Muslims attempt to identify traditions of tolerance and acceptance of homosexuality in the context of an again 'authentic' Islam which paradoxically is equally selectively constructed. In the quest for 'authenticity', or for building a new secular politicized sense of Muslimness it is clear that the idioms of choice and modernity are used extensively as we pointed out in Chapter 5. As Khan (2002) points out, the allegedly stable, timeless and fixed 'tradition' many are looking for are in fact context contingent, and their putative constancy is actually a matter of ideological projects emerging from the current moment. Existing networks and rituals are incorporated in novel ideological and political projects while traditional authority, ethnic or local or Islamic can easily be relativized in the context of a polyphonic universe opened up by the rich and diverse opportunity structure inherent in the process of construction a European Muslim identity.

In this context, any mention of European Muslims cannot refer to an overarching identity that represses or displaces all this diversity of experience, heritage and belief but rather to a context of interaction, of development of shared frameworks of experience, responses to challenges and opportunities and repertoires of social action and identification. It could be argued that European Muslims have embarked on a journey of discovery, where encounters, the identification of shared concerns and the engagement in collective action slowly sets in motion processes of convergence. In other words we are witnessing a process akin to that described by the British historian E. P. Thompson in his seminal work *The Making of the English Working Class* (1968).

As Thompson characteristically points out referring to the notion of class:

Sociologists who have stopped the time-machine and, with a good deal of conceptual huffing and puffing, have gone down to the engine-room to look, tell us that nowhere at all have they been able to locate and classify a class. They can only find a multitude of people with different occupations, incomes, status hierarchies, and the rest. Of course they are right, since class is not this or that part of the machine, but *the way the machine works* once it is set in motion – not this and that interest, but *the friction of interests* the movement itself, the heat, the thundering noise.... [U]ltimately, the definition can only be made in the medium of *time* – that is, action and reaction, change and conflict. When we speak of a class we are thinking of a very loosely defined body of people who share the same congeries of interests, social experiences, traditions and value system, who have a *disposition* to *behave* as a class, to define themselves in their actions and their consciousness in relation to other groups of people in class ways. But class itself is not a thing, it is a happening.

(1965: 357; original emphasis)

It is precisely this deafening noise generated by the conversations and debates among European Muslims, the friction that is inherent in encounters of relative strangers, the anarchic script of this polyphony, the happening that we set up to study.

Talking about the emerging Muslim public spaces obviously is not something that can be accomplished through this study alone. We are essentially dealing with the product of the collective action of Europeans who identify themselves as Muslim in a variety of ways and engage in the construction of cultural and other networks, utilize and create particular media in particular ways and are involved in processes of cultural exchange. We are also dealing with a fluid and continuously evolving terrain, whose contours and morphology are constantly redefined through complex processes of negotiation, interaction and contestation, both at the local and transnational level. In this context, locality and local experience is framed within a broader transnational network and the latter is localized (made sense in terms of its local manifestations). What is more, it is a space where participants are agonizingly seeking ways of overcoming what they perceive to be under- and mis-representation or alienation. It provides the means for 'inhabiting' local and translocal/transnational domains by rendering these familiar in terms of sounds, images, negating and overcoming absences and silences.

Paraphrasing Benedict Anderson, the European Muslim identity, still a project in progress, can be seen as a process of imagining a community, a geographically and culturally dispersed set of political coordinates held together by a shared collection of narratives, identities and symbols. It is through an investment in these frames of reference and belief – these constant 'imaginings' of the life and identity of European Muslims – that the sense of commonality underpinning citizenship and the sense of belonging to a transnational community emerges. To this end, the project in question relies on a rich array of cultural practices for their reproduction. The analysis that has preceded indicates that it is these and practices that can successfully straddle the transnational and the local that can articulate these dimensions in the translocal space. The capacity to mobilize emotional and colloquial aspects of European Muslim experience and to relate to the experiential frames of Europe's Muslims makes possible the (re)production of identities, solidarities and agency.

Notes

Introduction

1. For example, in their study of young Muslim people in Oldham and Rochdale, Thomas and Sanderson (2011) found that being Muslim is by far the most important form of identity among their informants. Similarly Maliepaard and Phalet (2012) in their study of Dutch-Turkish youth found that the latter considered being Muslim by far the most important aspect of their identity – a quite interesting conclusion given the systematic, yet on occasion ambiguous, attempt of the Turkish state to decouple nation and religion during the best part of the last eight decades (see Özkırımlı and Sofos 2008). established a correlation between the media coverage of Western military involvement in the Middle East and the strengthening of expressions of identification by young Muslims as such. Finally, the Pew Global Attitudes Project (Pew 2006: 10) findings seem to confirm these conclusions.

1 Muslims in Europe: Balancing between Belonging and Exclusion

1. This distinction was explicitly articulated back in 1991 by the then candidate for the French presidency Jacques Chirac in what became known as *le bruit et l'odeur* (the noise and smell) speech as it referred to the noise and smell emanating from families of Muslim and black African immigrants. In it, Chirac contrasted the latter with immigrants of the post-war era, most of which left the European South and Poland, suggesting that they were far more easily assimilable. Chirac obviously had a specific political agenda in the conjuncture of the French presidential election but his argument was not novel or confined to that particular context. The discourse of the unmanageable character of Muslim immigration has resurfaced on many occasions in many different European societies at the official and everyday level.

2. Salman Rushdie's *The Satanic Verses* was published by Viking Penguin in July 1988. The book, a work of fiction, recounted a number of episodes from the life of Prophet Muhammad, some of which painted him in a way that challenged orthodox representations of his person, representing him as a confused individual surrounded by followers of dubious qualities. Its irreverent stance towards the person of the Prophet but also its deconstructive approach towards the formative era of Islam were soon identified by Muslim activists and leaders and sparked mobilizations against the book that often culminated in violent acts such as bombings and arson

against companies and persons associated with the book. Although established accounts of the controversy focus on the passionate and violent reaction of 'pious' or fanatical Muslims to the offensive way in which the Prophet Muhammad was represented, or on the fatwā issued by Iran's supreme leader, Ayatollah Ruhollah Khomeini, inviting Muslims to kill Rushdie, what is more important, as we will argue later on, is the sense of injustice that many Muslims – pious and non-pious alike – in Europe and beyond experienced at the time. In this sense, the *Satanic Verses* were seen by many Muslims in Europe not so much as an assault against the Prophet but as an assault against them and against their position in European societies. What is more, the official and dominant reactions to the anger and, often violence, of some were perceived as largely dismissive of Muslims as a whole and of their cultures which were represented as lesser, belated and partial. As Malik (2010) suggests, the main effect of the controversy was the polarization of public debate dividing 'Muslims from Westerners along the fault line of culture'. As we will argue later, the controversy over Salman Rushdie's book *Satanic Verses*, just as a chain of subsequent high-profile controversies, represented a constitutive moment in the process of formation of a European Muslim identity or, at least, of a widespread consciousness among Muslims in Europe sharing aspirations, concerns and challenges.

3. The *Affaire du foulard* refers to a series of disputes around the right of Muslim women to wear headscarves in public places, especially schools in France. Premised on the view that the headscarf was not a mere clothing item but a religious or quasi-religious symbol, the Collège Gabriel Havez in Creil suspended three female students when the latter refused to remove their headscarves in October 1989 as their attire was deemed incompatible with the principle of *laïcité* that is supposed to inspire public education. A month later the *Conseil d'État* found that wearing a scarf was not incompatible to the *laïcité* of public education. In December, the then minister of education Lionel Jospin intervened and issued a statement that reignited the controversy, declaring that schools had the discretion and responsibility of determining whether wearing of the scarf in schools was to be allowed. Following this rather ambiguous statement, the principal of Noyon's Collège Pasteur suspended a number of female students, while parents of one of the previously affected students initiated legal procedures against the school. Soon, the headscarf issue mobilized Muslims and non-Muslims alike; teachers in various schools held strikes against students wearing headscarves in school premises; Muslim parents became more vociferous while the government issued yet another statement effectively ignoring the earlier verdict of the *Conseil d'État* and stressing the importance of upholding the principle of *laïcité* in public schools. In September 1994, the 'François Bayrou memo' attempted to distinguish between 'acceptable', 'discreet' religious symbols and 'ostentatious' ones (including the headscarf), which were to be banned in public establishments. This new government intervention

sparked protests among students against the effective ban on the head-scarf. Since 1994 the headscarf remained an important rallying point for advocates of secularism, human rights but also Muslim religious activism and provided an arena for debate and confrontation. To date over one hundred female students have been sanctioned for covering their hair, although several such measures have been annulled by the courts.

In Germany, the debate on the right of Muslim women to wear a headscarf has a fairly long history too. One of the first confrontations followed the decision of a Baden-Württemberg school not to employ a female applicant because she wore a veil. In July 1998, the regional government upheld the decision claiming that the *hijab* is a political symbol of female submission and not a religious requirement. In 2003 the issue of the *hijab* reached the Federal Constitutional Court which recognized the right of German *länder* to introduce bans (Cesari 2009; Statham 2004). Soon after, the Brandenburg government introduced a ban of all religious symbols for civil servants, and Baden-Württemberg introduced a *hijab* ban for teachers, which was, however, rejected by the court in July 2006 on the grounds that such a prohibition was discriminatory against Muslims, since veiled Catholic nuns were not forbidden to teach in the state's schools (Cesari 2009). As this last case indicates, the debate in Germany has focused on abstract concerns regarding the submission of women to patriarchal structures, sadly without paying attention to the affected women's personal choices. And, in other instances, Muslim women clearly constitute the main targets of secular drives to expunge religious symbols from public spaces. We discuss these issues in more detail in Chapter 6 of this volume.

4. Islamophobia is a relatively new term, at least in the sense of being used in the social sciences to refer to a set of attitudes and predispositions – the 'dread or hatred of Islam and therefore, to the fear and dislike of all Muslims' but also to a set of practices – discriminating against Muslims by excluding them from economic, social and public life (The Runnymede Trust 1997). Our use of the term is informed by this definition that links the realm of attitudes and action. Fred Halliday introduced an alternative and somewhat awkward term – anti-Muslimism – which we consider more accurate as it refers to Muslims and not to Islam and therefore pinpoints the target of islamophobia – real people. As Halliday very aptly stresses, anti-Muslimism is not premised on theological objections or religious differences but on a 'hostility to *Muslims*, to communities of people whose sole or main religion is Islam, and whose Islamic character, real or invented, forms one of the objects of prejudice' (1996). We will nevertheless adopt the convention and we will be using the term *Islamophobia* throughout this book when referring to such repertoires of attitudes and action.

5. Van Gogh was an outspoken critic of the multicultural policies of the Netherlands, particularly with reference to the efforts made to accommodate Muslim immigrants. He frequently referred to Muslims as 'goat-fuckers' in his radio show and cooperated with Somali-born Ayaan Hirsi

Ali – a Dutch MP and vocal critic of the 'backwardness of Islam' – turning her script into the ten-minute long film *Submission*, exploring the violence against women in Islam. The film proved controversial and Van Gogh and Hirsi Ali received death threats. Mohammed Bouyeri murdered Van Gogh as he was cycling to work on 2 November 2004 by shooting him eight times and afterwards stabbing him in the chest. Bouyeri left a five-page note accusing the West and Van Gogh's collaborator in the film *Submission*, Ayaan Hirsi Ali, of contempt towards Islam and Muslims. Van Gogh's murder caused a public outcry and renewed calls towards the government to review its multicultural policies.

6. The *Jyllands-Posten* or Muhammad cartoons controversy was sparked by the publication of 12 caricatures on the theme of the prophet Muhammad in the Danish conservative daily *Jyllands-Posten* on 30 September 2005. The newspaper culture editor, Flemming Rose, justified the publication of the caricatures on the grounds of the need to have a debate on the nature of Islam as a religion and system of cultural values as well as of the importance of addressing the predominant Western culture of encouraging or imposing self-censorship among intellectuals when they touch upon difficult issues (Muhammeds Ansigt, *Jyllands Posten* 30 September 2005, p. 3 and Rose, F. (2005) 'Face of Muhammed', *Jyllands-Posten*. URL (consulted February 2006), http://www.jp.dk/kultur/artikel: aid=3293102/. Danish Muslim organizations found the caricatures offensive – some argued that the conflation of the prophet with terrorism or bigotry was offensive, some suggested that depicting the prophet is tantamount to blasphemy, while others suggested that this was a racist attack against Danish Muslims. The controversy soon transcended Denmark's borders with protests in both the West and Muslim countries and a proposed boycott of Danish products and newspapers in 49 countries reprinting the caricatures in the name of free speech. The controversy was seen by many as the product of the failed multiculturalist project in the West, whereas it brought to the foreground of public debate the tension between the right to engage in critical free speech and the responsibility not to demean or denigrate the other while doing so.

7. The first high-profile instance of 'Islamic' terrorism was the 1995 bombings carried out by the *Armed Islamic Group* (GIA), after they decided to extend their activities from Algeria to France. These comprised a series of gas bomb attacks in Metro and RER stations, and a car bomb attack at a Jewish school in Lyon between July and October 1995. Six years later, on 11 September 2001, 19 Muslim men hijacked four passenger jets and executed four coordinated suicide attacks in New York and the Washington DC areas flying two of those airplanes into the World Trade Center complex in New York and one into the Pentagon building in Arlington, Virginia. al-Qaeda's leader, Osama bin Laden, claimed responsibility for the attacks accusing the United States of supporting Israel, and imposing crippling sanctions against Iraq. The United States responded to the attacks externally by launching the War on Terror and invading Afghanistan to depose the Taliban, which had harboured al-Qaeda and

internally by introducing the Patriot Act – a major overhaul of the web of legislation protecting civil liberties. In the morning of 11 March 2004, a number of explosions in Madrid's commuter train system killed 191 people and wounded 1800. The attacks were traced back to a local terrorist cell claiming affiliation to al-Qaeda. Finally, in the morning of 7 July 2005 four Muslim men carried out a series of coordinated suicide attacks in London's public transport system targeting the underground railway and a bus killing 52 passengers and injuring about 700 more.

8. We should point out here that although we borrow the term *speaking Muslim* from Burgat, we use it somewhat differently. For Burgat, the term refers to 'have recourse in a privileged and sometimes ostentatious fashion to a lexicon or a vocabulary derived from Muslim culture'. Such a formulation implies a dualism between the means (adopting a Muslim vocabulary and of ways of deploying it) and the objective (protest, access to power, will to change the world) whose utility (revealing the diversity of the meaning of being Muslim) is obscured by its instrumentalism. We would therefore suggest an alternative use of 'speaking Muslim' that emphasizes experiencing and making sense of the world through the lens of 'being Muslim'. We elaborate on this point in Chapter 3.

9. It is interesting to note here that 'according to Europol statistics, only 3 attacks (failed, foiled or completed) have been carried out by people who were described as "Islamist" in 2010, compared to 160 undertaken by "separatists" and 45 by "left-wing groups" (TE-SAT 2011, "European Terrorism Situation and Trend Report", 2011, p. 36)' (in Özkırımlı 2012).

10. There is a vast and diverse debate on this issue. On 28 June 2006 the then UK Communities Secretary, Ruth Kelly, summarized the often rehearsed key argument against multiculturalism pointing out that in her opinion 'we have moved from a period of uniform consensus on the value of multiculturalism, to one where we can encourage that debate by questioning whether it is encouraging separateness'. Interestingly, the 'moment of truth' for exponents of this argument, the point at which such a verdict became possible was predominantly linked with the perceived resistance of Europe's Muslims to integration or assimilation, depending on one's point of view.

11. Rabasa et al. point out on the issue of the visibility of Muslim radicals 'By and large, radicals have been successful in intimidating, marginalizing or silencing moderate Muslims – those who share the key dimensions of democratic culture – to varying degrees' (2007: 1).

12. Here we see discourse in the way understood by Michel Foucault (1972, 1980), as transcending the common sense distinction between language, thought and action. According to this definition, discourse comprises constellations of statements working together which 'refer to the same object, share the same style and support a strategy... a common institutional... or political drift or pattern' (Cousins and Hussain 1984: 84–85). Discourse is the means of creating the *social*, a vehicle for the construction of thought and action, self and other. Discourse constructs its subject and delimits the ways in which it can be constructed.

13. To be fair, others attempt to disengage the theme of conflict from binaries that perpetuate Orientalist hierarchies and power relations and articulate a more sober narrative. Sniderman and Hagendoorn, for example, talk about 'ways of life colliding', but hasten to clarify that they have in mind, not irreconcilable conflicts, but

> genuine differences about what is right and wrong embedded˙ in a larger context of common ground. The points of difference, though sharp, are limited; the area of agreement, though not complete, is large.
>
> (2007: 9)

Their criticisms are directed, not towards European Muslims and their cultures, but towards multiculturalism which, in their opinion, accentuates awareness of cultural differences between mainstream and minorities, foments prejudice, undercuts support for cultural pluralism and undermines tolerance.

14. Zarka, Taussig and Fleury 2004: 159–162. In their editorial introductions to each section of this 733-page volume, Zarka, Taussig and Fleury present a comprehensive and coherent view of Islam as a problem. See especially 1–14, 159–162, 221–223, 241–243, 319–322, 397–400, 467–470, 515–517, 559–602 and 665–667.

15. Among the permutations of this discourse of territorial threat is that of the *inverse colonization* of Europe. For example, shortly after the riots of November 2005, a Gaullist deputy, Jérôme Rivière, said in obvious anguish that France was undergoing a process of 'colonization in reverse'. There is, he suggested, 'a threshold of immigration beyond which a country looks in the mirror and no longer recognizes itself'. 'France has been, for over a millennium, a country of Judeo-Christian heritage. Speaking for myself, I do not want it to become a land of Islam' (Rivière 2010).

16. Lacan, speaking about the *point de capiton* defined it as 'the point of convergence that enables everything that happens in this discourse to be situated retroactively and prospectively' (Lacan, Seminar III, 267–268). In other words, the *point de capiton* constitutes the centre, so to speak, upon which meaning is anchored, which inflects the various elements that comprise it.

17. The *Euston Manifesto* is a group of left-wing academics, journalists and activists based in the United Kingdom, named after its 2006 declaration of principles by a group. The manifesto calls for 'the reconfiguration of progressive opinion' by 'drawing a line between forces on the Left that remain true to its authentic values, and currents that have lately shown themselves rather too flexible about these values'. The group criticized quarters within the left which are critical of particular actions of Western governments such as the military presence in Iraq, or which 'conceal prejudice against the Jewish people behind the formula of "anti-Zionism"' and called for the Left to define itself 'against those for whom the entire progressive democratic agenda has been subordinated to a blanket and simplistic "anti-imperialism" and/or hostility to

the current US administration' ('The Euston Manifesto', 29 March 2006 http://eustonmanifesto.org/the-euston-manifesto/).
18. See also Miera and Sala Pala (2009: 396).
19. *Aporia* is a term derived from classical rhetoric. Originally from the Greek word απορία, meaning 'lack or resources', 'doubt' or 'difficulty', Chakravorty Spivak uses the term in a dual sense, denoting both lack of resources, both material and symbolic, that would enable the *subaltern* to articulate a voice and a profound state of indecision. For an extensive discussion of the concept of aporia and of the subaltern position of minorities, see Chakravorty Spivak (1988: 271–313).
20. Among these see Hunter (2002), Yazbeck Haddad (2002), Maréchal, Allievi, Dassetto and Nielsen (2003), Mandaville (2001), Cesari (2004), Allievi and Nielsen (2003), Nielsen (1995), Modood, Triandafyllidou and Zapata-Barrero (2006), Cesari and McLoughlin (2005).

2 Islam in Europe: A Genealogy

1. Indeed, 'Caucasia', as the broader region on both sides of the Caucasus was being referred to by the Ottomans (and is still referred to in contemporary Turkey – *Kafkasya*), had been seen as one of the 'valiant sons of Islam', to use the words of Bediuzzaman Said Nursî (also known as Kurdi), an Islamic theologian, born in 1876 in the city of Bedlîs in what is today Southeastern Turkey or Northern Kurdistan (Said Nursî 1908:121–32). This belief is illustrated in his conversation with a Russian policeman in Tbilisi, today the capital of Georgia, a predominantly Christian Orthodox country. Saidi Nursî climbed the hill known as Shaykh Sanan Tepesi, which views the city of Tbilisi and valley of the river of Kura. When a Russian policeman approached him, he asked him, 'Why are you studying the land with such attention?' Saidi Nursî replied: 'I am planning my medrese', implying that even the non-Muslim parts of Caucasia were undisputed parts of the imaginary geography of the *Dar-al-Islam*.

   However, it should be pointed out that, apart from these, residual, topographies, recent political events such as the break-up of the Soviet Union and the emergence of a host of Central Asian republics with predominantly Muslim populations, or the Chechen independence movement, have also played a role in the re-imagination of *Dar-al-Islam*. As our research findings indicate (see Chapter 4 in this volume) the violent suppression of the Chechen independence movement by the Russian Federation military has given this small Caucasian republic a significant place in European Muslim topographies of Islam.

2. Such notions derive from the political organization of the early Islamic world into *caliphates* which claimed to express the unity of the community of believers. The head of the caliphate (Caliph) traditionally based his authority and legitimacy on the claim of being a successor to prophet Muhammad's political authority. From the time of Muhammad until 1924, a number of dynasties claimed the leadership of the *Ummah* including the Umayyads, the Abassids, the Fatimids and finally the Ottomans.

The Turkish Republic, established on the ruins of the Ottoman empire under Mustafa Kemal Atatürk, officially abolished the last caliphate in 1924 bringing to an end a long tradition of Islamic political universalism. However, there have been renewed calls in the Muslim world for the reestablishment of the Caliphate, although the exact meaning and 'shape' of such an institution in an era where the nation state is institutionalized is unclear.

Among the various proponents of the caliphate today one needs to mention the *Muslim Brotherhood*, one of the largest and most influential Islamic groups in the world, which advocates pan-Islamic unity and the implementation of *sharia* although it, too, organizationally has followed and accepted the divides institutionalized by modern nation states. Other organizations include the Pakistani *Tanzeem-e-Islam* and the *Hizb ut-Tahrir* (Party of Liberation), an offshoot of the *Muslim Brotherhood*, which is active in 40 countries in Central Asia, Europe and the Arab world. *Hizb ut-Tahrir* has a more specific vision as it considers the caliphate as an alternative governing system whose principles are embedded in the Qur'an and the teachings of the prophet Muhammad, and envisages its establishment as a culmination of a process of political change, marked by the overthrow of national governments in the Muslim world.

It is also interesting to note that *Taliban* leader, Mohammad Omar, used the caliphic title 'Commander of the Faithful' (*Ameer al-Mumineen*) in order to add legitimacy to his leadership, albeit not claiming the leadership of the entire *Ummah*. In one of his messages Osama bin Laden has called for Muslims to 'establish the righteous caliphate of our umma' (Lawrence 2005: 121), thus giving the caliphate a prominent place in the al-Qaeda imaginary. A more detailed discussion on the importance and role of the caliphate in European Muslim imaginaries can be found in Chapter 4 of this volume.

3. The 'memory', or rather the recognition of the Muslim presence in medieval Spain and Portugal has, until the death of General Francisco Franco and the demise of his regime in the mid- to late 1970s, been represented as a short episode in a long and continuous history of a Christian nation. Official history had not, until then, shed light on the gaps and absences in the established historical narrative, including questions regarding how a temporary invasion of the Iberian Peninsula could have left such a durable presence in terms of architecture, town planning, irrigation and, of course, on daily life and material culture after the Reconquista. In fact, as Harvey (2005) points out, Spanish identity has been premised on its representation as antithetical to Islam:

> Still nowadays in Spain, in dozens of towns and cities, there are enacted annually pageants of 'Moors and Christians'. These take a variety of forms, but one unvarying feature is that the Christians eventually triumph, not the Moors. It would be a profound mistake to see these pageants as mere opportunities for dressing up, still less as shows put on for tourists. Tourists may or may not be present, but the street

theatre of *Moros y Cristianos* makes a powerful public statement about the identity of Spain's citizens; an identity that was arrived at in combat with the national enemy, the Moor. Spain's national patron, Saint James, has the epithet *Matamoros* ('Moor killer'). The swaggering finery in which the 'Moors' are arrayed in these pageants only serves to underline the triumph of the Christians who overthrew them.

4. A band of Arab corsairs established a small foothold at Fraxinetum, in Provence; others raided and plundered cities and monasteries along the Mediterranean coasts of Europe, making occasional ventures inland, capturing Brindisi in 838 and even sacking Saint Peter's in Rome in 846, San Vincenzo and the monastery of Monte Cassino in 881. These incursions however, just as the Iberian Peninsula conquest, were not part of a coordinated effort to conquer Europe. The Muslim world was increasingly fragmented, both politically and religiously, and these raids by pirates and fortune-seekers were the fruits of individual ambition and greed, not of a planned Muslim expansion (for more details see Setton and Baldwin 2006: 40–53).

5. Saracen was a term widely used in Europe during the medieval era. Its original use in both Greek and Latin referred to a pagan people who lived in desert areas in or around the Sinai Peninsula region and the northern Hijaz (Daniel 1979, Retso 2003). Byzantine texts refer to the Muslim invaders of the Eastern Roman empire as Saracens and by the twelfth century, *Saracen* had become synonymous with *Muslim* in Medieval Latin literature (Tolan 2002). The alternative term historically used to denote Muslim peoples, 'Moor' is derived from the Latin *Mauri*, referring to the North African populations prior to the Muslim conquest of the region and, eventually, to the medieval Muslim inhabitants of Morocco, western Algeria, western Sahara, Mauritania, the Iberian Peninsula, Sicily and Malta. Here, we use the terms that original sources used to describe the Muslim peoples that were encountered by medieval European societies.

6. Indeed under the rule of Roger II (1130–1154), William I (1154–1166) and William II (1166–1189) Christianity and Islam coexisted peacefully. But with the death of William II and the eventual ascendance of the Hohenstaufen dynasty, Muslim Sicilians saw their condition and treatment by the authorities worsen. Muslim revolts in 1224 and 1243 were violently suppressed and the Muslim population of the island were exiled.

7. Nielsen describes in some detail the process of Muslim settlement in Germany, Britain, France and other parts of western Europe between the fifteenth and twentieth centuries (pp. 5–9). From the limited contact and settlement of war defectors in East Central Europe in the thirteenth century to the more intensified and massive establishment of Muslim communities in Europe in the post-war period, this has certainly been a multifaceted process characterized by different degrees of continuity and consistency in different regions. The establishment of Muslim communities in western Europe has similarly been the product of movement of labour, refugees and defectors. Populations were received in a variety of different ways: welcomed on occasion, feared and isolated in others.

8. This labour-led Muslim migration to Europe is in stark contrast to Muslim migration to the United States of America, which predominantly originates in family- or village-based immigration, educational migration and the growth of Islam among the African-American community.

9. Germany instituted a formal guest worker programme (*Gastarbeiterprogramm*). On a smaller scale, the Netherlands and Belgium put in place a similar *gastarbeider* scheme. In the case of Germany, as many guest workers decided not to return to their 'native' countries, they made use of the 'residence authorization' legal framework (*Aufenthaltsberechtigung*) to bring their spouses and dependants to Germany. For at least a couple of decades, the very same framework allowed their German-born offspring to stay in Germany without, however, the right to obtain German citizenship. Reunification legislation has varied considerably in different European countries but the overall effect of the relevant legal frameworks was the arrival and settlement of a second wave of migrants – many from Muslim countries and predominantly female or young (Cesari 2004: 14).

10. For more details on the different 'return' packages and legal frameworks in France and Germany as well as their effectiveness, see Cesari (2004: 14).

11. For example, in a climate of perceived adversity, declaring one's Muslim affiliation is not always a preferred course of action when answering the relevant census question. In addition, there are no sufficient data to provide accurate information on the provenance of undocumented migrants.

12. So whereas in 1971 Dutch population data indicate that the ratio of Muslim men to women from Turkey and North Africa was 9:1, by 1977 the ratio had become 4:3 (cf. Nielsen 2004: 63).

13. The Runnymede Trust (1997).

14. Mandaville (2007: 292) estimates Europe's Muslim population at 'over twenty million'. Other estimates include Nielsen 2004, Hunter 2002.

15. Samuel Huntington (1993, 1996) and Bernard Lewis (2002, 2004) are among the most renowned scholars who have argued that Islam as a religion and a culture is incompatible with liberal, democratic Western values. Similarly, in his 12 September 2006 lecture at the University of Regensburg, Pope Benedict XVI argued that, in contrast to Christianity which has from the outset been inextricably linked with 'rationality', Islam is impervious to such bounds. And, referring to the candidacy of Turkey for European Union membership in an interview he gave to Le Figaro in August 2004, Josef Ratzinger, prior to his election as Pope Benedict XIV, stated that 'Europe is a cultural and not a geographical continent. It is united by its culture which gives it a common identity. The roots which formed ... this continent are those of Christianity' and that Turkey had been 'always in contrast with Europe' and that to include it in the European Union would be a mistake, implicitly arguing that Turkey's Islamic heritage was incompatible to his notion of Europe. In these formulations, Christianity, which Enlightenment thinkers considered to be superstition and juxtaposed to rationality, is extricated from these binary

divisions and recast as consonant with the rational outlook of Enlighten-ment Europe. Islam, on the other hand, is not treated in a similar way but remains allied to superstition and backwardness.

16. In an interview with *Le Monde* (9 November 2002), Giscard d'Estaing, likened Turkey's entry to the European Union to 'the end of Europe' as, he pointed out, Turkey has 'a different culture, a different approach, a differ-ent way of life'. Although this was not made explicit at the time, Giscard d'Estaing's aversion towards Turkish membership of the EU has largely been attributed to the fact that the overwhelming majority of Turks are Muslim, hence non-European.

17. Interestingly, Nursi envisaged a 'Japanese' model for the development of the *Dar-al-Islam*. He advised his followers to emulate the Japanese in acquiring civilization, for by taking only the virtues of civilization from the Europeans, they would preserve their national customs, the leaven of every nation's continuance, but leave behind the undesirable. Refer-ring explicitly to Europe, Nursi (1908) rather cryptically claimed 'Europe is pregnant with Islam and will give birth to an Islamic Nation', Sukran Vahide (2001: 19–20).

18. For a very interesting reading of Ramadan's work and the relevant debate, see Andrew F. March, 'Liberal Citizenship and the Search for Overlapping Consensus: The Case of Muslim Minorities', *Philosophy & Public Affairs* 34, no. 4 (Fall 2006), pp. 373–42.

3 Who Are the European Muslims?

1. It should also be pointed out that Muslim communities have used, or been encouraged to adopt broader than ethnic self-representation strate-gies for the very same reasons. So in France, Muslims originating in the Maghreb have been addressed as *Maghrebins* and have, to some extent, adopted strategically appropriate discourses and practices whenever that was more appropriate or expedient. Also, in the United Kingdom, South Asian Muslims have used the idiom of 'Asianness' together with non-Muslim South Asians when 'numbers made sense'. Having said that, we should stress that such 'choices' are not solely determined by some instru-mental logic but are the product of complex processes which include emotional attachments, shared experiences as well as rational choice calculations.

2. Thus some governments prefer, encourage or facilitate the organization, representation, consultation of ethnic groups, for example, although others have tended to privilege the organization of faith communities. For example, in the aggressively secular system of the French Republic, ethnicity provided a more appropriate means of identification and rep-resentation as opposed to religion – Islam has only recently become an acceptable framework for the organization and representation of French Muslims albeit in a very limited way in the form of the official *Conseil Francais du Culte Musulman* and the independent *Communaute Francaise*

de Confession Musulmane whereas in the context of the Netherlands, the consociational system which leaves room for different faiths to gain official recognition and resources, Islam has been a preferred vehicle for access to institutional and material resources.

3. Baumann (1996: 123) identifies such divides in the local context of Southall West London in his study of the construction of community and culture in demotic and dominant discourses. He points out the divisions between Sunni and Shi'a Muslims, or between Muslims and members of the Ahmadiyya movement and their distinct associational and religious lives stressing that what may appear to the unsuspecting outsider to be a seamless unity could often be a highly fractious construct with no resonance to those who are supposed to be its members.

4. See, for example, the BBC's reports on the cost of translation services provided by local and health authorities to (Muslim migrant) individuals who cannot otherwise access important and often needed services, which represented those in need of translation as unwilling to integrate, thus decontextualizing the inability of some of them – mainly women – to speak English from community and patriarchal power relations and ignoring their possible vulnerability once the voice given to them through translation services is withdrawn (Mark Easton 2006).

5. For an excellent discussion of subjectivity and agency in such contexts, see Mahmood (2005: 1–39).

6. Dassetto estimated in the early 1990s that approximately 60 per cent of Europe's Muslims could be called 'Muslims' on the basis of their ethnic or cultural roots (Ansari 2005: 145; Dassetto 1996).

7. Shireen Hunter's edited book *Islam, Europe's Second Religion*, reflects a combination of this interdisciplinarity with what we would claim to be a casual definition of European Islam which, in effect, amounts to a non-definition. Admittedly, this does not reduce its usefulness as its agenda is much broader, notably

> to trace the history and process of Muslim immigration to and implantation in various European countries; to provide an ethnic, sectarian, and socioeconomic profile of Europe's Muslim communities – with special attention to identifying patterns of commonality and diversity; to measure the social and economic progress of Muslim communities and the level of their political participation; and to analyze the patterns of interaction within Europe's Muslim communities and between them and the broader Islamic world, especially their home countries.
>
> (Hunter 2002: xvii)

In the introduction of the volume, Hunter stresses that over the past few decades 'Islam has peacefully emerged as Europe's second largest religion after Christianity' and points out that today 'at least 15 million people in Western Europe adhere to the Muslim faith' (xiii), but there is very little in terms of evidence to substantiate this as a considerable logical leap is required from being able to trace one's origins in a 'Muslim' country to translating this into 'adhering to the Muslim faith' as we argue in the course of this chapter.

8. Having said that, extremely influential and significant work had already appeared as early as in the 1980s, such as Anwar (1984, 1985) and Gerholm and Lithman (1988).

9. Interestingly, the controversy and suspicion surrounding the various BME community mapping projects funded by the United Kingdom's *Prevent Agenda Framework* (designed to combat radicalization and terrorism) is illustrative of the implicit definitions of Muslims and other 'foreigners' as suspected or potential terrorists and of the agendas inherent in population 'counting' or charting projects.

10. Although British policies towards minorities have been quite complex, it would not be inaccurate to say that the logic of ethnic compartmentalization upon which British colonial administration was premised has also left its indelible mark on the theory and practice of minority policy in the United Kingdom itself. Thus, from local authority consultation practices to education and even adoption services, migrants and their descendants were 'ethnicized' as they had to be classified on the basis of a quite exhaustive system of ethnic categorization. It is only in the 2001 census that respondents were given the option to identify themselves in terms of their religion.

11. The Netherlands has most often opted to deal with migrant populations in terms of their religious affiliation, most probably as religious communities have been prominent in the Dutch consociational system.

12. The French response to diversity has until recently been the most typical example of this although the French government attempted to engage with its Muslim population by establishing a Muslim Council and therefore recognizing the reality of the ground as well as attempting to create and co-opt a Muslim elite. We will attempt to assess the merits and shortcomings of this endeavour in Chapters 3 and 4.

13. As we have already argued in the previous chapter, the figures are notoriously imprecise, as most western European countries (with the exception of Austria, the Netherlands, Switzerland and, as of 2001, the United Kingdom) do not collect data on the religion of residents. As a result, the available data are based on various sources estimating the number of migrants from countries where Islam is the most important religion. But even then, the inadequacy of the existing calculations is difficult to ignore. Characteristically, in June 2006 the London-based Turkish press expressed surprise at the Office for National Statistics figures according to which there are currently only 52,893 Turkish residents in England and Wales, in sharp contrast to both common sense observations and the data provided by the Turkish Embassy and the Representative Office of the self-styled Turkish Republic of Northern Cyprus, according to which the number is closer to 270,000 (İngiltere'de 53 bin Türkiyeli yaşiyor! *Londra Gazete*, 15 June 2006, pp. 1 and 17).

14. For example, French law prohibits the insertion of questions about religion in the national census, and other authorities interpret secularism

in a similar way. Thus, schools and local authorities often refuse to even contemplate investigating the religious backgrounds and, by extension, potential needs of their populations. Despite this lack of reliable data a figure of four million (roughly 7 per cent of the population of 59.6 million) is the most common estimate of the number of Muslims in France. French government figures on the country's Muslim population are based on extrapolations from the country's population with North-African, West African and Turkish origins.

15. It is characteristic to see that, in some European countries, the discourse on Muslims is not just coupled with that of immigration; in Sweden and Austria it is quite often a discourse about foreigners (Anwar, Blaschke and Sander 2004): 251–259; Jim Heintz, 'Immigrants Outsiders in Sweden' *AP*, 5 October 1998. Che Sidanius (1998) 'Immigrants in Europe: The Rise of a New Underclass', *The Washington Quarterly*. Vol. 21, No. 4, Autumn.

16. Our proposed definition of what it means to be a European Muslim as outlined in this chapter is informed by theories of identity formation developed within the fields of social movement research, and what we could call constructivist strands within the sociology and social psychology of identity and of nationalism. As such, our discussion of Muslim identity formation reflects a broader discussion on identity formation in general that has developed within these fields.

17. On the notion of equivalence, see Laclau and Mouffe (1985: 127–134). Equivalence constitutes a discursive trope that is crucial in processes of collective identity formation. For example, an array of different social groupings hitherto defined through the differences that separate them can be transformed into part of a broader grouping insofar as an underlying commonality among them is constructed discursively. As long as this construction is effective, it dissimulates the differences or renders them into variations of the underlying commonality. Equivalence exists only through subverting the differential character of the elements it defines as equivalent. Laclau and Mouffe suggest that equivalence works through the negative reference to an 'other', or put differently, through juxtaposing self and other.

18. During the end of our fieldwork in the area, radical Muslim groups sought the limelight of publicity by resorting to 'symbolic action'. More precisely, in 2010, through a series of 'happenings' heavy with symbolism, a local Muslim group had tried to rally local Muslim opinion behind turning areas of Waltham Forest into Sharia-controlled zones, free of alcohol, gambling, drugs, smoking and homosexuality. One of the leading figures of the campaign, the charismatic Abu Izzadeen has on various occasions suggested that sharia would also mean an end to men and women mixing in public in a deliberate attempt to draw symbolic boundaries between conservative segments of the local Muslim community and the non-Muslim population that was likely to be alarmed by such an initiative. The campaign, however, did not amount to much more than producing large numbers of highly visible stickers proclaiming the sharia-controlled

zone and sticking them on shop fronts, bus stops and other public spaces, combined with occasional public events where campaigners would outline their vision of sharia zones. The highly confrontational character of the campaign, the identification of its audience exclusively as the existing Muslim community and the lack of any dialogue with other community groups made it clear that this was effectively a demarcation exercise that sought, not so much to identify a sharia-governed locality but to polarize and draw boundaries between 'Muslims' and 'non-Muslims'.

19. Indeed, the politics regarding the use of urban space are extremely intricate and quite often are hijacked by extremist forces Muslim and non-Muslim alike. For example, the plans of *Tablighi Jamaat* to build a mosque with a capacity of 12,000 worshippers (widely called Mega Mosque) in West Ham have provided the opportunity for a British National Party-inspired e-petition to 10 Downing Street as well as broader concerns by the local community including several local Muslims.

4 Space, Place and Social Action: European Muslim Geographies

1. Discussing the complexity of the phenomenon of globalization, Appadurai identifies certain fundamental disjunctures between economy, culture and politics. An elementary framework for exploring such disjunctures can revolve around the relationship between five dimensions of global cultural flow which he terms: (a) ethnoscapes; (b) mediascapes; (c) technoscapes; (d) finanscapes; and (e) ideoscapes. He uses the common suffix '-scape' to indicate

> first of all that these are not objectively given relations which look the same from every angle of vision, but rather that they are deeply perspectival constructs, inflected very much by the historical, linguistic and political situatedness of different sorts of actors: nation-states, multinationals, diasporic communities, as well as sub-national grouping and movements (whether religious, political or economic), and even intimate face-to-face groups, such as villages, neighborhoods and families. Indeed, the individual actor is the last locus of this perspectival set of landscapes, for these landscapes are eventually navigated by agents who both experience and constitute larger formations, in part by their own sense of what these landscapes offer. (1996)

According to Appadurai, 'ethnoscape', denotes the landscape of persons who, through moving transnationally constitute the shifting world in which we live: tourists, immigrants, refugees, exiles, guestworkers and others and the networks they construct through their activities. Similarly, 'technoscape' refers to the global dispersal of technology and the way it moves at high speeds across boundaries. 'Finanscapes' refers to the ever shifting landscape of currency markets, national stock exchanges and fund transfers globally. Related to these landscapes are what he calls 'mediascapes' and 'ideoscapes', which refer specifically to the production and dissemination of information and ideas, master and counter-narratives that traverse the globe and are taken up, modified and domesticated in different local and translocal contexts.

2. Despite the diversity of the ways 'phenomenological geography' is understood the concept generally refers to the production of place and place-based communities through the practices of social individuals. For a sympathetic yet critical discussion of the concept see Moores (2006).

3. The term *Information and Communication Technologies* refers to the integration of telecommunications (telephone lines and wireless signals), computers as well as the relevant software which enables users to access, store, transmit and process information.

4. As our observation findings indicate, this relative ease with new media and communications technologies is the product of considerable investment in terms of money and time by many Muslim community organizations, mosques and families. In all major cities that are home to sizeable Muslim communities, young people are offered training courses in a variety of contexts in order to become ICT-literate, partly in order to provide them with a head start in the job market. But there is evidence that this is also clearly a grievance-driven process, as the frustration with the available mainstream media diet briefly outlined above.

5. Studies of diasporic radio, for example (Echchaibi 2002; Hargreaves 2001; Tsagarousianou 2001) reveal that listeners often appreciate the psychological proximity and immediacy the medium can have. Interactive content in the case of Beur FM (Echchaibi 2002), one of the most prominent French radio stations catering for the country's large Maghrebi/Maghrebi-descended community, or of Ramadan Radio (Tsagarousianou 2001), has been identified as particularly significant as audiences often found that they reflect an intimate knowledge of the community they address or, according to Drijvers (1992: 199), 'a clear insight into the social stratification of the communities they are attempting to serve'.

6. Syria, for example, boasted a small but successful industry for real-time, strategy games such as the very successful *Quraish* (released in 2005 by Syrian *Akar Media*) while Jordan has also enjoyed small successes in the digital media sector such as studio *Quirkat's* highly successful *Arabian Lords* (*Sadat al-sahra'*), a real-time strategy game developed in 2007 with US *BreakAway Games*.

5 The Politics of Contestation and the Construction of Injustice

1. *Zakat* is the giving of a fixed portion of one's wealth as a tax for charity and one of the Five Pillars of Islam. For a more specific historical analysis of the concept of *zakat*, see Bonner (2005).

2. *Hizb-ut-Tahrir* is a transnational political organization active in numerous countries and one of the most active Islamic political organizations in Britain. It emphasizes the primacy of Muslim over national identities and has often attracted criticism because of its alleged function as a radicalizing force among Britain's Muslim community. See Hamid (2007).

3. Ansari (2005), through his study of attitudes to jihad, terrorism and martyrdom among British Muslims, also recognizes the complexity and ambivalence inherent in the interpretations of his respondents. Although he points out that they seem to glorify these acts, he nevertheless recognizes that they were decoupling the horrific acts of terror from the reasons that prompted them to commit them. We think that the responses of our informants largely reflect this ambiguity but also suggest that many European Muslims deconstruct the notion of martyrdom into its violent and its symbolic/communicative dimensions.

6 Spaces of Identity and Agency and the Reconfiguration of Islam

1. In her excellent discussion of *Multiculturalism without Culture* Anne Phillips (2007) provides a concise account of the relevant debate from a feminist perspective. Phillips herself stresses that minority culture group members should not be seen only through the prism of rigid versions of multiculturalism that prioritize a reified notion of culture. Instead, she suggests, they should be seen as social individuals possessing autonomy. This formulation is not part of a strategy for the abolition of multiculturalism; rather, as she herself points out, 'It is time for elaborating a version of multiculturalism that dispenses with reified notions of culture, engages more ruthlessly with cultural stereotypes, and refuses to subordinate the rights and interests of women to the supposed traditions of their culture' (Phillips 2007: 72).

2. *Musulmans Progressistes de France* is an organization that brings together people who work towards a more tolerant, open and inclusive Islam. Its founder Ludovic-Mohamed Zahed told us that the project included creating safe, inclusive spaces for Muslims that are marginalized from mainstream Islamic institutions to pray, meditate and come together. Since the interview, Zahed went on to establish *Homosexuels Musulmans 2 France* (http://www.homosexuels-musulmans.org/), an organization that seeks to express 'brothers and sisters [that] are trying to [reconcile] traditions, religious beliefs, human spirituality, with their sexual preference that falls within the area of privacy' (http://www.homosexuels-musulmans.org/gay_muslims.html, last accessed 1 April 2013). In line with the commitment of the two organizations to open up new inclusive spaces, the first 'inclusive' Friday prayers took place in Paris on 30 November 2012.

7   Is There a Space for European Muslims?

1. Cesari very aptly points out that this form of politics may also involve 'what Irving Goffman calls "contact terrorism": using Islamic symbols, clothing, or behavior to play on the Other's fear of and repulsion for Islam' (2008: 176).
2. Dassetto estimated in the early 1990s that approximately 60 per cent of Europe's Muslims could be called 'Muslims' on the basis of their ethnic or cultural roots (Ansari 2005: 145; Dassetto 1996).

References

Abbas, T. (ed.) (2005) *Muslim Britain: Communities under Pressure*. London: Zed Books.

Abu-Lughod, L. (1991) 'Writing Against Culture.' In R.G. Fox (ed.) *Recapturing Anthropology: Working in the Present*. Santa Fe, NM: School of American Research Press, pp. 137–162.

Abu-Lughod, L. (2005) *Dramas of Nationhood: The Politics of Television in Egypt*. Chicago: University of Chicago Press.

Abumalham, M. (ed.) (1995) *Comunidades islámicas en Europa*. Madrid: Editorial Trotta.

Ahmad, F. (2001) 'Modern Traditions? British Muslim Women and Academic Achievement.' *Gender and Education* 13(2), pp. 137–152.

Ahmad, F. (2012) 'Graduating Towards Marriage? Attitudes Towards Marriage and Relationships among University-Educated British Muslim Women.' *Culture and Religion: An Interdisciplinary Journal* 13(2), pp. 193–210.

Ahmad, F., T. Modood and S. Lissenburgh (2003) *South Asian Women and Employment in Britain: The Interaction of Gender and Ethnicity*. London: PSI.

Ahmed, A. (1999) *Islam Today: A Short Introduction to the Muslim World*. London: I.B. Tauris.

Alexander, J. et al. (2004) *Cultural Trauma and Collective Identity*. Berkeley: University of California Press.

Allli, R. (2000) 'Questions à la Conscience Musulmane en Europe.' *Islam de France* (8), pp. 29–40.

Allievi, S. (1999a) 'Les conversions à l'Islam. Redéfinition des frontières identitaires entre individu et communauté.' dans Félix Dassetto (ed.) *Paroles d'Islam, Individus, sociétés et discours dans l'islam européen contemporain*. Paris: Maisonneuve et Larose.

Allievi, S. (1999b) *Les Convertis à l'Islam. Les Nouveaux Musulmans d'Europe*. Paris: L'Harmattan.

Allievi, S. (1999c) 'Pour une Sociologie des Conversions. Lorsque des *Europé*ens deviennent Musulmans.' *Social Compass* 46(3), pp. 283–300.

Allievi, S. (2009) *Conflicts over Mosques in Europe. Policy Issues and Trends*. London: Alliance Publishing Trust.

Allievi, S. and J.S. Nielsen (eds.) (2003) *Muslim Networks and Transnational Communities in and across Europe*. Boston: Brill.

AlSayyad, N. and M. Castells (eds.) (2002) *Muslim Europe or Euro-Islam*. Lanham and London: Lexington Books.

Aminzade, R and D. McAdam (2001) 'Emotions and Contentious Politics.' In R. B. Aminzade et al. *Silence and Voice in the Study of Contentious Politics*. Cambridge: Cambridge University Press, pp. 14–50.

Amiraux, V. (1997) 'Turkish Islamic Associations in Germany and the Issue of European Citizenship.' In S. Vertovec and C. Peach (eds.) *Islam in Europe. The Politics of Religion and Community.* Basingstoke: Macmillan.

Anderson, B. (1983) *Imagined Communities. Reflections on the Origin and Spread of Nationalism.* London: Verso.

Anderson, B. (1992) 'Long-Distance Nationalism: World Capitalism and the Rise of Identity Politics: The Wertheim Lecture.' Amsterdam: Centre for Asian Studies. URL (consulted 2 October 2011), http://www.iias.nl/asia/wertheim/?q=lectures.

Anderson, J.W. (1999) 'The Internet and Islam's New Interpreters.' In D. F. Eickelman and J. W. Anderson (eds.) *New Media in the Muslim World: The Emerging Public Sphere.* Bloomington: Indiana University Press, pp. 41–56.

Anderson, J.W. (1999) 'New Media, New Publics: Reconfiguring the Public Sphere of Islam.' *Social Research* 70(3), pp. 887–906.

Ansari, H. (2005) 'Attitudes to Jihad, Martyrdom and Terrorism among British Muslims.' In T. Abbas (ed.) *Muslim Britain: Communities under Pressure.* London. Zed Books.

Antes. P and C. Hewer (1994) 'Islam in Europe.' In S. Gill, G. D'Costa and U. King (eds.) *Religion in Europe. Contemporary Perspectives.* Kampen: Kok Pharos.

Anthias, F. and N. Yuval-Davis (1992) *Racialized Boundaries: Race, Nation, Gender, Colour and Class and Anti-racist Struggle.* London: Routledge.

Anwar, M. (1984) *Social and Cultural Perspectives on Muslims in Western Europe.* Research Paper 24. Birmingham: Centre for the Study of Islam and Christian-Muslim Relations. Selly Oak Colleges.

Anwar, M. (1985) 'Who are the Muslims in Europe?' *Impact International* 15(4).

Anwar, M. (1994) *Young Muslims in Britain.* Markfield: Islamic Foundation.

Anwar, M., J. Blaschke and A. Sander (2004) *State Policies Towards Muslim Minorities. Sweden, Great Britain and Germany.* Berlin: Edition Parabolis.

Appadurai, A. (1996) *Modernity At Large: Cultural Dimensions of Globalization.* Minneapolis: University of Minnesota Press.

Babès, L. (2000) 'L'identité Islamique Européenne selon Tariq Ramadan.' *Islam de France* (8), pp. 5–20.

Babès, L. (2004) 'Norme et autorité religieuse chez les jeunes musulmans de France.' In M. Cohen, J. Joncheray and P. Luizard (eds.) *Les Transformations de'l autorité religieuse.* Paris: L'Harmattan, pp. 199–214.

Basit, T.N. (1996) 'Obviously I'll have an Arranged Marriage': Muslim Marriage in the British Context. *Muslim Education Quarterly* 13, pp. 4–19.

Basit, T.N (1997) *Eastern Values; Western Milieu: Identities and Aspirations of Adolescent British Muslim Girls.* Aldershot: Ashgate.

Ballard, R. (1996) 'Islam and the Construction of Europe.' In W.A.R Shadid and P.S. van Koningsveld (eds.) *Muslims in the Margin: Political Responses to the Presence of Islam in Western Europe.* Kampen: Kok Pharos.

Baumann, G. (1996) *Contesting Culture: Discourses of Identity in Multi-ethnic London.* Cambridge: Cambridge University Press.

Bednarz, D. and R. Kreuel (1998) 'Allah-Mania.' In *Der Spiegel* special 1, Hamburg, pp. 110–113.

Bendix, R. (1997) *In Search of Authenticity: The Formation of Folklore Studies.* Madison, WI: The University of Wisconsin Press.

Berger, P. and T. Luckmann (1971) *The Social Construction of Reality: A Treatice in the Sociology of Knowledge.* London: Penguin.

Berman, P. (2003) *Terror and Liberalism.* NY: W. W. Norton & Company.

Bhachu, P. (1996) 'The Multiple Landscapes of Transnational Asian Women in the Diaspora.' In V. Amit-Talai and C. Knowles (eds.) *Re-situating Identities: The Politics of Race, Ethnicity and Culture*, Ontario: Broadview Press, pp. 283–303.

Bradby, H. (1999) 'Negotiating Marriage: Young Punjabi Women's Assessment of their Individual and Family Interests.' In R. Barot, H. Bradley and S. Fenton (eds.) *Ethnicity, Gender and Social Change*, Basingstoke: Macmillan, pp. 152–166.

Billig, M. (1995) *Banal Nationalism.* London; Thousand Oaks, CA: Sage.

Bistolfi, R. and F. Zabbal (1995) *Islams d'Europe – Integration ou Insertion Communautaire?* Paris: L'Aube.

Blaschke, J. (2004) 'Tolerated but Marginalised – Muslims in Germany.' In Parabolis Verlagsabteilung im Europäischen Migrationszentrum (eds.) *State Policies towards Muslim Minorities. Sweden, Great Britain and Germany.* Kempten, pp. 41–197.

Blommaert, J. and J. Verschueren (1992) *Het Belgische Migrantendebat.* Antwerp: IprA.

Bonner, M. (2005) 'Poverty and Economics in the Qur'an.' *Journal of Interdisciplinary History* 35(3), pp. 391–406.

Bowman, G. (2003) 'Constitutive Violence and the Nationalist Imaginary. Antagonism and Defensive Solidarity in Palestine and Former Yugoslavia.' *Social Anthropology* II (3), pp. 319–340.

Brah, A. (1996) *Cartographies of Diaspora: Contesting Identities.* New York, NY: Routledge.

Brice, M.A.K. (2010) *A Minority within a Minority: A Report on Converts to Islam in the United Kingdom.* London: Faith Matters.

Broder, H. (2006) *Hurra, wir kapitulieren! Von der Lust am Einknicken.* Berlin: wjs-Verlag.

Bunt, G. (2000) *Virtually Islamic: Computer-Mediated Communication and Cyber-Islamic Environments.* Cardiff: University of Wales Press.

Bunt, G. (2009) *iMuslims: Rewiring the House of Islam.* London: Hurst.

Burgat, F. (2008) *Islamism in the Shadow of al-Qaeda.* Austin: University of Texas Press.

Burman, T. (1994) *Religious Polemic and the Intellectual History of the Mozarabs.* Leiden & New York: Brill.

Castells, M.J.L. Qui and A. Sey (eds.) (2007) *Mobile Communication and Society: A Global Perspective.* Massachusetts: MIT University Press.

CENSIS. (2002) *36° Rapporto sulla situazione sociale del Paese.* Rome: Centro Studi Investimenti Sociali.

Cesari, J. (1999) 'Pluralism in the Context of Globalization. European Muslim Youth.' *ISIM Newsletter* 2.

Cesari, J. (2003) 'Muslim minorities in Europe: the silent revolution.' In: J. Esposito & F. Burgat (eds.) *Modernising Islam: Religion in the Public Sphere in the Middle East and in Europe*, London: Hurst, pp. 251–269.

Cesari, J. (2004) *When Islam and Democracy Meet: Muslims in Europe and in the United States*. Basingstoke: Palgrave Macmillan.

Cesari, J. (2008) 'Muslims in Western Europe after 9/11: Local and Global Components of the Integration Process.' In G. Motzkin and Y. Fischer (eds.) *Religion and Democracy in Contemporary Europe*. London: Alliance Publishing Trust, pp. 153–167.

Cesari, J. (2009) *The Securitisation of Islam in Europe*. Challenge Research Paper No. 14. Paris: CEPS.

Cesari, J. and S. McLoughlin (eds.) (2005) *European Muslims and the Secular State*. Aldershot: Ashgate.

Choueiri, Y.M. (1990) *Islamic Fundamentalism*. London: Printer Publishers.

Coffé, H. (2005) 'The Adaptation of the Extreme Right's Discourse: The Case of the Vlaams Blok.' *Ethical Perspectives: Journal of the European Ethics Network* 12(2), pp. 205–230.

Cohen, N. (2005) *I Still Fight Oppression* Observer, 7 August.

Conway, G. (1997) *Islamophobia: A Challenge for Us All*. London: The Runnymede Trust.

Cousins, M. and A. Hussain (1984) *Michel Foucault*. Basingstoke: Macmillan.

Dale, A., N. Shaheen, E. Fieldhouse and V. Kalra (2002a) 'Labour Market Prospects for Pakistani and Bangladeshi Women.' *Work, Employment and Society* 16(1), pp. 5–26.

Dale, A., N. Shaheen, E. Fieldhouse and V. Kalra (2002b) 'Routes into Education and Employment for Young Pakistani and Bangladeshi Women in the UK.' *Ethnic and Racial Studies* 25(6), pp. 942–68.

Danforth, L. (1995) *The Macedonian Conflict: Ethnic Nationalism in a Transnational World*. Princeton: Princeton University Press.

Daniel, N. (1979) *The Arabs and Mediaeval Europe*. London: Longman.

Dassetto, F. (1996) *La construction de L'Islam européen, Approche Socioanthropologique*. Paris: l'Harmattan.

Dassetto, F. (1996) Paroles d'islam : individus, sociétés et discours dans l'islam européen contemporain. Paris : Maisonneuve et Larose.

De Certeau, M. (1984) *The Practice of Everyday Life*. Berkeley: The University of California Press.

Dubisch, J. (1995) *In a Different Place: Pilgrimage, Gender, and Politics at a Greek Island Shrine*. Princeton, NJ: Princeton University Press.

Dwyer, C. (1999) 'Veiled Meanings: British Muslim Women and the Negotiation of Differences.' *Gender, Place and Culture* 6(1), pp. 5–26.

De Certeau, M. (1984) *The Practice of Everyday Life*. Berkeley: The University of California Press.

Delanty, G. (1995) *Inventing Europe*. Basingstoke: Macmillan.

Deltombe, T. (2005) *L'Islam Imaginaire; La construction Médiatique de l'Islamophobie en France, 1975–2005*. Paris: La Découverte.

Douwes, D. (ed.) (2001) Naar Een Europese Islam? Amsterdam: Mets & Schilt.

Drijvers, J. (1992) 'Community Broadcasting: A Manifesto for the Media Policy of Small European Countries.' *Media, Culture and Society* 14, pp. 193–201.

Easton, M. (2006) 'Cost in translation' at http://news.bbc.co.uk/1/hi/uk/6172805.stm (last accessed 27 May 2013)

Echchaibi, N. (2002) '(Be)longing Media: Minority Radio Between Cultural Retention and Renewal.' *Javnost/the Public* 9(1), pp. 37–50.

Eickelman, D.F. and J. Piscatori (2004) *Muslim Politics*. Princeton: Princeton University Press.

Emerson, M. (ed.) (2011) *Interculturalism: Europe and its Muslims in Search of Sound Societal Models*. Brussels: Centre for European Policy Studies.

Erik, J. (2005) 'From Vlaams Blok to Vlaams Belang: The Belgian Far-Right Renames Itself.' *West European Politics* 28(3), pp. 493–502.

Esposito, J.L. (1992) The Islamic Threat: Myth or Reality? Oxford: Oxford University Press.

Esposito, J.L. (1997) Political Islam: Radicalism, Revolution or Reform. Boulder, Co: Lynne Rienner Publishers.

Esposito, J.L (2002). What Everyone Needs to Know about Islam. Oxford: Oxford University Press.

Esposito, J.L. and J.O. Voll (2001) Makers of Contemporary Islam. Oxford: Oxford University Press.

Esposito, J.L. and D. Mogahed. (2007) *Who Speaks for Islam? What a Billion Muslims Really Think*. NY: Gallup Press.

European Monitoring Centre on Racism and Xenophobia (2006) *Muslims in the European Union: Discrimination and Islamophobia*. Vienna: EUCM.

Eyerman, R. (1994) *Between Culture and Politics: Intellectuals in Modern Society*. Cambridge: Polity.

Fassmann, H. and R. Münz (1992) 'Patterns and Trends of International Migration in Western Europe.' *Population and Development Review* 18(3), pp. 457–480.

Foucault, M. (1972) *The Archaeology of Knowledge*. London: Routledge.

Foucault, M. (1980) *Power/Knowledge: Selected Interviews and Other Writings 1972–1977*. edited by C. Gordon. London: Harvester.

Fraser, N. (1995) 'From Redistribution to Recognition? Dilemmas of Justice in a "Postsocialist" Age.' *New Left Review* 212, pp. 68–93.

Gaffney, P. (1994) *The Prophet's Pulpit: Islamic Preaching in Contemporary Egypt*. Berkeley: University of California Press.

Gamson, W.A. (1992) *Talking Politics*. Cambridge: Cambridge University Press.

Gamson, W.A. (1995) 'Constructing Social Protest.' In Hank Johnston and Bert Klandermans (eds.) *Social Movements and Culture*. London: UCL Press.

Gerholm, T. and Y.G. Lithman. (1988) *The New Islamic Presence in Western Europe*. London and New York: Mansell.

Giddens, A. (1984) *The Constitution of Society*. Cambridge: Polity Press.

Goffman, E. (1974) *Frame analysis: An Essay on the Organization of Experience*. London: Harper and Row.

Goldberg, A. (2002) 'Islam in Germany.' In S. Hunter (ed.), *Islam, Europe's Second Religion: The New Social, Cultural, and Political Landscape*, Westport, CT: Praeger. pp. 29–50.

Göle, N. (2011) *The Lure of Fundamentalism and the Allure of Cosmopolitanism*. Princeton, NJ: Markus Wiener Publishers.

Gunner, G. (1999) *Att slakta ett får i Guds namn. Om religionsfrihet och demokrati*. Stockholm: Fakta info direkt.

Hale, G. (1998) *Making Whiteness*. New York: Vintage.

Hall, S. (1992) 'The West and the Rest: Discourse and Power.' In S. Hall and B. Gieben (eds.) *Formations of Modernity*. Cambridge: Polity Press, pp. 275–331.

Hall, S. (ed.) (1997) *Representation: Cultural Representations and Signifying Practices*. London: Sage Open University.

Halliday, F. (1996) *Islam and the Myth of Confrontation*. London: I.B. Tauris.

Hamid, S. (2007) 'Islamic Political Radicalism in Britain: The Case of Hizb-ut-Tahrir.' In T. Abbas (ed.) *Islamic Political Radicalism: A European Perspective*. Edinburgh: Edinburgh University Press, pp. 145–159.

Hannigan, J.A. (1991) 'Social Movement Theory and the Sociology of Religion: Toward a New Synthesis.' *Sociological Analysis* 52(4), pp. 311–331.

Hargreaves, A.G. (2001) 'Media Effects and Ethnic Relations in Britain and France.' In R. King and N. Wood (eds.) *Media and Migration: Constructions of Mobility and Difference*. London/New York: Routledge, pp. 23–37.

Harvey, L.P. (2005). *Muslims in Spain 1500 to 1614*, Chicago: University of Chicago Press.

Heintz, J. (1998) 'Immigrants Outsiders in Sweden' *AP*, October 5.

Hirschkind, C. (2006) *The Ethical Soundscape: Cassette Sermons and Islamic Counterpublics*. New York: Columbia University Press.

Hollander, E. and J. Stappers (1992) 'Community Media and Community Communication.' In N. Jankowski, O. Prehn and J. Stappers (eds.) *The People's Voice: Local Radio and Television in Europe*. London: John Libby, pp. 16–26.

Horrie, C. & P. Chippindale. (2003) *What is Islam? A Comprehensive Introduction*. London: Virgin.

Hunter, S.T. (ed.) (2002) *Islam, Europe's Second Religion: The New Social, Cultural, and Political Landscape*. Westport, CT: Praeger.

Huntington, S.P. (1996) *The Clash of Civilizations and the Remaking of World Order*. New York, NY: Simon and Schuster.

Husband, C. (1994) 'The Political Context of Muslim Communities' participation in British Society.' In B. Lewis and D. Schnapper (eds.) *Muslims in Europe*. London: Pinter, pp. 79–97.

Juul Petersen, M. (2011) *For Humanity or for the Umma? Ideologies of Aid in Four Transnational Muslim NGOs*. Copenhagen: University of Copenhagen.

Kepel, G. (1987) *Les Banlieues de l'Islam: Naissance d'une Religion en France*. Paris: Editions du Seuil.

Kepel, G. (2004) *The War for Muslim Minds: Islam and the West.* Cambridge, Mass: Harvard University Press.

Khan, M. (2005) 'Belgium's Muslim Beggars,' http://www.brookings.edu/research/opinions/2005/12/15islamicworld-khan (last accessed 27 May 2013).

Khan, S. (2000) *Muslim Women' Crafting a North American Identity.* Gainsville, FL: University of Florida Press.

Khan, S. (2002) *Aversion and Desire: Negotiating Muslim Female Identity in the Diaspora.* Toronto: Womens' Press.

Kitzinger, J. (1994) 'The Methodology of Focus Groups: The Importance of Interaction between Research Participants.' *Sociology of Health & Illness* 16(1), pp. 103–121.

Klausen, J. (2005) *The Islamic Challenge: Politics and Religion in Western Europe.* Oxford: Oxford University Press.

Laclau, E. and C. Mouffe (1985) *Hegemony and Socialist Strategy.* London: Verso.

Lash, S. and J. Urry. (1994) *Economies of Signs and Space.* London: Sage.

Lawrence, B. (2005). *Messages to the World. The Statements of Osama bin Laden.* London: Verso.

Leggewie, C. (1993). *Alhambra : der Islam im Westen.* Reinbek bei Hamburg: Rowohlt.

Leveau, R. and S. Hunter. (2002), 'Islam in France.' In S. Hunter (ed.), *Islam, Europe's Second Religion: The New Social, Cultural, and Political Landscape,* Westport, CT: Praeger, pp. 3–28.

Lewis, B. (2002) *What Went Wrong? Western Impact and Middle Eastern Response.* Oxford: Oxford University Press.

Lewis, B. (2007) *Europe and Islam.* Washington DC: American Enterprise Institute Press.

Lewis, B. and D. Schnapper (eds.) (1994) *Muslims in Europe.* London: Pinter.

Lewis, P. (2007) *Young, British and Muslim.* London and New York: Continuum.

Mahmood, S. (2005) *Politics of Piety. The Islamic Revival and the Feminist Subject.* Princeton, NJ: Princeton University Press.

Maliepaard, M. and K. Phalet (2012) 'Social Integration and Religious Identity Expression among Dutch Muslims: The Role of Minority and Majority Group Contact.' *Social Psychology Quarterly* 75(2), pp. 131–148.

Malik, K. (2010) *From Fatwa to Jihad: The Rushdie Affair and Its Aftermath.* Melville House.

Mamdani, M. (2004) *Good Muslim, Bad Muslim.* New York: Pantheon Books.

Mandaville, P. (2001) *Transnational Muslim Politics: Reimagining the Umma.* London: Routledge.

Mandaville, P. (2002) *Transnational Muslim Politics: Reimagining the Umma.* London: Taylor and Francis.

Mandaville, P. (2007) *Global Political Islam.* London: Routledge.

Maréchal, B. (ed.) (2002) *L'Islam et les musulmans dans l'Europe élargie: radioscopie – A Guidebook on Islam and Muslims in the Wide Contemporary Europe.* Louvain-la-Neuve, Académia-Bruylant.

Maréchal, B., S. Allievi, F. Dassetto and J. Nielsen (eds.) (2003) *Muslims in the Enlarged Europe*. Leiden: Brill.

Massey, D. (1994) *Space, Place and Gender*. Minneapolis: University of Minnesota Press.

Médine (2005) 'How Much More French Can I Be?' *Time Magazine*. 6 November in http://www.time.com/time/magazine/article/0,9171, 1126720,00.html (last accessed 13 May 2013).

Melucci, A. (1985) 'The Symbolic Challenge of Contemporary Movements.' *Social Research* 52, pp. 789–816.

Melucci, A. (1988) 'Getting Involved: Identity and Mobilization in Social Movements.' In B. Klandermans, H. Kriesi and S. Tarrow (eds.) *From Structure to Action: Comparing Social Movement Research Across Cultures*. Greenwich, CT: JAI Press, pp. 329–338.

Melucci, A. (1995) 'The Process of Collective Identity.' In H. Johnston and B. Klandermans (eds.) *Social Movements and Culture*. Minneapolis: University of Minnesota Press.

Melucci, A. (1996) *Challenging Codes: Collective Action in the Information Age*. Cambridge: Cambridge University Press, pp. 41–63.

Mehrländer, U. (1978) 'Bundesrepublik Deutschland.' In E. Gehmacher, D. Kubat and U. Mehrländer. (eds.) *Ausländerpolitik im Konflikt*. Bonn: Bundesminister für Arbeit und Sozialordnung, pp. 115–139.

Metcalfe, B.D. (ed.) (1996) *Making Muslim Space in North America and Europe*. Berkeley: University of California Press.

Miera, F. and V. Sala Pala (2009) 'The Construction of Islam as a Public Issue in Western European Countries through the Prism of the Muhammad Cartoons Controversy: A Comparison between France and Germany.' *Ethnicities* 9(3), pp. 383–408.

Millwood-Hargrave, A. (2002) *Multi-cultural Broadcasting: Concept and Reality*. Report by the BBC, BSC, ITC and RA. URL (consulted 2 October 2011), http://www.ipa.co.uk/ documents/Multicultural_ Broadcasting.pdf.

Minority Rights Group (2005) 'World Directory of Minorities and Indigenous Peoples.' http://www.minorityrights.org/?lid=1907 (last accessed 28 June 2013).

Mitchell, T. (1991) *Colonising Egypt*. Berkeley: University of California Press.

Modood, T., A. Triandafyllidou and R. Zapata-Barrero (eds.) (2006) *Multiculturalism, Muslims and Citizenship*. Routledge.

Moores, S. (2006) 'Media Uses and Everyday Environmental Experiences: A Positive Critique of Phenomenological Geography.' *Particip@tions* 3(2), http://www.participations.org/volume%203/issue%202%20-%20special/3_02_moores.htm (last accessed 12 January 2013).

Moscovici, S. (1981) *L'Age des foules: un traité historique de psychologie des masses*. Paris: Fayard.

Nauck, B. (1994) 'Changes in Turkish Migrant Families in Germany.' In Bernard Lewis and Dominique Schnapper (eds.) *Muslims in Europe*. London: Pinter, pp. 130–147.

Neal, A. G. (1994) *National Trauma and Collective Memory: Major Events in the American Century.* Armonk, NY: M.E. Sharpe.

Neumann, I. (1999) *Uses of the Other: The 'East' in European Identity Formation.* Minneapolis: University of Minnesota Press.

Nielsen, J.S. (2004) *Muslims in Western Europe.* Columbia University Press.

Nielsen, J.S. (1999) *Towards a European Islam.* Basingstoke: Macmillan.

Nonneman, G., T. Niblock and B. Szajkowski (eds.) (1996) *Muslim Communities in Europe.* Reading: Ithaca.

Nursî, Bediüzzaman Said. (1960) *Kastamonu Lahikasi.* Istanbul, Sinan Matbaasi.

Open Society Institute, European Union Monitoring and Advocacy Program. (2007) *Muslims in the Netherlands* (last consulted on 12 November 2009), http://www.eumap.org/topics/minority/reports/eumuslims/background_ reports/download/netherlands/netherlands.pdf.

Open Society Institute. (2010) *Muslims in Europe: A Report on 11 EU Cities.* New York, London and Budapest: Open Society Institute.

Özkırımlı, U. (2012) 'And People's Concerns were Genuine. Why Didn't We Listen More? Nationalism, Multiculturalism and Recognition in Europe.' *Journal of Contemporary European Studies* 20, 3.

Özkırımlı, U. and S.A. Sofos (2008) *Tormented by History: Nationalism in Greece and Turkey.* London: Hurst & Co and New York: Columbia University Press.

Parekh, B. (1998) 'Integrating Minorities.' In T. Blackstone, B. Parekh and P. Sanders (eds.) *Race Relations in Britain, A Developing Agenda,* London: Routledge.

Parekh, B. (2000) *Rethinking Multiculturalism: Cultural Diversity and Political Theory.* Basingstoke: Palgrave Macmillan.

Peele, G, (2006) 'The Politics of Multicultural Britain.' In P. Dunleavy et al. (eds.), *Developments in British Politics 8,* Basingstoke: Palgrave Macmillan.

Peterson, A. (2011) 'The Long Winding Road to Adulthood : A Risk-filled Journey for Young People in Stockholm's Marginalized Periphery.' *Young* 19(3), pp. 271–289.

Pew Social Attitudes Survey. (2006) *Muslims in Europe.* Washington, DC: Pew Global.

Phillips, A. (2007) *Multiculturalism without Culture.* Princeton, NJ: Princeton University Press.

Piela, A. (2011) 'Beyond the Traditional-Modern Binary: Faith and Identity in Muslim Women's Online Matchmaking Profiles.' *CyberOrient* 5(1), http://www.cyberorient.net/article.do?articleId=6219 (accessed 21 August 2011).

Poole, E. (2002) *Reporting Islam: Media Representations of British Muslims.* London: I.B. Tauris.

Powers, S. (2008) 'Examining the Danish Cartoon Affair: Mediatized Cross-cultural Tensions?' *Media, War & Conflict* 1.

Pryce-Jones, D. (2004) 'The Islamization of Europe?' *Commentary,* 31 December 2004. URL (consulted 2 October 2011), http://www. commentarymagazine.com/article/the-islamization-of-europe/.

Rabasa, A., C. Benard, L.H. Schwartz and P. Sickle. (2007) *Building Moderate Muslim Networks*. Santa Monica, CA: Rand Corporation.

Rachedi, N. (1994) 'Elites of Maghrebin Extraction in France.' In B. Lewis and D. Schnapper (eds.) *Muslims in Europe*. London: Pinter, pp. 67–78.

Ramadan, T. (1999) *To Be a European Muslim: A Study of Islamic Sources in the European Context*. Leicester: Islamic Foundation.

Ramadan, T. (2000) *Les Musulmans dans la Laïcité, responsabilités et droits des musulmans dans les sociétés occidentales*. Lyon: Tawhid.

Ramadan, T. (2001) *Islam, the West, and the Challenges of Modernity*. Leicester: Islamic Foundation.

Rath, J. (2005) 'Against the Current. The Establishment of Islam in the Netherlands.' *Canadian Diversity* 4(3), pp. 31–34.

Rath J., K. Groenendijk and R. Penninx (1991) 'The recognition and institutionalisation of Islam in Belgium, Great Britain and the Netherlands.' *New Community* 18(1), pp. 101–114.

Rath, J., R. Penninx, K. Groenendijk and A. Meyer (2001) *Western Europe and its Islam. The Social Reaction to the Institutionalization of a 'New' Religion in the Netherlands, Belgium and the United Kingdom*. Leiden/Boston/Tokyo: Brill.

Retso, J. (2003) *The Arabs in Antiquity: Their History from the Assyrians to the Umayyads*. London: Routledge.

Rivière, J. (2010) 'Le multiculturalisme des imbéciles.' URL (consulted 2 October 2012), http://blog.jeromeriviere.fr/spip. php?article33.

Rose, F. (2005) 'Face of Muhammed.' *Jyllands-Posten*. URL (consulted 5 February 2006), http://www.jp.dk/kultur/artikel:aid=3293102/.

Roy, O. (1994) 'Islam in France: Religion, Ethnic Community or Social Ghetto?' In B. Lewis and D. Schnapper (eds.) *Muslims in Europe*. London: Pinter, pp. 54–66.

Roy, O. (1999) *Vers un Islam européen*. Paris: Edition Esprit.

Roy, O. (2004) *Globalised Islam: The Search for a New Ummah*. London: Hurst.

Roy, O. (2007) *Secularism Confronts Islam*. NY: Columbia University Press.

Rushdie, S. (1989) *The Satanic Verses*. London: Viking Penguin.

Ryan, C. and W.A. Gamson 'The Art of Reframing Political Debates.' *Contexts* 5(1), pp. 13–18.

Safran, N (1961). *Egypt in Search of Political Community*. Cambridge (Mass): Harvard University Press.

Said, E.W. (1978) *Orientalism*. New York: Pantheon Books.

Said, E.W. (1993) *Culture and Imperialism*. New York: Vintage Books.

Said, E.W. (2001) 'The Clash of Ignorance.' *The Nation*, 22 October.

Sander, Å. (1993) *I vilken utsträckning är den svenske muslimen religiös? Någraöverväganden kring problematiken med att ta reda på hur många muslimer som deltar i verksamheten vid de muslimska 'församlingarna' i Sverige*. Göteborg: KIM-Rapport, nr. 14, Göteborgs universitet.

Sander, Å. (1996a) 'The Status of Muslim Communities in Sweden.' In G. Nonneman, T. Niblock and B. Szajkowski (eds.) *Muslim Communities in the New Europe*. Reading: Ithaca, pp. 269–289.

Sander, Å. (1996b) 'Sweden and Norway.' In F. Dasseto and Y. Conrad (eds.) *Musulmans en Europé Occidentale. Bibliographie commentée/Muslims in Western Europe. An Annotated Bibliography*. Paris: L'Harmattan, pp. 151–173.

Sander, Å. (1997) 'To What Extent is the Swedish Muslim Religious?' In S. Vertovec and C. Peach (eds.) *Islam in Europe: The Politics of Religion and Community*. London: Macmillan, pp. 269–289.

Sander, Å. (2004) 'Muslims in Sweden.' In M. Anwar et al. (eds.) *State Policies towards Muslim Minorities: Sweden, Great Britain and Germany*. Berlin: Edition Parabolis (http://www.emz-berlin.de/projekte_e/pj20_1E.htm).

Sauer, M. and A. Goldberg. (2001) *Die Lebenssituation und Partizipation Türkischer Migranten in Nordrhein-Westfalen*. Hamburg: Zentrum für Türkeistudien, Lit Verlag.

Scannell, P. (1996) *Radio, Television and Modern Life: A Phenomenological Approach*. Oxford: Blackwell.

Schiffauer, W. (1999) *Islamism in the Diaspora. The fascination of political Islam among second generation German Turks*, at http://www.transcomm.ox.ac.uk/working%20papers/Schiffauer_Islamism.PDF (last accessed November 2011).

Schmidt, G. (2012) ' "Grounded" Politics: Manifesting Muslim Identity as a Political Factor and Localized Identity in Copenhagen.' *Ethnicities* 12, pp. 603–622.

Sfeir, A. (2001) *Les réseaux d'Allah. Les filières Islamistes en France et en Europe*. Paris: Plon.

Shadid, W.A.R. and P.S. van Koningsveld (1995) *Religious Freedom and the Position of Islam in Western Europe. Opportunities and Obstacles in the Acquisition of Equal Rights*. Kok Pharos, Kampen.

Shadid, W.A.R and P.S. van Koningsveld (1996) *Muslims in the Margin: Political Responses to the Presence of Islam in Western Europe*. Kampen: Kok Pharos Publishing House.

Shapiro, M.J. (1997) *Violent Chartographies; Mapping Cultures of War*. Minneapolis: University of Minnesota Press.

Shildrick, T. (2006) 'Youth Culture, Subculture and the Importance of Neighbourhood.' *Young* 14(1), pp. 61–74.

Sidanius, C. (1998) 'Immigrants in Europe: The Rise of a New Underclass.' *The Washington Quarterly* 21(4).

Skovgaard-Petersen, J. and B. Gräf (eds.) (2009) *Global Mufti: The Phenomenon of Yusuf-al-Qaradawi*. London: Hurst.

Southern, R.W. (1962). *Western Views of Islam in the Middle Ages*. Cambridge (Mass): Harvard University Press.

Spivak, G.C. (1988) 'Can the Subaltern Speak?' In G. Nelson and L. Grossberg (eds.) *Marxism and the Interpretation of Culture*. Basingstoke: Macmillan, pp. 271–315.

Sreberny, A. and A. Mohammadi (1994) *Small Media, Big Revolution: Communication, Culture, and the Iranian Revolution*. Minneapolis: University of Minnesota Press.

Statham, P. (2004) 'Resilient Islam: Muslim Controversies in Europe.' *Harvard International Review* 26, 3.

Sunier, T. and A. Meyer (1996) 'Religion.' In H. Vermeulen (ed.) *Immigrant Policy for a Multicultural Society. A Comparative Study of Integration, Language and Religious Policy in Five Western European Countries.* Brussels: Migration Policy Group.

Taysir Dabbagh, N. (2005) *Suicide in Palestine: Narratives of Despair.* Northampton, Mass: Olive Branch Press.

Thompson, E. P. (1968) *The Making of the English Working Class.* Harmondsworth: Penguin.

Thomas, P. and Sanderson, P. (2011) 'Unwilling Citizens? Muslim young people and national identity.' *Sociology* 45(6), pp. 1028–1044.

Tibi, B. (2006) 'Europeanizing Islam or the Islamization of Europe.' In Peter Katzenstein (ed.) *Religion in an Expanding Europe.* Cambridge: Cambridge University Press.

Tilly, C. (2004) 'Foreword' In Q. Wiktorowicz (ed.) *Islamic Activism.* Indiana University Press.

Tolan, J.V. (2002) *Saracens: Islam in the Medieval European Imagination.* New York: Columbia University Press.

Toynbee, P. (2005) *In the Name of God,* Guardian, 22 July 2005.

Tribalat, M. (1996) *De l'Immigration à l'Assimilation: Enquête sur les Populations d'Origine Étrangère en France.* Paris: Editions de la Découverte.

Tsagarousianou, R. (2001) 'Ethnic Community Media, Community Identity and Citizenship in Contemporary Britain.' In Nick Jankowski and Ole Prehn (eds.) *Community Media in the Information Age: Perspectives, Findings and Policy.* New Jersey: Hampton Press.

Tsagarousianou, R. (2007) *Diasporic Cultures and Globalization.* Maastricht: Shaker.

Tsagarousianou, R. (2008) 'Narrating the Diaspora: Diasporic Audiences and the Construction of Diasporic Experience.' *Journalism & Communication Review.*

Tsagarousianou, R. and S. Sofos (2010) 'The Voice Behind the Veil.' URL (consulted 2 October 2012), http://europeanmuslims.blogspot.se/2010/07/voice-behind-veil-by-roza.html.

Turner, V. (1974) *Dramas, Fields and Metaphors: Symbolic Action in Human Society.* Ithaca: Cornell University Press.

Urry, J. (2000) *Sociology Beyond Societies: Mobilities for the Twenty-First Century.* London: Routledge.

van der Bie, R. (2009) 'Kerkelijkheid en kerkelijke diversiteit, 1889–2008.' In H. Schmeets and R. Van der Bie (eds.) *Religie aan het begin van de 21ste eeuw.* Den Haag/Heerlen: Centraal Bureau voor de Statistiek, pp. 13–25.

Vertovec, S. and C. Peach (eds.) (1997) *Islam in Europe: The Politics of Religion and Community.* Basingstoke: Macmillan.

Vertovec, S. and A. Rogers. (eds.) (1998) *Muslim European Youth: Reproducing Ethnicity, Religion, Culture.* Aldershot: Ashgate.

Volpi, Frédéric. (2010) *Political Islam Observed.* NY: Columbia University Press.

Waardenburg, J.D.J. (1988) 'The Institutionalization of Islam in the Netherlands, 1961–86.' In T. Gerholm and Y.G. Lithman (eds.) *The New Islamic Presence in Western Europe*. London and New York: Mansell Publishing, pp. 8–31.

Waardenburg, J.D.J. (1991) 'Muslim Associations and Official Bodies in some European Countries.' In W.A.R. Shadid and P.S. Koningsveld (eds.) *The Integration of Islam and Hinduism in Western Europe*. Kampen: Kok Pharos.

Werbner, P. (1994) 'Islamic Radicalism and the Gulf War: Lay Preachers and Political Dissent among British Pakistanis.' In B. Lewis and D. Schnapper (eds.) *Muslims in Europe*. London: Pinter, pp. 97–115.

Werbner, P. (2002) *Imagined Diasporas among Manchester Muslims*. Santa Fe, NM: School for American Research Press.

White, J.B. (2002) *Islamist Mobilization in Turkey: A Study in Vernacular Politics*. Seattle: University of Washington Press.

Wiktorowicz, Q. (ed.) (2004) *Islamic Activism*. Indiana University Press.

Wieviorka, Michel (1995) *The Arena of Racism*. London: Sage.

Virilio, P. (1991) *Lost Dimension*. Los Angeles: Semiotext(e).

Yazbeck-Haddad, Y. (ed.) (2002) *Muslims in the West: From Sojourners to Citizens*. New York: Oxford University Press.

Yükleyen, Ahmet (2012) *Localizing Islam in Europe: Turkish Islamic Communities in Germany and the Netherlands*. Syracuse, NY: Syracuse University Press.

Zarka, Yves Charles, Sylvie Taussig, Cynthia Fleury and Michèle Tribalat (eds.) (2004) *L'islam en France: Difficile tolérance*. Paris: Presses Universitaires de France.

Zebiri, Kate (2008) *British Muslim Converts; Choosing Alternative Lives*. Oxford: Oneworld.

Index

Printed and bound by CPI Group (UK) Ltd, Croydon, CR0 4YY